PRACTICAL CORE SOFTWARE SECURITY

As long as humans write software, the key to successful software security is making the software development program process more efficient and effective. Although the approach of this textbook includes people, process, and technology approaches to software security, **Practical Core Software Security: A Reference Framework** stresses the people element of software security, which is still the most important part to manage as software is developed, controlled, and exploited by humans.

The text outlines a step-by-step process for software security that is relevant to today's technical, operational, business, and development environments. It focuses on what humans can do to control and manage a secure software development process using best practices and metrics. Although security issues will always exist, students learn how to maximize an organization's ability to minimize vulnerabilities in software products before they are released or deployed by building security into the development process.

The authors have worked with Fortune 500 companies and have often seen examples of the breakdown of security development lifecycle (SDL) practices. The text takes an experience-based approach to apply components of the best available SDL models in dealing with the problems described above. Software security best practices, an SDL model, and framework are presented in this book. Starting with an overview of the SDL, the text outlines a model for mapping SDL best practices to the software development life cycle (SDLC). It explains how to use this model to build and manage a mature SDL program. Exercises and an in-depth case study aid students in mastering the SDL model.

Professionals skilled in secure software development and related tasks are in tremendous demand today. The industry continues to experience exponential demand that should continue to grow for the foreseeable future. This book can benefit professionals as much as students. As they integrate the book's ideas into their software security practices, their value increases to their organizations, management teams, community, and industry.

About the Authors

Dr. James Ransome, PhD, CISSP, CISM is a veteran chief information security officer (CISO), chief security officer (CSO), and chief production security officer (CPSO), as well as an author and co-author of numerous cybersecurity books.

Anmol Misra is an accomplished leader, researcher, author, and security expert with over 16 years of experience in technology and cybersecurity.

Mark S. Merkow, CISSP, CISM, CSSLP has over 25 years of experience in corporate information security and 17 years in the AppSec space helping to establish and lead application security initiatives to success and sustainment.

PRACTICAL CORE SOFTWARE SECURITY
A Reference Framework

James F. Ransome

Anmol Misra

Mark S. Merkow

CRC Press
Taylor & Francis Group
Boca Raton London New York

CRC Press is an imprint of the
Taylor & Francis Group, an **informa** business

AN AUERBACH BOOK

First Edition published 2023
by CRC Press
6000 Broken Sound Parkway NW, Suite 300, Boca Raton, FL 33487-2742

and by CRC Press
4 Park Square, Milton Park, Abingdon, Oxon, OX14 4RN

CRC Press is an imprint of Taylor & Francis Group, LLC

ISBN: 978-1-032-33314-4 (hbk)
ISBN: 978-1-032-27603-8 (pbk)
ISBN: 978-1-003-31907-8 (ebk)

DOI: 10.1201/9781003319078

Typeset in Adobe Garamond Pro
by DerryField Publishing Services

Dedications

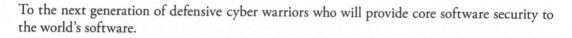

To the next generation of defensive cyber warriors who will provide core software security to the world's software.

— James Ransome

To software security professionals committed to building secure software.

— Anmol Misra

This book is dedicated to the next generation of application security professionals to help alleviate the struggle to reverse the curses of defective software, no matter where they show up.

— Mark Merkow

Dedications

Contents

List of Figures

List of Tables

Preface

The age of the software-driven machine has taken significant leaps over the last few years. Human tasks, such as those of fighter pilots, stock-exchange floor traders, surgeons, industrial production and power-plant operators that are critical to the operation of weapons systems, medical systems, and key elements of our national infrastructure, have been or are rapidly being taken over by software. This is a revolutionary step in the machine whose brain and nervous system is now controlled by software-driven programs taking the place of complex nonrepetitive tasks that formerly required the use of the human mind. This has resulted in a paradigm shift in the way the state, military, criminals, activists, and other adversaries can attempt to destroy, modify, or influence countries, infrastructures, societies, and cultures. This is true even for corporations, as we have seen increasing cases of cyber corporate espionage over the years. The previous use of large armies, expensive and devastating weapons systems and platforms, armed robberies, the physical stealing of information, violent protests, and armed insurrection are quickly being replaced by what is called cyber warfare, crime, and activism.

In the end, the cyber approach may have just as profound effects as the techniques used before in that the potential exploit of software vulnerabilities could result in:

- Entire or partial infrastructures being taken down, including power grids, nuclear power plants, communication media, and emergency response systems.
- Chemical plants modified to create large-yield explosions and/or highly toxic clouds.
- Remote control, modification, or disablement of critical weapon systems or platforms.
- Disablement or modification of surveillance systems.
- Criminal financial exploitation and blackmail.
- Manipulation of financial markets and investments.
- Murder or harm to humans through the modification of medical support systems or devices, surgery schedules, or pharmaceutical prescriptions.
- Political insurrection and special-interest influence through the modification of voting software, blackmail, or brand degradation though website defacement or underlying web application takedown or destruction.

A side effect of the cyber approach is that it has given us the ability to do the above at a scale, distance, and degree of anonymity previously unthought of from jurisdictionally protected locations through remote exploitation and attacks. This gives governments, criminal groups, and activists the ability to proxy prime perpetuators to avoid responsibility, detection, and political fallout.

Although there is much publicity regarding network security, the real Achilles heel is the (insecure) software that provides the potential ability for total control and/or modification of a target, as described above. The criticality of software security as we move quickly toward this new age of tasks previously relegated to the human mind being replaced by software-driven machines cannot be underestimated. It is for this reason that we have written this book. In contrast, and for the foreseeable future, software programs are and will be written by humans. This also means that new software will keep building on legacy code or software that was written prior to security being taken seriously, or before sophisticated attacks became prevalent. As long as humans write the programs, the key to successful security for these programs is in making the software development program process more efficient and effective. Although the approach of this book includes people, process, and technology approaches to software security, we believe that the people element of software security is still the most important part to manage as long as software is developed, controlled, and exploited by humans. What follows is a step-by-step process for software security that is relevant to today's technical, operational, business, and development environments, with a focus on what humans can do to control and manage the process in the form of best practices and metrics. We will always have security issues, but this book should help in minimizing them when software is finally released or deployed. We hope you enjoy our book as much as we have enjoyed writing it.

About the Book

This book outlines a step-by-step process for software security that is relevant to today's technical, operational, business, and development environments. The authors focus on what humans can do to control and manage a secure software development process in the form of best practices and metrics. Although security issues will always exist, this book will teach you how to maximize your organization's ability to minimize vulnerabilities in your software products before they are released or deployed, by building security into the development process. The authors have worked with Fortune 500 companies and have often seen examples of the breakdown of security development lifecycle (SDL) practices. In this book, we take an experience-based approach to applying components of the best available SDL models in dealing with the problems described above, in the form of an SDL software security best practices model and framework. *Practical Core Software Security: A Reference Framework* starts with an overview of the SDL and then outlines a model for mapping SDL best practices to the software development life cycle (SDLC), explaining how you can use this model to build and manage a mature SDL program.

This is as much a book for your personal benefit as it is for your academic and organization's benefit. Professionals who are skilled in secure software development and related tasks are in tremendous demand today, and we continue to see exponential demand that will continue to grow for the foreseeable future. As you integrate these ideas into your daily duties, your value increases to your company, your management, your community, and your industry.

Although security is not a natural component of the way industry has been building software in recent years, the authors believe that security improvements to development processes are possible, practical, and essential. They trust that the software security best practices and model presented in this book will make this clear to all who read the book, including executives, managers, and practitioners.

Audience

This book is targeted toward students in higher education programs within the business or engineering discipline and anyone who is interested in learning about software security in an enterprise environment, including:

- Product Security and Quality Executives
- Software Security Architects
- Security Consultants
- Software Development Engineers
- Enterprise SDLC Program Managers
- Chief Information Security Officers
- Chief Technology Officers
- Chief Privacy Officers whose companies develop software

If you want to learn about how software security should be implemented in developing enterprise software, this is a book you don't want to skip.

Support

Errata and support for this book are available on the CRC Press website.

Structure

This book is divided into nine chapters. Chapter 1 provides an introduction to the topic of software security and why it is important that we get it right the first time. Chapter 2 introduces the challenges of making software secure and the SDL framework. Chapters 3 through 8 provide mapping of our SDL with its associated best practices to a generic SDLC framework. Chapter 9 describes how to adapt our reference framework to your environment successfully by applying solutions proposed in Chapters 3 through 8. Each chapter includes learning objectives, along with multiple choice questions and exercises to provide hands-on practice using a case study to develop a custom SDL. Answers to the multiple-choice questions are found in Appendix B. Each chapter logically builds on prior chapters to help you paint a complete set of practical steps that lead to secure application software and responsive, secure development practices that predictably and reliably produce high-quality and provably secure applications.

Assumptions

This book assumes that a reader is familiar with the basics of software development (and methodologies) and basic security concepts. Knowledge of the SDL, different types of security testing, and security architecture is recommended but not required. For most topics, we gently introduce readers to the topic before diving deep into that particular topic.

Acknowledgments

I would like to thank all the team members, partners, collaborators, and coauthors who have worked with me over the years and who continue to evangelize that cyber security must start at the source, which is software. I would also like to thank Anmol and Mark for collaborating with me on this book and the Taylor & Francis Group and Derryfield Publishing Services for bringing this project our way.

— James Ransome

I want to thank everyone who has supported me over the years. And I want to thank Mark Merkow for collaborating with James Ransome and me on the book. I would also like to thank the Taylor & Francis Group and the Derryfield Publishing Services team for their help with the manuscript.

— Anmol Misra

I can't thank James and Anmol enough for the awesome opportunity to work on this book— it's been a pleasure and a joy!

I also want to thank the teams at the Taylor & Francis Group and Derryfield Publishing Services for the privilege of working with some of the best professionals in the business!

— Mark Merkow

About the Authors

Dr. James Ransome, PhD, CISSP, CISM is the Chief Scientist for CYBERPHOS, an early-stage cybersecurity startup. He is also a member of the board of directors for the Bay Area Chief Security Officer Council.

Most recently, James was the Senior Director of Security Development Lifecycle Engineering for Intel's Product Assurance and Security (IPAS). In that capacity, he led a team of SDL engineers, architects, and product security experts to drive and implement security practices across the company. Prior to that, James was the Senior Director of Product Security and PSIRT at Intel Security (formerly McAfee).

James's career includes leadership positions in the private and public sectors. He served in three chief information security officer (CISO) roles at Applied Materials, Autodesk, and Qwest Communications and four chief security officer (CSO) positions at Pilot Network Services, Exodus Communications, Exodus Communications—Cable and Wireless Company, and Cisco Collaborative Software Group. Before entering the corporate world, He worked in government service for 23 years supporting the U.S. intelligence community, federal law enforcement, and the Department of Defense.

James holds a PhD (https://nsuworks.nova.edu/gscis_etd/790/) in Information Systems, specializing in Information Security; a Master of Science Degree in Information Systems; and graduate certificates in International Business and International Affairs. He taught Applied Cryptography, Advanced Network Security, and Information Security Management as an Adjunct Professor in the Nova Southeastern University's Graduate School of Computer and Information Science (SCIS) Information Security Program. The graduate school is designated as a National Center of Academic Excellence in Information Assurance Education by the U.S. National Security Agency and the Department of Homeland Security.

James is a Certified Information Security Manager (CISM), a Certified Information Systems Security Professional (CISSP), and a Ponemon Institute Distinguished Fellow.

He has authored or coauthored 14 cyber-related books and is currently working on his 15th.

— James Ransome

Anmol Misra is an accomplished leader, researcher, author, and security expert, with over 16 years of experience in technology and cybersecurity.

His engineering, security, and consulting background makes him uniquely suited to drive the adoption of disruptive technologies. He is a team builder focused on mentoring and nurturing high-potential leaders, fostering excellence, and building industry partnerships. He is known for his pragmatic approach to security.

As Senior Director—Infrastructure Security, Anmol is responsible for cloud and information security at Autodesk. Before Autodesk, he managed security and compliance for Collaboration Cloud at Cisco. As part of Ernst & Young's (EY's) Advisory Services, before Cisco, he helped Fortune 500 companies define and execute strategy; build and implement secure, scalable solutions; and achieve regulatory compliance.

Anmol is one of the two authors of *Android Security: Attacks and Defenses* and *Core Software Security: Security at the Source*. He is also a contributing author of *Defending the Cloud: Waging Warfare in Cyberspace*. His books are used by leading universities worldwide to teach security. He has taught security to students and professionals alike, and his work has been cited by research papers in prestigious journals, including journals published by the ACM and the IEEE.

— Anmol Misra

Mark S. Merkow, CISSP, CISM, CSSLP has over 25 years of experience in corporate information security and 17 years in the AppSec space helping to establish and lead application security initiatives to success and sustainment. Mark is a faculty member at the University of Denver, where he works developing and instructing online courses in topics across the Information Security spectrum, with a focus on secure software development. He also works as an advisor to the University of Denver's Information and Computing Technology Curriculum Team for new course development and changes to the curriculum and for Strayer University as an advisor to the undergraduate and graduate programs in information security.

Mark has spent his IT career in a variety of roles, including application development, systems analysis and design, security engineering, and security management. Mark holds a Master of Science in Decision and Information Systems from Arizona State University (ASU), a Master of Education in Distance Education from ASU, and a Bachelor of Science in Computer Information Systems from ASU.

Mark has authored or coauthored 18 books on IT and has been a contributing editor to four others. Mark remains very active in the information security community, working in a variety of volunteer roles for the Phoenix Chapter of (ISC)², ISACA®, and OWASP®. You can find Mark's LinkedIn® profile at: linkedin.com/in/markmerkow

— Mark Merkow

Chapter 1

Introduction

CHAPTER OVERVIEW

Welcome to our book about what we still believe to be the most important topic in information security for the foreseeable future: software security. In the following sections, we will cover five major topics that highlight the need, value, and challenges of software security. This will set the stage for the remainder of the book, where we describe our model for software security: building security into your software using an operationally relevant and manageable security development lifecycle (SDL) that is applicable to all software development life cycles (SDLCs).

CHAPTER TAKE-AWAYS

- Describe the importance and need for software security.
- Understand the role of security within the software development life cycle (SDLC).
- Distinguish between quality and security attributes in code.
- Describe the fundamental goals of the security development lifecycle (SDL).
- Determine when and how to apply threat modeling and application risk analysis processes.

The rationale and the principles needed to achieve an effective software security program include:

1. **The importance and relevance of software security**. Software is critical to everything we do in the modern world and is behind our most critical systems. As such, it is imperative that it be secure by design. Most information technology (IT)-related security solutions have been developed to mitigate the risk caused by insecure software. To justify a software security program, the importance and relevance of the monetary costs and other risks for not building security into your software must be known, as well as the importance, relevance, and costs for building security in. At the end of the day, software security is as much a business decision as it is about avoiding security risks.

2. **Software security and the software development life cycle**. It is important to know the difference between what are generally known in software development as *software security* and *application security*. Although these terms are often used interchangeably, we differentiate between them because we believe there is a distinct difference in managing programs for these two purposes. In our model, *software security* is about building security into the software through a SDL in an SDLC, whereas *application security* is about protecting the software and the systems on which it runs after release.

3. **Quality versus secure code**. Although secure code is not necessarily quality code, and quality code is not necessarily secure code, the development process for producing software is based on the principles of both quality and secure code. You cannot have quality code without security or security without quality, and their attributes complement each other. At a minimum, quality and software security programs should be collaborating closely during the development process; ideally, they should be part of the same organization and both part of the software development engineering department. We will discuss this organizational and operational perspective later in the book.

4. **The three most important SDL security goals**. At the core of all software security analysis and implementation are three core elements of security: *confidentiality, integrity,* and *availability,* also known as the C.I.A. model. To ensure high confidence that the software being developed is secure, these three attributes must be adhered to as key components throughout the SDL.

5. **Threat modeling and attack surface validation**. The most time-consuming and misunderstood part of the SDL is threat modeling and attack surface validation. In today's world of Agile development, you must get this right or you will likely fail to make your software secure. Threat modeling and attack surface validation throughout the SDL will maximize your potential to alleviate post-release discovery of security vulnerabilities in your software product. We believe this function to be so important that we have dedicated a SDL section and a separate chapter to this topic.

1.1 The Importance and Relevance of Software Security

Although dated, the following statements are still relevant and highlight the security challenges that still exist in many software development organizations today. The 2005 U.S. President's Information Technology Advisory Committee (PITAC) report stated: "Commonly used software engineering practices permit dangerous errors, such as improper handling of buffer overflows, which enable hundreds of attack programs to compromise millions of computers every year."[1] This happens mainly because "commercial software engineering today lacks the scientific underpinnings and rigorous controls needed to produce high-quality, secure products at acceptable cost."[2]

The Gartner® Group reports that more than 70 percent of current business security vulnerabilities are found within software applications rather than the network boundaries.[3] A focus on application security has thus emerged to reduce the risk of poor software development, integration, and deployment. As a result, software assurance quickly became an information assurance (IA) focus area in the financial, government, and manufacturing sectors to reduce the risk of unsecure code: Security built into the software development life cycle makes good business sense.

A U.S. Department of Homeland Security 2006 Draft, "Security in the Software Lifecycle," states the following:

> The most critical difference between secure software and insecure software lies in the nature of the processes and practices used to specify, design, and develop the software . . . correcting potential vulnerabilities as early as possible in the software development lifecycle, mainly through the adoption of security-enhanced process and practices, is far more cost-effective than the currently pervasive approach of developing and releasing frequent patches to operational software.[4]

At the RSA® 2011 USA conference, cloud security issues were highlighted, but very little discussion was devoted to addressing the problem; however, at the 2012 conference, it was all about addressing the security issues in the cloud that had been so aptly identified the year before. The same thing happened in 2012, starting with a few key conferences, and continued with a major focus on discussing solutions for software security in 2013. For example, in early 2012, *Information Week* identified "Code gets externally reviewed" as one of the 10 security trends to watch in 2012,[5] and stated that "this business mandate is clear: Developers must take the time to code cleanly, and eradicate every possible security flaw before the code goes into production." There was also a popular security article published on March 1, 2012, titled "To Get Help with Secure Software Development Issues, Find Your Own Flaws," which highlighted panel discussions at RSA 2012 in San Francisco.[6] This panel did a great job of identifying some of the critical issues but did not address solving the software security challenges that it identified. However, things started to change mid-year 2012: The agenda for the Microsoft® inaugural Security Development Conference, held in May 2012,[7] was less about Microsoft and more about bringing secure software development thought leadership together and in three separate tracks to include "security engineering," "security development lifecycle (SDL) & business," and "managing the process" to discuss solutions to the most important security issue in industry—secure software development. This trend continued with the blackhat® USA 2012 Conference,[8] the RSA 2013 Conference,[9] and the 2013 Microsoft Security Development Conference.[10]

Think about it: What really causes a majority of the information security problems we have today? What is the primary target of hackers, cybercriminals, and nation-state cyber warriors? It is insecure code. What has quickly become the highest unnecessary cost to software development? It is flaws arising from insecure code in software products that have already been released to the market. When these flaws are discovered and/or exploited, they cause interruptions in current product development cycles to fix something that should have been fixed during the development of the product that has the flaw; they cause delays in product release dates because individuals or teams working on current products are pulled off cycle to fix issues in a previously released product; and they result in vulnerability scope creep because vulnerabilities discovered in one product may affect the security of others in web, Software-as-a-Service (SaaS), and cloud applications. They also create legal issues, reputation degradation, and public relations nightmares, such as those experienced by Sony®, Symantec®, and RSA over several years. They can also result in significant liability to the company. In an age of extensive regulations governing privacy and exposure of data, this quickly adds up even for big corporations. The point here is that even as the high-tech world, its consumers, customers, regulators, and the media have started to realize that not only is it imperative to fix software security problems, there is, in fact, a way to solve these issues in the form of a structured security software development life cycle or framework, such that all eyes will be on those who develop software code, particularly code that is used in critical and sensitive applications to see if the developers are adhering to this practice within their own environment—whether it be traditional/Waterfall, Scrum/Agile, or a blended development methodology.

Every sector of the global economy, from energy to transportation, finance, and banking, telecommunications, public health, emergency services, water, chemical, defense, industrial, food, agriculture, right down to the postal and shipping sectors, relies on software. Anything that threatens that software, in effect, poses a threat to our lives. Because of all the potential harm that could occur from exploitation of coding defects, the product not only has to work right (*quality*), it also has to be secure (*security*). Hence, we believe the title and content of this book addresses perhaps the most critical challenge we face in information and cyber security over the next few years.

Many believe that you can just fix software vulnerabilities after the product has been developed and be done with it. This is not that easy, however, because the cost to fix vulnerabilities increases over the SDLC, as shown in Figure 1.1, and most security activities happen post-release, including code audits, remediation, bug fixes, required patches, and also hacking. In a cloud environment, there may be multiple versions of an application running and it is often a challenge to fix security vulnerabilities across all of them. Exposure in one version of an application in a cloud environment can result in exploitation of all of them unless there are stringent network segmentation controls in place. Even these might prove to be insufficient in the event of sophisticated attacks.

The cost associated with addressing software problems increases as the lifecycle of a project matures (see Figure 1.1). In 1988, Barry Boehm stated that defects found in the field cost 50–200 times as much to correct as those corrected earlier.[11] Years later, Boehm stated that this ratio was 5:1 for small noncritical systems.[12] Data presented by Fortify in 2008 indicate that the cost of correcting security flaws at the requirements level is up to 100 times less than the cost of correcting security flaws in fielded software.[13] No matter what numbers are used, it is clear from the references above and others used in industry that there are substantial cost savings to fixing security flaws early in the development process rather than fixing them after software is fielded. For vendors, the cost is magnified by the expense of developing and

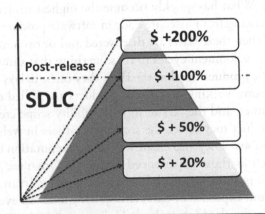

Figure 1.1   Cost to address software problems mapped to SDLC phases.

patching vulnerable software after release and can be a costly way of securing applications. Furthermore, patches are not always applied by owners/users of the vulnerable software; and patches can contain yet more vulnerabilities.[14] We have seen patches that fix one security problem but open (or re-open) other security issues. Companies are not always able to give each patch (fix) the attention it deserves, or it may not go through the regular software development life cycle, resulting in more security problems than the patch/fix is designed to mitigate.

For a number of years, the information security industry has focused on network and application security, assuming that software is secure and their security controls are all that is needed, instead of actually protecting organizations against software security failures. As we review the security development lifecycle and its associated best practices in this book, it should be clear that the network and application should come later in a comprehensive and layered defense-in-depth security program, and that software security should be considered the first step in the information security lifecycle, not the last. In a nutshell, network and application security programs are more about compensating controls, but it is only through addressing security at the source that we can really address problems.

1.2 Software Security and the Software Development Life Cycle

One significant area of confusion in the security industry over the years has been a misunderstanding of the difference between software security and application security. Gary McGraw has provided an excellent description of the difference between the two:

> On one hand, **software** security is about building secure software: designing software to be secure; making sure that software is secure; and educating software developers, architects, and users about how to build security in. On the other hand, **application** security is about protecting software and the systems that software runs in a post-facto, only after development is complete.[15]

Software security has come a long way since first attacks on a reasonably large scale started to materialize toward the end of the 1980s. Software back then was written without much thought for security (e.g., UNIX code, TCP/IP stack). After the advent of Microsoft Windows® and then the Web, attacks started increasing in sophistication and frequency, and thus it became necessary to look at software security. Industry started to look for short-term fixes through various "add-ons." These resulted in anti-virus, firewalls, anti-spyware, and so on. However, the real issue—how code was being developed and written—was not addressed. This started to change only in the last decade when SDL practices started to be taken seriously. Many enterprises impacted by software security defects (e.g., Microsoft) started to look seriously at how to build security in software code by improving software development practices. This resulted in recommended SDL practices from academia and software giants such as Microsoft. We now had the theory and guidelines on how to build security into the code from the start and thus lessen the possibility of software loopholes that could be exploited by attackers.

Confidentiality, integrity, and availability are the three primary goals that the industry considers to be of the utmost importance in any secure software development process. What the developers do to protect, enforce, and ensure these primary goals will equate to the "justifiably high confidence" part of the secure code definition. A developer can write very efficient code that is easy to maintain and reusable; however, if that code allows an unauthorized user to access the application's assets, then that code is either exposed or it is not, and there is no second chance for getting it right.

SDLs should not be confused with the standard software development life cycle. SDL methodology, as the name suggests, is really aimed at developing *secure* software, not necessarily *quality* software. As defined in the IT Law Wiki, the "Security Development Lifecycle is a software development process used to reduce software maintenance costs and increase reliability of software concerning software security related bugs."[16] In January 2002, many Microsoft software development groups prompted "security pushes" to find ways to improve existing security code. Under this directive, the Trustworthy Computing (TwC) team formed the concepts that led to the Microsoft Security Development Lifecycle. Established as a mandatory policy in 2004, the Microsoft SDL was designed as an integral part of the software development process at Microsoft.[17] The term SDL has been used by others since then—both for representing the Microsoft process and as a generic term for the process defined in the IT Law Wiki link above. Our use of the term SDL throughout this book will be to represent a secure development process composed of software security best practices based on comparative research on Microsoft's SDL and alternative models developed since 2004; the authors' experience and research into what does and does not work in most current development organizations; and the business realities of today's development austerity requirements coupled with the increasing demands for securing code at the source with relevant, cost-effective, and realistic software security practices.

The goals of SDL are twofold: The first goal is to reduce the number of security vulnerabilities and privacy problems; the second goal is to reduce the severity of the vulnerabilities that remain. There are industry standards that define what needs to be done in software development, such as ISO®/IEEE™, which define the primary phases of a traditional software development approach to software engineering. The elements of an SDL are typically very adaptive and are incorporated into the standard development life cycle for an organization.

Static analysis and threat modeling are among the tools used to develop secure code. Static analysis tools use a technique called "Taint Analysis" to look for unfiltered or unsanitized inputs (the scourge of software security) in application code. The greatest promise of static analysis tools derives from their ability to identify many common coding defects related to poor software development hygiene. Unfortunately, implementation bugs created by developer errors are often only part of the problem. Static analysis tools cannot evaluate design and architectural flaws. They cannot identify poorly designed cryptographic libraries or improperly selected algorithms, and they cannot point out *design problems* that might cause confusion between authentication and authorization. They also cannot identify passwords or magic numbers embedded in code. Static analysis tools can, however, peer into more of a program's dark corners with less fuss than dynamic analysis, which requires actually running the code. Static analysis also has the potential to be applied before a program reaches a level of completion at which testing can be meaningfully performed. The earlier security risks are identified and managed in the software development life cycle, the better!

Although these SDL practices have been good in theory, when applied to enterprises, results have been mixed. There are multiple reasons for this. Legacy code still forms a large codebase of our software industry, so going back in time and applying these practices is very difficult. Software outsourcing or off-shoring is another area where these practices are difficult to implement efficiently. Software developers and companies often work under tight deadlines to put a product out before competition, and thus software security has typically taken a back seat. There is a lack of management commitment to effectively implement SDL practices in such a fast-moving environment in which software security is often done as an afterthought.

Even though some security practices are common to both software and application security, such as penetration testing, source code scanning, security-oriented testing, and security education, there is no substitute for integrating security into the software development life cycle. The human element of the process is key to the success of any security development process and requires very seasoned software security architects and engineers to be successful. Threat modeling, applying principles such as *least privilege* and *defense in depth,* is perhaps the most understood, important, and needed element of the software development life cycle and requires human expertise and not tools to accomplish. One must also gather the real security requirements for a system and consider compliance, safety issues, contractual requirements, what data the application will process, and business risk.

Training is another critical element of the SDL that requires the human element. Training helps to reduce the cost of security, and an effective training program will motivate your development team to produce more secure software, with fewer problems and with more efficiency and cost effectiveness. It should be emphasized that no point solutions will provide a single solution for software security; rather, a holistic defense-in-depth approach is required, including a blend of people, process, and technology with a heavy emphasis on people. Although tools can parse through large quantities of code rapidly, faster than a human could, they are no replacement for humans. For the foreseeable future, software security will still be considered an art, but the art can be augmented through process and technology, and contrary to myths perpetrated by some practitioners, the art can be taught through proper mentorship by seasoned software security architects and engineers. These are the team members who have the experience, can think like an adversary, and do it throughout the development process, which is a key element for the success of any SDL. Some authors differentiate between secure-coding best practices and secure-design principles; we will address both in the software security best practices presented in this book and leverage the experience of the seasoned architects and engineers identified above to accomplish this.

Software security requires a focused effort to be successful and is not a natural outcome of conventional software development processes, even from development groups that have good traditional "quality" practices. Software security, however, should be a key of a mature quality program. As we will explain in this book, secure code does not necessarily mean quality code, and quality code does not necessarily mean secure code, but the foundation of software applications and the development processes that produce them should be based on common best practices of both quality code and secure code.

1.3 Quality Versus Secure Code

The foundation of software applications, and the development processes that produce them, is based on the common best principles of quality code and secure code. These principles are the driving force behind the concepts and design of industry best practices. To produce secure code that will stand the test of time, you must learn how to incorporate these principles into the development process. Remember that secure code is not necessarily quality code, and quality code is not necessarily secure code.[18]

Secure code does not mean quality code: You must know how to write quality code before you can write secure code. A developer can write very secure code that authorizes and authenticates every user transaction, logs the transaction, and denies all unauthorized requests; however, if the code does not return expected results, then even this very secure code may never see the light of day. Software quality characteristics are not the same as security. Quality is not measured in terms of confidentiality, integrity, and availability, but rather in terms of ease of use and whether it is reusable and maintainable.[19]

Quality code does not mean secure code: A developer can write efficient code that is easy to maintain and reusable, but if that code allows an unauthorized user to access the application's assets, then the code is of no use. Unlike software quality, software security is not subjective. Sensitive information is either exposed or it is not, and there is no second chance to get it right. Ultimately, quality, security, and maintainability are the three primary goals the industry considers to be of the upmost importance in any secure software development process.[20]

You cannot have quality without security or security without quality. These two attributes complement each other, and both enhance overall software product integrity and market value. Good developers should be able to identify what quality factors are in software and how to code them. Likewise, good developers should know how the software they develop can be attacked and what the weakest areas are in the software; if the code allows an unauthorized user to access the application's assets, then that code is either exposed or it's not, and there is no second chance to get it right.[21]

1.4 The Three Most Important SDL Security Goals

Any competent developer can write very efficient code that is maintainable and easy to reuse; however, if the code allows an unauthorized user to access the application's assets, then that code is not secure. Unfortunately, security is still an area that is often either overlooked or minimally applied during the software development life cycle. There are three minimum goals that that the information security industry considers of primary importance for an SDL:

1. Confidentiality
2. Integrity
3. Availability

These three goals are generally referred to collectively by the acronym C.I.A. It is generally accepted that if the developers ensure, enforce, and protect C.I.A. throughout the software development life cycle through generally accepted practices, this will justify high confidence that the code is secure.

Information security, confidentiality, integrity, and availability are defined as follows in *44 U.S.C., Sec. 3542:*

Information security: The protection of information and information systems from unauthorized access, use, disclosure, disruption, modification, or destruction in order to provide confidentiality, integrity, and availability.

Confidentiality: Preserving authorized restrictions on information access and disclosure, including means for protecting personal privacy and proprietary information.

Integrity: Guarding against improper information modification or destruction, and includes ensuring information non-repudiation and authenticity.

Availability: Ensuring timely and reliable access to and use of information.[22]

Confidentiality, availability and integrity combined provide information security.

Confidentiality is achieved by keeping unauthorized users (human or software) from accessing confidential information. By maintaining confidentiality, the software will be considered trustworthy. Authorization and authentication are the two properties that support confidentiality in that *authorization* ensures that the user has the appropriate role and privilege to view data, and *authentication* ensures that the user is who he or she claims to be and that the data come from the appropriate place. The integrity of the application is defined by the way in which the application accepts, transmits, and stores data. The data must remain unchanged by unauthorized users and remain very reliable from the data entry point all the way to the database and back. Data encryption, digital signatures, and public keys are just some examples of how to maintain integrity and confidentiality. Excluding any scheduled downtimes, availability refers to the percentage of time a system or software is available during its normally scheduled hours of operations. As key components of software security, the lack of confidentiality, availability, and integrity will degrade the reputation of the product, resulting in both loss of reputation and loss of sales. In the end, software security is as much about a good business process as it is about quality.

1.5 Threat Modeling and Attack Surface Validation

Threat modeling and attack surface validation are perhaps the most time-consuming, misunderstood, and difficult parts of the SDL. They require the attention of the most seasoned and experienced person of the software security team: the software security architect. The idea behind threat modeling is simply to understand the potential security threats to the system, determine risk, and establish appropriate mitigations (What? How bad is it? How can it be fixed?). When it is performed correctly, threat modeling occurs early in the project lifecycle and can be used to find security design issues before code is committed. This can lead to significant cost savings because issues are resolved early in the development life cycle. Threat modeling also helps businesses manage software risk, creates awareness of security dependencies and assumptions, and provides the ability to translate technical risk into business impact. The bottom line is that the earlier security risks are identified and managed in the software life cycle, the better.

The correct way of doing threat modeling requires getting into the mind of the hacker, and this takes a special breed of software security professional: one who can think like a hacker and imagine all the ways that an adversary could attack or exploit the software. It is thus a slightly different way to test applications. Although quality assurance professionals can do security testing and can typically discover some vulnerabilities, they usually have the customers' thoughts in mind rather than those of the hacker. In many cases, companies do not have this talent internally and have to hire third-party contractors to do this work.

A U.S. Data and Analysis Center for Software (DACS) October 2008 report, "Enhancing the Development Lifecycle to Produce Secure Software: A Reference Guidebook on Software Assurance," defines a threat to a software-intensive system as "any actor, agent, circumstance, or event that has the potential to cause harm to that system or to the data or resources to which the system has or enables access."[23] A threat can be categorized based on its intentionality. For example, a threat can be unintentional, intentional but non-malicious, or malicious; a malicious threat is assumed to be intentional. Although threats in all three categories have the potential to compromise the security of software, only malicious threats are realized by attacks. The DACS report also states:

> The majority of attacks against software take advantage of, or exploit, some vulnerability or weakness in that software; for this reason, "attack" is often used interchangeably with "exploit," though the Build Security In Attack Pattern Glossary makes a clear distinction between the two terms, with attack referring to the action against the targeted software and exploit referring to the mechanism (e.g., a technique or malicious code) by which that action is carried out.

Modeling software is a way to envision the interactions of the proposed software within its intended environment. The better the model reflects the intended environment, the more useful the modeling approach becomes. Therefore, secure software design and development benefits from modeling that explicitly incorporates security threats. As described in the DACS 2007 Software Security Assurance State-of-the-Art Report (SOAR), "[T]he primary issues in modeling are doing it well; doing it thoroughly enough; and knowing what to do with the results (e.g., how to transform the analysis into a metric and/or otherwise usable decision point." Combining the concepts of threats and modeling, the report defines threat modeling as "a methodical approach for assessing and documenting the weaknesses of security risks associated with an application. It allows a development team to identify the highest risk components by approaching security from the perspective of an adversary who has specific goals in attacking an application."[24]

Given the normal constraints of time and resources, it is not possible to test all code in an application. However, at a minimum, testing should cover the entry points and exit points of an application that may be accessible to an attacker, commonly referred to as the application's *attack surface*. Accessibility increases the attack surface. For example, code that is restricted to local access by an administrator has a smaller attack surface than code exposed to remote access by an anonymous user.

The attack surface should be fully tested by exercising all the code paths in an application that are part of the attack surface. The elements of the attack surface can be identified with the use of scanning tools, such as port scanning tools for open ports, and code analysis tools to locate the portions of the code that receive input and send output. It may even be necessary to develop custom tools, for example, to locate entry points specific to a custom application. The minimum attack surface is typically defined early in the software development life cycle and measured again through the later phases. It is often helpful to formally define and measure the attack surface before testing. As we will discuss later in the book, although tools will be useful at this stage of analysis, a human element is still required, and it will take the expertise of the seasoned software security architect described above.

1.6 Summary

Software is only as secure as the quality and relevance of the best practices that the software development team uses. Software security must be built in from the very start. It must be a critical part of the design from the very beginning and included in every subsequent development phase all the way through fielding a complete system. Correcting vulnerabilities as early as possible in the SDLC through the adoption of security-enhanced processes and practices is far more cost effective than attempting to diagnose and correct such problems after the system goes into production. This will greatly reduce the need to patch the software to fix security holes discovered by others after release of the product, which will degrade the reputation and credibility of the vendor and adversely impact it financially. Today, we are seeing an increased need for security in software development in that security requirements, design, and defensive principles have to be worked into the traditional SDLC and, most important, in choosing security development practices that embrace this need throughout all the activities of the SDLC.

We have worked with Fortune 500 companies and have often seen examples of breakdowns in SDL practices. In this book, we take an experience-based approach to applying components of the best available SDLs models in dealing with the problems described above in the form of an SDL software security best practices model and framework. We shall begin by giving an overview of the security development lifecycle and then outline a model for mapping SDL best practices to the software development life cycle and how you can use this to build a mature SDL program. Although security is not a natural component of the way industry has been building software in recent years, we believe that security improvements to development processes are possible, practical, and essential, and we trust that the software security best practices and model presented in this book will make this clear to all who read this book, whether you are an executive, manager, or practitioner.

Chapter Quick-Check

1. The costs to remediate security flaws once a software product is released can run as much as _____ times the costs to remediate them while still in development:

   a. 50
   b. 100
   c. 500
   d. 1500

2. Defective software is:

   a. A network security problem
   b. An operating system security problem
   c. A user-caused problem
   d. A software development and engineering problem

3. The three goals of the security development lifecycle are:

   a. Reliability, efficiency, and maintainability
   b. Speed, quality, and continuous releases

    c. Confidentiality, integrity, and availability

    d. Availability, reliability, and portability

4. Threat modeling and attack surface analysis is most effective when it's conducted:

    a. Post-release

    b. During product inception/product backlog development

    c. During integration testing phase(s)

    d. Prior to code development/commitment

Exercises

1. Visit the Significant Cyber Incidents site at the Center for Strategic and International Studies for a timeline of significant cyber incidents since 2006. As you read through these attacks, consider how a security development lifecycle and secure development practices could have prevented these attacks or mitigated the damage from them. Are there any specific types of attacks that require an intervention or change to the SDL? How would you prioritize those changes?

2. The migration of applications, infrastructure, platforms, and administration to cloud computing has forced a myriad of changes across IT departments. How does this migration affect software planning, development, testing, and implementation from the security perspective? What needs to be preserved? What needs to be reimagined?

3. Education and awareness of software security are cornerstones for an effective program since development teams are responsible for securing all the code they produce. How would you convince IT development management that their teams need to be properly prepared for their security responsibilities?

References

1. President's Information Technology Advisory Committee. (2005). "Cybersecurity: A Crisis of Prioritization," Executive Office of the President, National Coordination Office for Information Technology Research and Development, 2005, p. 39. Retrieved from https://www.nitrd.gov/pubs /pitac/pitac_report_cybersecurity_2005.pdf

2. Ibid.

3. Aras, O., Ciaramitaro, B., and Livermore, J. (2008). "Secure Software Development—The Role of IT Audit." *ISACA Journal,* vol. 4, 2008, pp. 45–48. Retrieved from https://www.isaca.org /resources/isaca-journal/past-issues

4. U.S. Department of Homeland Security. (2006). "Security in the Software Lifecycle: Making Software Development Processes—and Software Produced by Them—More Secure," DRAFT Version 1.2, p. 13. Retrieved from https://resources.sei.cmu.edu/asset_files/WhitePaper/2006_019_001_52113.pdf

5. Schwartz, M. (2012). "10 Security Trends to Watch in 2012." Retrieved from https://www.dark reading.com/vulnerabilities-threats/10-security-trends-to-watch-in-2012

6. Parizo, E. (2012). "To Get Help with Secure Software Development Issues, Find Your Own Flaws." Retrieved from http://searchsecurity.techtarget.com/news/2240129160/To-get-help-with -secure-software-development-issues-find-your-own-flaw

7. Taft, D. (2012). "Microsoft Holds Security Development Conference." Retrieved from https://www .eweek.com/security/microsoft-holds-security-development-conference/

8. blackhat.com. (2013). Black Hat USA 2012 Conference webpage, July 21–26, 2012, Las Vegas, NV. Retrieved from http://www.blackhat.com/html/bh-us-12

9. The OWASP Foundation. (2013). "Approaching Secure Code. Where do I start?" RSA 2013. Retrieved from https://owasp.org/www-pdf-archive/MASTER-RSA2013-v3.pdf

10. Microsoft Corporation. (2012). Registration Open for 2013 Security Development Conference: Calling All IT Security Professionals. Retrieved from https://news.microsoft.com/2012/12/18/registration-open-for-2013-security-development-conference-calling-all-it-security-professionals/

11. Boehm, B., and Papaccio, P. (1998). "Understanding and Controlling Software Costs." *IEEE Transactions on Software Engineering,* vol. 14, no. 10, October 1988, pp. 1462–1477.

12. Beohm, B., and Basili, V. (2001). "Software Defect Reduction Top 10 List." *Computer,* vol. 34, no. 1, January 2001, pp. 135–137.

13. Meftah, B. (2008). "Business Software Assurance: Identifying and Reducing Software Risk in the Enterprise," 9th Semi-Annual Software Assurance Forum, Gaithersburg, MD, October 2008. https://buildsecurityin.us-cert.gov/swa/downloads/Meftah.pdf

14. Viega, J., and McGraw, G. (2006). *Building Secure Software: How to Avoid Security Problems the Right Way.* Boston, MA: Addison-Wesley.

15. McGraw, G. (2006). *Software Security: Building Security In*, p. 20. Boston, MA: Addison-Wesley.

16. IT Law Wiki. (2012). "Security Development Lifecycle Definition." Retrieved from http://itlaw.wikia.com/wiki/Security_Development_Lifecycle

17. Microsoft Corporation. (2021). "About the Microsoft SDL." Retrieved from https://www.microsoft.com/en-us/securityengineering/sdl/about#:~:text=The%20Microsoft%20Security%20Development%20Lifecycle%20%28SDL%29%20was%20an,the%20software%20development%20process%20at%20Microsoft%20in%202004

18. Grembi, J. (2008). *Secure Software Development: A Security Programmer's Guide.* Boston, MA: Course Technology.

19. Ibid.

20. Ibid.

21. Ibid.

22. United States Government. (2006). "44 U.S.C., SEC. 3542: United States Code, 2006 Edition," Supplement 5, Title 44; CHAPTER 35 – COORDINATION OF FEDERAL INFORMATION POLICY, SUBCHAPTER III – INFORMATION SECURITY, Sec. 3542 – Definitions. Retrieved from http://www.gpo.gov/fdsys/pkg/USCODE-2011-title44/pdf/USCODE-2011-title44-chap35-subchapIII-sec3542.pdf

23. Goertzel, K., et al., for Department of Homeland Security and Department of Defense Data and Analysis Center for Software. (2008). "Enhancing the Development Life Cycle to Produce Secure Software: A Reference Guidebook on Software Assurance," Version 2, October 2008. Retrieved from https://www.academia.edu/1383839/Enhancing_the_Development_Life_Cycle_to_Produce_Secure_Software_A_Reference_Guidebook_on_Software_Assurance

24. Goertzel, K., et al. (2007). "Software Security Assurance: State-of-the-Art Report (SOAR)," July 2007. Retrieved from https://www.researchgate.net/publication/279351339_Software_Security_Assurance_A_State-of-Art_Report_SAR

Chapter 2

The Security Development Lifecycle

CHAPTER OVERVIEW

We start this chapter by introducing the concept of overcoming the challenges of making software secure using a security development lifecycle (SDL). There will be further discussions of the models, methodologies, tools, human talent, and metrics for managing and overcoming these challenges. We will close with a discussion of the mapping of our SDL with its associated best practices to a generic software development life cycle (SDLC), which will be the subject of the next six chapters, followed by a chapter mapping our SDL best practices to several of the most popular software development methodologies.

There is still a need for better static and dynamic testing tools and a formalized security methodology integrated into SDLCs that is within the reach of a majority of software development organizations. In the past decade or so, the predominant SDL models have been out of reach for all but the most resource-rich companies. Our goal in this book is to create an SDL based on leveraged minimal resources and best practices rather than requiring resources that are out of reach for a majority of software security teams.

CHAPTER TAKE-AWAYS

- Explain the underlying challenges in creating secure software as they exist in processes, talent, and technology.
- Distinguish between the industry maturity models used for measuring the progress of software security programs and the metrics needed for measuring progress.
- Compare and contrast various industry standards, guidance, and best practices for secure software development programs.

- Understand the need for specialized development team roles that enable secure software development success.
- Explore the various implementations of software development life cycles and methodologies, along with the steps needed to convert them into a security development lifecycle.

2.1 Overcoming Challenges in Making Software Secure

As mentioned in Chapter 1, SDLs are the key step in the evolution of software security and have helped to bring attention to the need to build security into the software development life cycle. In the past, software product stakeholders did not view software security as a high priority. It was believed that a secure network infrastructure would provide the level of protection needed against malicious attacks. In recent history, however, network security alone has proved inadequate against such attacks. Users have been successful in penetrating valid channels of authentication through techniques such as Cross-Site Scripting (XSS), Structured Query Language (SQL) injection, and buffer overflow exploitation. In such cases system assets were compromised and both data and organizational integrity were damaged. The security industry has tried to solve software security problems through stopgap measures. First came platform security (OS security), then came network/perimeter security, and now application security. We do need defense-in-depth to protect our assets, but fundamentally it is a software security flaw and needs to be remediated through an SDL approach.

The SDL has as its base components all of the activities and security controls needed to develop industry and government-compliant and best practices–hardened software. A knowledgeable staff as well as secure software policies and controls are required in order to truly prevent, identify, and mitigate exploitable vulnerabilities within developed systems.

Not meeting the least of the activities found within the SDL provides an opportunity for misuse of system assets from both insider and outsider threats. Security is not simply a network requirement, it is now an information technology (IT) requirement, which includes the development of all software for the intent to distribute, store, and manipulate information. Organizations must implement the highest standards of development in order to ensure the highest quality of products for its customers and the lives that they protect.

Implementation of an SDL program ensures that security is inherent in good enterprise software design and development, not an afterthought included later in production. Taking an SDL approach yields tangible benefits such as ensuring that all software releases meet minimum security criteria, and that all stakeholders support and enforce security guidelines. The elimination of software risk early in the development cycle, when vulnerabilities are easier and less expensive to fix, provides a systematic approach for information security teams to collaborate with during the development process.

The most well-known SDL model is the Trustworthy Computing Security Development Lifecycle (or SDL), a process that Microsoft® has adopted for the development of software that needs to withstand a malicious attack. Microsoft's SDL[1] has been evolving for over a decade and is considered the most mature of the top three models. Other popular SDL models are the BSIMM SSDL Touchpoints,[2] the OWASP® Code Review Guide,[3] and the Cisco® Secure Development Lifecycle (Cisco SDL).[4]

The Microsoft SDL also has a Security Development Lifecycle (SDL) Optimization Model[5] designed to facilitate gradual, consistent, and cost-effective implementation of the SDL by development organizations outside of Microsoft. The model helps those responsible for integrating security and privacy in their organization's software development life cycle to assess their current state and to gradually move their organizations toward adoption of the proven Microsoft program for producing more secure software.

The SDL Optimization Model enables development managers and IT policy makers to assess the state of the security in development. They can then create a vision and roadmap for reducing customer risk by creating more secure and reliable software in a cost-effective, consistent, and gradual manner. As it moves through the maturity levels of the SDL Optimization Model, your organization's executive commitment to the goals and results of SDL will increase from tentative acceptance to a strong mandate.[6]

2.2 Software Security Maturity Models

Over the years, two popular software security maturity models have been developed and continue to mature at a rapid rate. One is BSIMM,[7] and the other is the OWASP Open SAMM.[8] BSIMM is short for Building Security In Maturity Model. The BSIMM is a study of real-world software security initiatives organized so that you can determine where you stand with your software security initiative and how to evolve your efforts over time. It is a set of best practices developed by analyzing real-world data from nine leading software security initiatives and creating a framework based on common areas of success. There are 12 practices organized into four domains. These practices are used to organize the 122 BSIMM activities.

By studying what the nine initiatives were doing, BSIMM's creators were able to build a best practices model that is broken down into 12 categories that software makers can follow:

1. Strategy and Metrics
2. Compliance and Policy
3. Training
4. Attack Models
5. Security Features and Design
6. Standards and Requirements
7. Architecture Analysis
8. Code Review
9. Security Testing
10. Penetration Testing
11. Software Environment
12. Configuration and Vulnerability Management[9]

The 12th release of BSSIM was published in 2021.[10]

The OWASP Software Assurance Maturity Model (SAMM™) is a flexible and prescriptive framework for building security into a software development organization. Covering more than typical SDLC-based models for security, SAMM enables organizations to self-assess their security assurance program and then use recommended roadmaps to improve in a way that is aligned to the specific risks facing the organization. Beyond that, SAMM enables the creation of scorecards for an organization's effectiveness at secure software development throughout the typical governance, development, and deployment business functions. Scorecards also enable management within an organization to demonstrate quantitative improvements through iterations of building a security assurance program.[11]

2.3 ISO/IEC 27034—Information Technology—Security Techniques—Application Security

In 2011, the International Organization for Standardization (ISO®)/International Electrotechnical Commission (IEC®) published Part 1 of 6 of the ISO/IEC 27034-1:2011 standard for Application Security.[12] The standard offers a concise, internationally recognized way to get transparency into a vendor/supplier's software security management process. It was designed to be flexible enough to align with diverse engineering organizations but specific enough to address real-world risk. It has now been published and is similar to the ISO/IEC 27001 for IT Security in that both customers and partners will expect compliance. As a standard for software security from an international body and not a vendor, it is also not tied to specific technology. Parts 2–7 are composed of the following: Part 2, Organization Normative Framework; Part 3, Application Security Management Process; Part 4, Application Security Validation; Part 5, Protocols and Application Security Control Data Structure; Part 6, Security Guidance for Specific Applications; Part 7, Assurance Prediction Framework.[13] Over the years, as organizations (and their customers) started paying attention to information security, the security and compliance industry came up with a plethora of attestations, certifications, and methodologies. These standards/attestations all claimed to be unique in the way they would measure the security posture of an organization. Competition and marketing hype drove confusion, with different organizations standardizing on different attestations. The authors have seen organizations pushing their customers (in most cases, other companies) to adopt their recommended attestation. For Fortune 500 companies this meant getting multiple attestations/certifications as a proof of security posture. It didn't help that most of these attestations/certifications focused on "compliance controls" or "policy-based security." The situation became worse with regulations such as SOX, GLBA, Safe Harbor, and HIPAA adding to the confusion. Companies often went for a set of certifications—one each for compliance, security, privacy, credit card, physical security, and so on.

The ISO/IEC developed the ISO/IEC 27001 (incorporating ISO/IEC 17799, which had been the previous *de facto* ISO standard for information security). It is an information security management system (ISMS) standard that specifies a management system intended to bring information security under formal management control. It mandates specific requirements that need to be met when an organization adopts the standard. The standard addresses information security holistically and encompasses everything from physical security to compliance. Industry has enthusiastically adopted the practices, and ISO/IEC 27001 is the leading standard for an information security management system (ISMS) today. Most of the controls from other standards can be mapped back to ISO/IEC 27001. This has enabled organizations to consolidate multiple security efforts under one standard, pursue a single framework with holistic security in mind, and collect metrics in a consistent manner to measure and govern security in an organization.

The authors see the landscape for software security (and SDL) as similar to what it was for information security as a whole a few years ago, before ISO/IEC 27001 came along. There are multiple SDL methodologies (open and proprietary), each claiming to be better than the next. Confusion prevails over the best way to accomplish software security in an organization. Applying any one framework to an organization either requires the organization to adopt different processes or to customize an SDL framework that will work in their environment. With the coming of ISO/IEC 27034, the authors see consolidation on a software security standards/framework as the ISO/IEC 27001 has done for information security. Even in its infancy, there is awareness of the importance of ISO/IEC 27034. Microsoft declared its SDL methodology to be in conformance with ISO/IEC 27034-1 shortly after its release.[14] We expect to see similar results for other frameworks in the near future.

The ISO/IEC 27034 standard provides guidance to help organizations embed security within their processes that help secure applications running in the environment, including application life cycle processes. It is a risk-based framework to continuously improve security through process integrating/improvements in managing applications. It takes a process approach by design.

The authors' recommended SDL framework can be mapped to ISO/IEC 27034 frameworks. We will lay out relevant mapping with ISO/IEC 27034 in Chapter 9.

2.4 Other Resources for SDL Best Practices

There are other sources for SDL best practices, and some of the most popular are described below.

2.4.1 SAFECode

The Software Assurance Forum for Excellence in Code (SAFECode) is a nonprofit organization dedicated to increasing trust in information and communications technology products and services through the advancement of effective software assurance methods. SAFECode is a global, industry-led effort to identify and promote best practices for developing and delivering more secure and reliable software, hardware, and services. It is meant to provide a foundational set of secure development practices that have been effective in improving software security in real-world implementations by SAFECode members across their diverse development environments. These are the "practiced practices" employed by SAFECode members, which we identified through an ongoing analysis of members' individual software security efforts. By bringing these methods together and sharing them with the larger community, SAFECode hopes to move the industry beyond defining theoretical best practices to describing sets of software engineering practices that have been shown to improve the security of software and are currently in use at leading software companies.[15,16]

2.4.2 U.S. Department of Homeland Security Software Assurance Program

Since 2004, the U.S. Department of Homeland Security (DHS) Software Assurance Program has been involved in the development and management of the Build Security In (BSI) website, along with the CERT® Division of the Software Engineering Institute (SEI) at Carnegie Mellon University.[17] BSI content is based on the principle that software security is fundamentally a software engineering problem and must be managed in a systematic way throughout the SDLC.

The Department of Homeland Security Software Assurance (SwA) Program seeks to reduce software vulnerabilities, minimize exploitation, and address ways to improve the routine development and deployment of trustworthy software products. Consistent with the Open Government Directive, the program enables public–private collaboration in developing, publishing, and promoting the use of practical guidance and tools, fostering investment in more secure and reliable software. The DHS Software Assurance Program collaborates with the private sector, academia, and other federal departments and agencies to enhance the security of software life cycle processes and technologies through activities such as the Software Assurance Forum that it co-sponsors with the Department of Defense (DoD) and the National Institute of Standards and Technology (NIST). A key initiative funded by the DHS and the National Security Agency (NSA) is the Common Weakness Enumeration (CWE™). CWE is a joint effort of the DHS with the NSA and the software community, including the government, the private sector, and academia, with the MITRE Corporation providing technical leadership and project coordination. Over 800 software weaknesses have been identified and cataloged. More than 62 security products and services already use CWE in a compatible manner. With the aim of reducing the most significant exploitable programming errors, the SANS Institute, an active participant in the Software Assurance Forum, has promoted the Top 25 CWEs. SANS came up with the idea of focusing on the Top 25 CWEs, and this effort represents a community collaboration to prioritize the most exploitable constructs that make software vulnerable to attack or failure.[18] This promotes the DHS co-sponsored CWE efforts and plays off the "Top XXX" brand that SANS has built since 2001, starting with their Top 10—the first prioritized list of security problems that organizations should address.

The CWE is an important component of the DHS's Software Assurance Program. This list of errors brings CWE to a practical, actionable, and measurable focus that will enable people to make and demonstrate real progress. Public–private collaboration forms the foundation of the DHS SwA Program. CWE is a good example of the type of public–private collaboration the department has been advocating. Consistent with the Open Government Directive, the SwA Program's sponsorship of CWE enables community participation, collaboration, and transparency. CWE provides the requisite characterization of exploitable software constructs; thus, it better enables the needed education and training of programmers on how to eliminate all-too-common errors before software is delivered and put into operation. This aligns with the Build Security In approach to software assurance so that software is developed more securely on the front end, thereby avoiding security issues in the longer term. The CWE provides a standard means for understanding residual risks and thus enables more informed decision making by suppliers and consumers concerning the security of software.[19]

2.4.3 National Institute of Standards and Technology

The National Institute of Standards and Technology (NIST) continues to be of great value in providing research, information, and tools for both the government and corporate information security community. The following are some of the key areas in which NIST contributes to the software security community.

The NIST Software Assurance Metrics And Tool Evaluation (SAMATE) project is dedicated to improving software assurance by developing methods to enable software tool evaluations, measuring the effectiveness of tools and techniques, and identifying gaps in tools and methods. This project supports the Department of Homeland Security's Software Assurance Tools and R&D Requirements Identification Program—in particular, Part 3, Technology (Tools and Requirements): the identification, enhancement, and development of software assurance tools. The scope of the SAMATE project is broad, ranging from operating systems to firewalls, SCADA to web applications, source code security analyzers to correct-by-construction methods.[20]

NIST Special Publication (SP) 800-64, "Security Considerations in the System Development Life Cycle," has been developed to assist federal government agencies in integrating essential information technology security steps into their established IT system development life cycle. This guideline applies to all federal IT systems other than national security systems. The document is intended as a reference resource rather than as a tutorial and should be used in conjunction with other NIST publications as needed throughout the development of the system.[21]

The National Vulnerability Database (NVD) is the U.S. government repository of standards-based vulnerability management data represented using the Security Content Automation Protocol (SCAP). These data enable automation of vulnerability management, security measurement, and compliance. The NVD includes databases of security checklists, security-related software flaws, misconfigurations, product names, and impact metrics.[22] The NVD Common Vulnerability Scoring System (CVSS) provides an open framework for communicating the risk characteristics and impacts of IT vulnerabilities. Its quantitative model ensures repeatable accurate measurement while enabling users to see the underlying vulnerability characteristics that were used to generate the scores. Thus, the CVSS is well suited as a standard measurement system for industries, organizations, and governments that need accurate and consistent vulnerability impact scores. Two common uses of the CVSS are in prioritizing vulnerability remediation activities and in calculating the severity of vulnerabilities discovered on one's systems. The NVD provides CVSS scores for almost all known vulnerabilities. In particular, the NVD supports the CVSS Version 2 standard for all CVE vulnerabilities. The NVD provides CVSS "base scores" which represent the innate characteristics of every vulnerability. It does not currently provide "temporal scores" (scores that change over time due to events external to the vulnerability). However, the NVD does provide a CVSS score calculator to allow you to add temporal data and even to calculate environmental scores (scores customized to reflect the impact of the vulnerability on your organization). This calculator contains support for U.S. government agencies to customize vulnerability impact scores based on FIPS 199 system ratings. We will discuss the use of CVSS scores for managing software security later in the book.[23]

2.4.4 Common Computer Vulnerabilities and Exposures

The Common Computer Vulnerabilities and Exposures (CVE®) is a list of information security vulnerabilities and exposures that aims to provide common names for publicly known problems. The goal of CVE is to make it easier to share data across separate vulnerability capabilities (tools, repositories, and services) with this "common enumeration." Information security *vulnerability* is a mistake in software that can be used directly by a hacker to gain access to a system or network. See the Terminology page of the CVE website for a complete explanation of how this term is used in the CVE. An information security *exposure* is a mistake in software that allows access to information or capabilities that can be used by a hacker as a stepping-stone into a system or network. Using a common identifier makes it easier to share data across separate databases, tools, and services, which, until the creation of CVE in 1999, were not easily integrated. If a report from a security capability incorporates CVE Identifiers, you may then quickly and accurately access fix information in one or more separate CVE-compatible tools, services, and repositories to remediate the problem. With CVE, your tools and services can "speak" (i.e., exchange data) with each other. You will know exactly what each covers because CVE provides you with a baseline for evaluating the coverage of your tools. This means that you can determine which tools are most effective and appropriate for your organization's needs. In short, CVE-compatible tools, services, and databases will give you better coverage, easier interoperability, and enhanced security.

Bugtraq® IDs are identifiers for a commercially operated vulnerability database that are used in security advisories and alerts, as well as for discussions on the Bugtraq mailing list. CVE Identifiers are from an international information security effort that is publicly available and free to use. CVE Identifiers are used for the sole purpose of providing a common name. For this reason, CVE Identifiers are frequently used by researchers and the makers of security tools, websites, databases, and services as a standard method for identifying vulnerabilities and for cross-linking with other repositories that also use CVE Identifiers. A CVE Identifier will give you a standardized identifier for any given vulnerability or exposure. Knowing this identifier will allow you to quickly and accurately access information about the problem across multiple information sources that are CVE-compatible. For example, if you own a security tool whose reports contain references to CVE Identifiers, you may then access fix information in a separate CVE-compatible database. CVE also provides you with a baseline for evaluating the coverage of your tools.

The CVE list feeds the U.S. National Vulnerability Database (NVD), which then builds upon the information included in CVE entries to provide enhanced information for each CVE Identifier such as fix information, severity scores, and impact ratings. NVD also provides advanced searching features such as by individual CVE-ID; by OS; by vendor name, product name, and/or version number; and by vulnerability type, severity, related exploit range, and impact.

CVE is sponsored by the U.S. Department of Homeland Security. US-CERT is the operational arm of the DHS. US-CERT incorporates CVE Identifiers into its security advisories whenever possible and advocates the use of CVE and CVE-compatible products and services by the U.S. government and all members of the information security community. The MITRE Corporation maintains CVE and this public website, manages the compatibility program, and provides impartial technical guidance to the CVE Editorial Board throughout the process to ensure that CVE serves the public interest.[24,25]

2.4.5 SANS Institute Top Cyber Security Risks

The SANS Top Cyber Security Risks, formerly the SANS Twenty Most Critical Internet Security Vulnerabilities, is a consensus list of the most critical problem areas in Internet security that require immediate remediation if present on your systems. Step-by-step instructions and pointers to additional information useful for correcting these security flaws are included as part of the list. The SANS list includes CVE Identifiers to uniquely identify the vulnerabilities it describes. This helps system administrators use CVE-compatible products and services to make their networks more secure.[26-28]

2.4.6 U.S. Department of Defense Cyber Security and Information Systems Information Analysis Center (CSIAC)

In September 2012, the Data & Analysis Center for Software (DACS), Information Assurance Technology Analysis Center (IATAC), and Modeling and Simulation Information Analysis Center (MSIAC) were merged to create the Cyber Security and Information Systems Information Analysis Center (CSIAC). The CSIAC, one of eight Information Analysis Centers (IACs) sponsored by DTIC, performs the Basic Center of Operations (BCO) functions necessary to fulfill the mission and objectives applicable to the Department of Defense Research Development Test and Evaluation (RDT&E) and Acquisition communities' needs for cyber security, information assurance, knowledge management and information sharing, software-intensive systems engineering, and modeling and simulation.[29] In the past, the DACS has produced some great documents on software security and the SDL for the community, most notably, "Enhancing the Development Lifecycle to Produce Secure Software: A Reference Guidebook on Software Assurance" (2008)[30] and the joint IATAC/DACS report "Software Security Assurance: State-of-the-Art Report (SOAR)" (2008),[31] and we expect them to continue to do so under the umbrella of the CSIAC.

2.4.7 CERT, Bugtraq®, and SecurityFocus

In addition to the sources we have discussed so far, the Carnegie Mellon Computer Emergency Readiness Team (CERT),[32] Bugtraq,[33] and SecurityFocus[34] are three other sources to be aware of.

CERT provides timely alerts on security vulnerabilities as well as a weekly summarized bulletin on vulnerabilities ("CERT Cyber Security Bulletin"). Information in the bulletin includes CVSS scores as well as CVE IDs to uniquely identify vulnerabilities. The compilation is based on vulnerabilities recorded in the NIST NVD[35] over the previous week. We will be discussing the CVSS scoring process in more detail later in the book.

Bugtraq is an electronic security mailing list that provides information on security vulnerabilities as well as security bulletins and announcements from vendors. The list often contains additional information such as examples of exploitations as well as fixes for the issues identified. Bugtraq is part of Accenture®. There are other useful mailing lists as well, such as those dedicated to Microsoft, Linux®, IDS, and incidents.

2.5 Critical Tools and Talent

As with all security tasks, whether they are offensive or defensive in their approach, there is always a blend of process, technology, and people that is required to make it successful. So far, the processes and models that are available for software security have been discussed in this section. There are two elements of the technology (tool) side of the triad that will make or break you in terms of software security, and another on the people (talent) side.

2.5.1 *The Tools*

Three primary tools are basic to the SDL, which are categorized as fuzzing, static, and dynamic analysis tools. Although we will go over the details of the best practices for their use in the SDL later in the book, a high-level overview follows.

2.5.1.1 Fuzzing

Fuzz testing or fuzzing is a black-box software-testing technique that can be automated or semiautomated, which provides invalid, unexpected, or random data to the inputs of a computer software program. In other words, it finds implementation bugs or security flaws by using malformed/semi-malformed data injection in an automated fashion. Inputs to the software program are then monitored for exception returns such as crashes, failing built-in code assertions, and potential memory leaks. Fuzzing has become a key element in the testing for software or computer system security problems. Fuzz testing has a distinct advantage over other tools in that the test design is extremely simple and free of preconceptions about system behavior.

Fuzzing is a key element of software security and must be embedded in the SDL. There are many vendors to choose from in this space, and some developers even develop their own tools. As you will see later on in the book, the timing at which the fuzzing tools are used in the SDL is critical. It should also be noted that fuzzing is used for both security and quality assurance testing.

Fuzzing has recently been recognized as both a key element and a major deficiency in many software development programs, so much so that it is now a Department of Defense Information Assurance Certification and Accreditation Process (DIACAP) requirement.

2.5.1.2 Static Analysis

Static program analysis is the analysis of computer software that is performed without actually executing programs. It is predominantly used to perform analysis on a version of the source code; however, this kind of analysis may also be done on some form of the object code. In contrast, dynamic analysis is performed by actually executing software programs. Static analysis is performed by an automated software tool and should not be confused with human analysis or software security architectural reviews, which involve manual human code reviews, program understanding, and comprehension. When used properly, static analysis tools have a distinct advantage over human static analysis in that analysis can be performed much more frequently and with security knowledge generally superior to that of the standard software developer. It also frees up the time of seasoned software security architects or engineers so that they only need be brought in when absolutely necessary.

Static analysis, also known as static application security testing (SAST), identifies vulnerabilities during the development or quality assurance phase of a project. It provides line-of-code level detection that enables development teams to remediate vulnerabilities quickly.

The use of static analysis tools and your choice of the appropriate vendor for your environment is another technology factor key to your success. Any technology that beneficially automates any portion of the software development process should be welcome, but this software has become "shelf-ware" in many organizations because the right people and right process were not used in selecting the tool or tools. Not all tools in this space are created equal, and some are better at some languages than others, whereas others have great governance/risk/compliance (GRC) and metric analysis front ends. In some cases, you may have to use up to three different tools to be effective. In the end, you need to choose tools that support your language, are scalable, can be embedded with your development processes, and have minimum false positives.

Software development is a complex business, and anything you can do to make the process more repeatable, predictable, and reduce "friction" is a big win for most organizations. There are many benefits to using static analysis tools. The most important reasons include the following.

- Static analysis tools can scale. They can review a great deal of code very quickly, something humans cannot do very well.
- Static analysis tools don't get tired. A static analysis tool running for four straight hours at 2:00 a.m. is just as effective as if it runs during business hours. You can't say the same thing about human reviewers.
- Static analysis tools help developers learn about security vulnerabilities. In many cases, you can use these tools and educational resources from the vendor to educate your development teams about software security.

2.5.1.3 Dynamic Analysis

Dynamic program analysis is the analysis of computer software that is performed by executing programs on a real or virtual processor in real time. The objective is to find security errors in a program while it is running, rather than by repeatedly examining the code offline. By debugging a program in all the scenarios for which it is designed, dynamic analysis eliminates the need to artificially create situations likely to produce errors. It has a distinct advantage of having the ability to identify vulnerabilities that might have been false negatives and to validate findings in the static code analysis.

Dynamic analysis, also known as dynamic application security testing (DAST), identifies vulnerabilities within a production or production-ready application. These tools are used to quickly assess a system's overall security and are used within both the SDL and SDLC. The same advantages and cautions about using static analysis tools apply to dynamic analysis tools.

The timing of the use of SAST and DAST tools in the SDL is critical and takes place primarily in the design and development phase of the SDL we will be presenting later in this book, as shown in Figure 2.1.

2.5.2 The Talent

2.5.2.1 Software Security Architects

As mentioned in Chapter 1, qualified senior software security architects will make or break your software security program. On the people front, the most critical element of an effective software security program is a cadre of senior level 3 and 4 software security architects. These

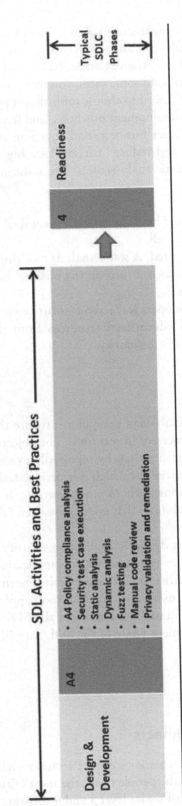

Figure 2.1 Design and development (A4) stage of the SDL activities and best practices.

are individuals who have 5 to 10 years of development/coding experience before they come into the security field and who are also experienced in the areas of software, networking, and cloud/SaaS architectural design.

These are not the typical folks in IT security who run tools; they are experienced architects who understand development and system architecture as well as they understand security. In addition, they must also have great political and people skills. These are the folks who are going to touch every element of the SDLC and SDL; they should be part of the sign-off process at each stage of the SDLC process, and they must be involved from pre-commit to post-release. They will make or break your software security practice and are key to its survival and success. Your senior software/application security architects are critical to handle product security escalations, train development team members, provide internal/external customer responses, and solve complex software/applications issues in SaaS and cloud environments.

Distinguishing between architectural drivers and other requirements is not simple, as it requires a complete understanding of the solution objectives. Software security architecture is an interactive process that involves assessment of the business value of system requirements and identifying the requirements that are most critical to the success of a system. These requirements include the functional requirements, the constraints, and the behavior properties of the solution, all of which must be classified and specified. These critical requirements are called *architectural drivers* because they shape the design of the system.

The security architect must figure out how, at the architectural level, necessary security technologies will be integrated into the overall system. In the cloud or SaaS environment, this includes network security requirements, such as firewalls, virtual private networks, etc. Architects explicitly document trust assumptions in each part of the system, usually by drawing trust boundaries (e.g., network traffic from outside the firewall is untrusted, but local traffic is trusted). Of course, these boundaries must reflect business requirements. For instance, high-security applications should not be willing to trust any unencrypted shared network media. Security requirements should come from the user. A typical job description for a seasoned software security architect might be as follows.

The software security architect is responsible for providing architectural and technical guidance to product security developers across all of Company X. The architect will design, plan, and implement secure coding practices and security testing methodology; ensure that practices meet software certification processes; drive the security testing of the products; test and evaluate security-related tools; and manage third-party vendors to meet those responsibilities above. Specific roles and responsibilities include the following:

- Drive overall software security architecture.
- Provide technical leadership in the comprehensive planning, development, and execution of Company X software security efforts.
- Work closely with product and engineering development teams to ensure that products meet or exceed customer security and certification requirements. This includes ensuring that the security architecture is well documented and communicated.
- Provide planning and input into the software engineering and product-development process related to security and sensitive to the constraints and needs of the business.
- Monitor security technology trends and requirements, such as emerging standards, for new technology opportunities.

- Develop and execute security plans. This may include managing joint development with third-party vendors, and providing guidance (with other departments) about the engineering and testing practices.
- Ensure, and create as needed, security policies, processes, practices, and operations to ensure reproducible development and high quality, while keeping costs under control.
- Engage in hands-on, in-depth analysis, review, and design of the software, including technical review and analysis of source code with a security perspective. Will include reviews of in-house developed code, as well as the review of technologies provided by third-party vendors.
- Provide a primary technical role in the security certifications process, including preparing extensive documentation and working with third-party evaluations.
- Provide training to staff, contractors, development, and quality assurance teams, and product/software security champions related to product security.
- Guide Company X software development teams through the Company X Security Development Lifecycle (SDL) for its SDLC by participating in design reviews, threat modeling, and in-depth security penetration testing of code and systems. These responsibilities extend to providing input on application design, secure coding practices, log forensics, log design, and application code security.

The software security architects are the cadre who will be critical in overseeing and training the efforts of software security champions that should be identified through a cross–business unit/software security education and awareness program. The architects will also spot and assess candidates for software security champions, as they are involved in various software product SDLs from concept commit to post-release.

2.5.2.2 Software Security Champions

Funding for corporate security departments—whether IT, physical, or software—is not likely to get any better in the foreseeable future, which means that you will have to be very judicious with your resources if you plan to be successful. As we implied earlier, seasoned software security architects are few and far between, and at best you will not likely be able to find and afford more than a handful in today's market. As you look at the SDL model used in this book or others referenced earlier in this chapter, you may be asking yourself how you can ever scale to this task given the resources that security software and the development teams working with them will have. The answer is that if you manage the software security team or have that function working for you, you will use the recruitment and leverage of software security champions (SSCs) to manage this daunting task. Candidates for this role should typically have a minimum of three to five years of software development experience; a passion for or background in software security; time to be trained in software security and on the centralized software security teams tools, plans, and processes; and, most important, must not only know how to develop (build) software but also how to deconstruct (take it apart) while "thinking like a hacker" regarding all possible paths or exploits (attack planes) that an adversary could take to exploit the software. Each product development organization should have at least one individual who has the technical capability to be trained as a software security champion and eventually as a junior software security architect to assist the centralized software security team in architecture security analysis/threat modeling. It is also important that SSCs be volunteers and not assignees who may lack the passion to succeed at this very challenging but rewarding role. Each business unit for software development within a company should have at least one SSC; for larger development organizations, it is preferable to have one for each tier product per business unit. A typical job description for a software security champion is as follows:

- SSCs must have a minimum of three to five years of software development experience; a passion for or background in software security; time to be trained in software security and on the centralized and business unit–specific software security tools, plans, and processes; and, most important, must not only know how to develop (build) software but also how to deconstruct it (take it apart) while "thinking like a hacker" regarding all possible paths or exploits (attack planes) that an adversary could take to exploit the software.
- Each product development organization will have one individual that has the technical capability to be trained as a software security architect to assist the centralized software security group in architecture security analysis/threat modeling. Ideally, each team should have an additional product security champion whose role is to assist as a change agent (more project/program–oriented individual) in addition to the technically oriented product security champion, if deemed necessary.
- Specific roles and responsibilities include:
  - Enforce the SDL: Assist the centralized software security group in assuring that the security tenets of confidentiality, integrity, availability, and privacy are adhered to in the SDL as part of the Company X SDLC.
  - Review: Assist the centralized software security team software security architects in conducting architecture security analysis, reviews, and threat modeling.
  - Tools Expert: Be the representative centralized software security team software security tool expert (e.g., static and dynamic, including fuzzing) within each development team, product group, and/or business unit.
  - Collocate: Be the eyes, ears, and advocate of the centralized software security team within each development team, product group, and business unit.
  - Attend Meetings: Participate in monthly phone meetings and, as budgets permit, twice-a-year face-to-face meetings, as members of a global Company X team of software security champions.

2.6 Principles of Least Privilege

In information security, computer science, and other fields, the principle of *least privilege* (also known as the principle of minimal privilege or the principle of least authority) requires that in a particular abstraction layer of a computing environment, every module (such as a process, a user, or a program, depending on the subject) must be able to access only the information and resources that are necessary for its legitimate purpose.[36,37]

Limiting the elevation of privilege is a significant part of threat modeling as a core component of the Architecture (A2) phase of our SDL, which we will discuss in Chapter 4. The concept of *elevation of privilege* is considered so important that it is the theme of a Microsoft Security Development Lifecycle card game designed to train developers and security professionals to quickly and easily find threats to software or computer systems.[38] An unauthorized privilege escalation attack takes advantage of programming errors or design flaws to grant the attacker elevated access to the network and its associated data and applications. These attacks can be either *vertical,* where the attacker grants himself privileges, or *horizontal,* where the attacker uses the same level of privileges he has already been granted, but assumes the identity of another user with similar privileges.

Ensuring least privilege prevents the disclosure of sensitive data and prevents unauthorized users from gaining access to programs or areas they were never meant to have. Software design should follow the principle of least privilege, and this is a critical element in software development. Limiting the level of privilege is critically important because the elevation of privilege can result in an attacker gaining authorizations beyond those granted to a normal user. For example, an attacker with general user privileges that are set for "read only" permissions may be able to hack the software to elevate his access to include "read and write." Facilitating least privilege requires that a user be given no more privilege than is necessary to perform a given task. During the design phase of the SDL/SDLC, you will need to determine the minimum set of privileges required to perform that job and restrict the user to a domain with those privileges and nothing more. Ensuring least privilege includes limiting not only user rights but also resource permissions such as CPU limits, memory, network, and file system permissions. This requires that multiple conditions have been met before granting permissions to an object because checking access to only one condition may not be adequate for strong security. For example, an attacker may be restricted from conducting a successful attack if he is able to obtain one privilege but not a second. Compartmenting software into separate components that require multiple checks for access can inhibit an attack or potentially prevent an attacker from taking over an entire system. Careful delegation of access rights can restrict attackers from successfully attacking software or a system. The minimum rights and access to the resource should be limited to the shortest duration necessary to perform the task.

2.7 Privacy

Protecting users' privacy is another important component of the SDL process and should be considered a system design principle of significant importance in all phases of the SDLC. Just as with a failure in security, a failure to protect the customer's privacy will lead to an erosion of trust. As more and more cases of unauthorized access to customers' personal information are disclosed in the press, the trust in software and systems to protect customers' data is deteriorating. In addition, many new privacy laws and regulations have placed an increased importance on including privacy in the design and development of both software and systems. As with security, software that has already progressed through the development life cycle can be very expensive to change; it is much less expensive to integrate privacy preservation methodologies and techniques into the appropriate phases of the SDLC to preserve the privacy of individuals and to protect personally identifiable information (PII) data. Some key privacy design principles included in Microsoft's SDL include the ability to provide appropriate notice about data that is collected, stored, or shared so that users can make informed decisions about their personal information; enable user policy and control; minimize data collection and sensitivity; and the protection of the storage and transfer of data.[39]

It is imperative that privacy protections be built into the SDLC through best practices implemented through the SDL. Ignoring the privacy concerns of users can invite blocked deployments, litigation, negative media coverage, and mistrust. We have incorporated privacy protection best practices into our SDL, which will be described in subsequent chapters.

2.8　The Importance of Metrics

In the words of Lord Kelvin, "If you cannot measure it, you cannot improve it."[40] This maxim holds true today as it applies to product security and the need to measure a software development organization's security posture accurately. Meaningful security metrics are critical as corporations grapple with regulatory and risk management requirements, tightening security budgets require shrewd security investments, and customers demand proof that security and privacy is being built into their products rather than through the historical post-release fixes.

Metrics tracking is like an insurance policy for your software projects and also assists in managing protection against vulnerabilities. As we have noted repeatedly, the cost of detecting a defect in successive stages of the SDLC is very high compared with detecting the same defect at the stage of the SDLC where the defect originated. Metrics can track these costs and provide significant help in various return-on-investment (ROI) calculations throughout the SDL/SDLC process. As shown in Figure 1.1, it costs little to avoid potential security defects early in development, especially compared to costing 10, 20, 50, or even 100 times that amount much later in development. A visual representation of the cost of fixing defects at different stages of the SDLC as part of the SDL process is given in Figure 2.2. It can be argued that the cost of preventing just one or two defects from going live is worth the cost of tracking metrics. The ability to foresee defects and remediate them is a good indicator of a healthy software security program, but quality metrics throughout the SDL/SDLC process can help in managing and often avoiding excessive remediation costs.

One goal of the SDL is to catch defects throughout the process as a multistaged filtering process rather than through a single activity or point in time, thus minimizing the remaining defects that lead to vulnerabilities. Each defect-removal activity can be thought of as a filter that removes some percentage of defects that can lead to vulnerabilities from the software product.[41] The more defect-removal filters there are in the software development life cycle, the fewer defects that can lead to vulnerabilities will remain in the software product when it is released. More important, early measurement of defects enables the organization to take corrective action early in the SDLC. Each time defects are removed, they are measured. Every defect-removal point becomes a measurement point. Defect measurement leads to something even more important than defect removal and prevention: It tells teams where they stand versus their goals, helps them decide whether to move to the next step or to stop and take corrective action, and indicates where to fix their process to meet their goals.[42] The SDL model that we will present in this book will focus on filtering out defects throughout the SDLC, with a particular focus on phases S1–S3 of our model (see Figure 2.3).

Security metrics can be an invaluable resource for assessing the effectiveness of an organization's software security program. Meaningful metrics can be used to continually improve the product security program's performance, substantiate regulatory compliance, raise the level of security awareness among management and stakeholders, and assist decision makers with funding requests. Without metrics, organizations are reduced to operating their product security programs under FUD: fear, uncertainty, and doubt.

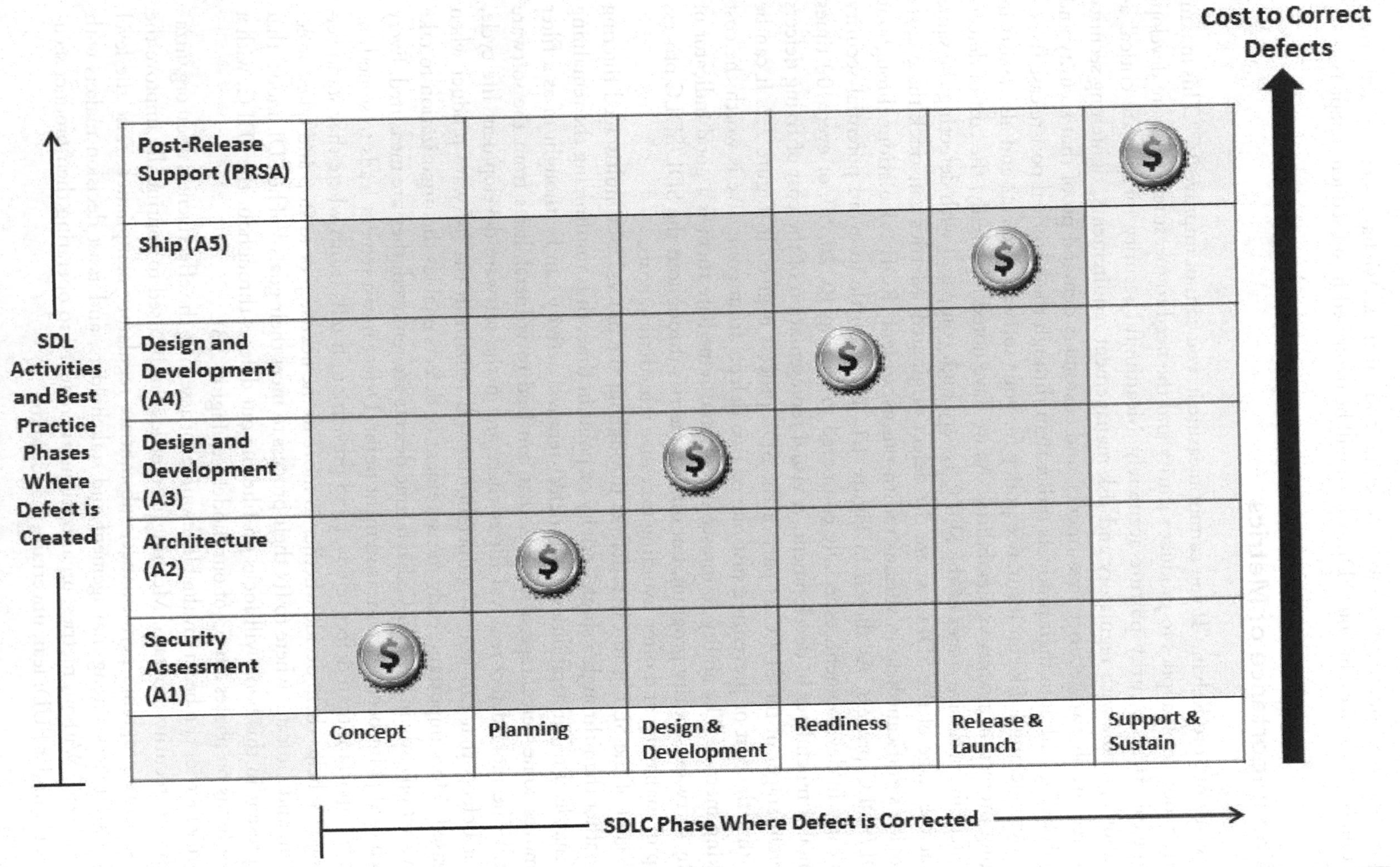

Figure 2.2 Visual representation of the cost of fixing defects at different stages of the SDLC as part of the SDL process.

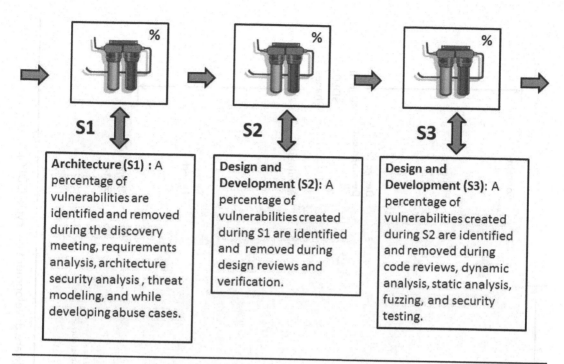

Figure 2.3 SDL phases S1–S3: defect identification and remediation filtering process.

Meaningful security metrics allow an organization to determine the effectiveness of its security controls. To measure the security posture of an organization effectively, product security must first ensure that the proper framework is in place in order to derive meaningful metric data. This includes a product security governance model suited to the entity's strategic and operational requirements. Such a model should support implementation of practical product security policies and procedures, consistent deployment of best practices and measures, and require strong executive management support across the organization. Best practices dictate a model under which security is managed as an enterprise issue—horizontally, vertically, and cross-functionally throughout the organization. This model is better suited to enable consistent monitoring, measurement, and reporting of an organization's product-security posture.

For security to be measured effectively, it must be managed effectively. As companies struggle to protect valuable information assets and justify risk-based decision making, a centralized metrics reporting mechanism is crucial for producing meaningful metrics and providing an ongoing assessment of the state of product security within a software development organization.

Rather than include a separate chapter on metrics in this book, our approach will be to include metrics in each step of the SDL model presented. This will cumulate in a discussion of the use of SDL metrics in managing the overall corporate software security program.

2.9 Mapping the Security Development Lifecycle to the Software Development Life Cycle

Whatever form of SDL you use, whether it is one that already exists, one you developed yourself, or a combination of both, you must map it to your current SDLC to be effective. Figure 2.4

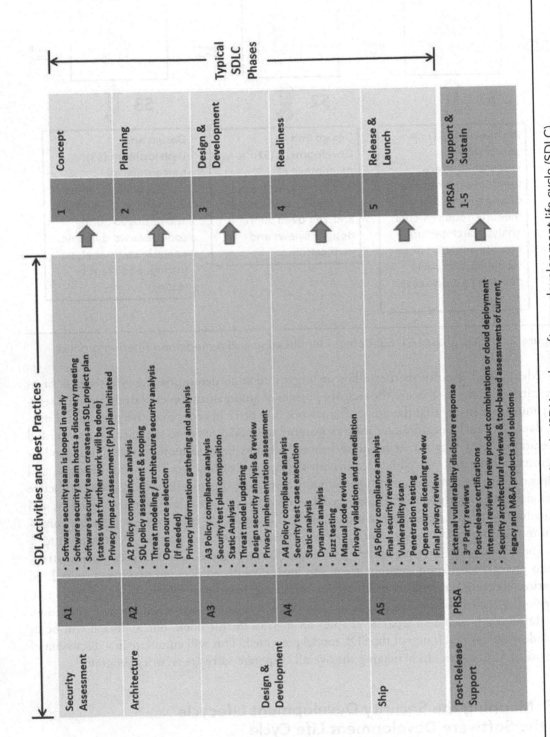

Figure 2.4 Mapping the security development lifecycle (SDL) to the software development life cycle (SDLC).

is an SDL activity and best practices model that the authors have developed and mapped to the typical SDLC phases. Each SDL activity and best practice is based on real-world experience and examples from the authors to showing the reader that security can be built into each of the SDLC phases—a mapping of security to the SDLC, if you will. If security is built into each SDLC phase, then the software has a higher probability of being secure by default, and later software changes are less likely to compromise overall security. Another benefit of this mapping is that you will have presumably worked with the owner(s) and stakeholders of the SDL, which will serve to build buy-in, efficiency, and achievable security in both the operational and business processes of the SDLC and will include the developers, product and program managers, business managers, and executives.

Subsequent chapters will describe each phase of the SDL presented in Figure 2.4 in detail. In addition, each phase is broken down individually in Figures 2.5 to 2.10.

Please note that, unlike some of the SDLs you may have seen before, we include post-release support activities and best practices in our SDL, as shown in Figure 2.10. We have included this because most software security teams or their equivalent, especially those in mid-sized or small companies, do not have the luxury of having an independent Product Security Incident Response Team (PSIRT)—a team dedicated solely to conduct security M&A assessments, third-party reviews, post-release certifications, internal reviews for new product combinations of cloud deployments, or review for legacy software that is still in use or about to be re-used. It takes some outside-the-box thinking to manage all of this with a small team. Later in the book, we will discuss leveraging seasoned software security architects, software security champions, specialized software, and third-party contractors to accomplish SDL goals and activities.

2.10 Software Development Methodologies

Earlier in the chapter we discussed the various SDLC models and provided a visual overview of our mapping of our SDL model to a generic SDLC. It should be noted, however, that multiple software development methodologies are used within the various SDLC models. Every software development methodology approach acts as a basis for applying specific frameworks to develop and maintain software and is less concerned with the technical side but rather the organizational aspects of the process of creating software. Principal among these development methodologies are the Waterfall model and Agile together with its many variants and spin-offs. The Waterfall model is the oldest and most well-known software development methodology. The distinctive feature of the Waterfall model is its sequential step-by-step process from requirements. Agile methodologies are gaining popularity in the industry, although they comprise a mix of traditional and new software development practices. You may see Agile or traditional Waterfall or maybe a hybrid of the two. We have chosen to give a high-level description of the Waterfall and Agile development models and a variant or two of each as an introduction to software development methodologies. In this book, we are providing a detailed framework in a Waterfall-type format, with associated lists that you can pick and choose from to meet the needs of your environment for full or partial upgrade software-development needs. In Chapter 9, we will show you how you can "build your own" SDL, building security into a process that is appropriate for your specific needs and environment, whether it be Agile, DevOps, Cloud, or a combination of two or more of these.

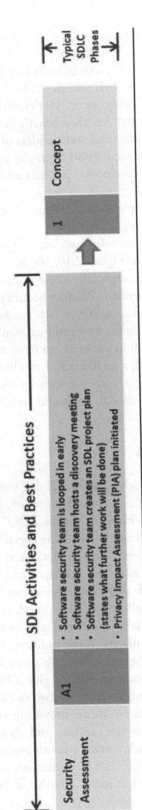

Figure 2.5 Chapter 3: Security Assessment (A1): SDL activities and best practices.

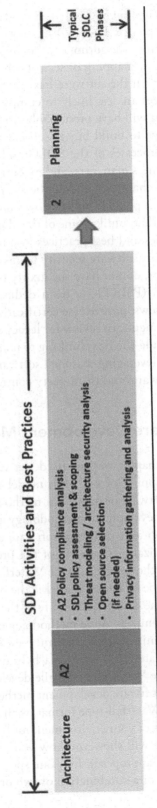

Figure 2.6 Chapter 4: Architecture (A2): SDL activities and best practices.

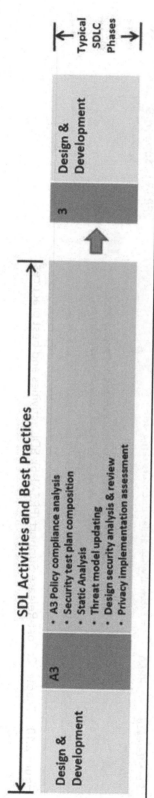

Figure 2.7 Chapter 5: Design and Development (A3): SDL activities and best practices.

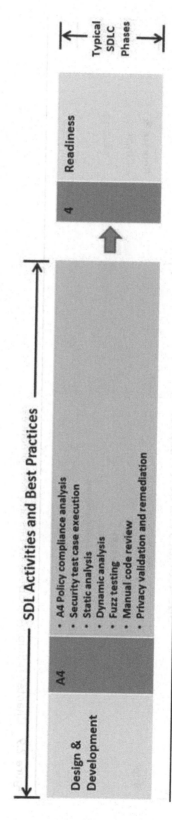

Figure 2.8 Chapter 6: Design and Development (A4): SDL activities and best practices.

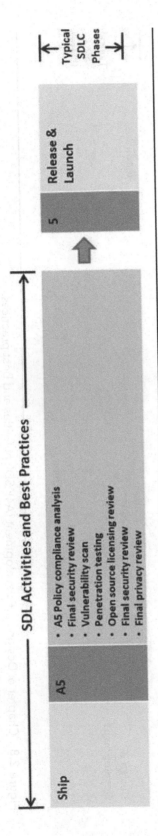

Figure 2.9 Chapter 7: Ship (A5): SDL activities and best practices.

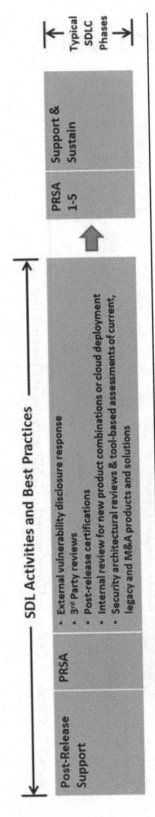

Figure 2.10 Chapter 8: Post-Release Support (PRSA1-5): SDL activities and best practices.

2.10.1 Waterfall Development

Waterfall development (see Figure 2.11) is another name for the more traditional approach to software development. This approach is typically higher risk, more costly, and less efficient than the Agile approach that will be discussed later in this chapter. The Waterfall approach uses requirements that are already known, each stage is signed off before the next commences, and it requires extensive documentation because this is the primary communication mechanism throughout the process. Although most development organizations are moving toward Agile methods of development, the Waterfall method may still be used when requirements are fully understood and not complex. Since the plan is not to revisit a phase using this methodology once it is completed, it is imperative that you do it right the first time: There is generally no second chance.

Although Waterfall development methodologies vary, they tend to be similar in that practitioners try to keep to the initial plan, do not have working software until very late in the cycle, assume they know everything upfront, minimize changes through a change control board (i.e., assume that change is bad and can be controlled), put most responsibility on the project manager (PM), optimize conformance to schedule and budget, generally use weak controls, and allow realization of value only upon completion. They are driven by a PM-centric approach under the belief that if the processes in the plan are followed, then everything will work as planned. In today's development environment, most of the above-mentioned items are considered negative attributes of the Waterfall methodology and are just a few of the reasons that industry is moving toward Agile development methodologies. The Waterfall approach may be looked on as an assembly-line approach, which may be excellent when applied properly to hardware but which has shortcomings in comparison to Agile when it comes to software development.

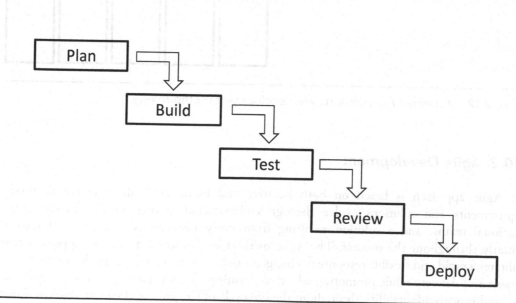

Figure 2.11   Waterfall software development methodology.

2.10.1.1 Iterative Waterfall Development

The iterative Waterfall development model (see Figure 2.12) is an improvement over the standard Waterfall model. This approach carries less risk than a traditional Waterfall approach but is more risky and less efficient than the Agile approach. In the iterative Waterfall method, the overall project is divided into various phases, each executed using the traditional Waterfall method. Dividing larger projects into smaller identifiable phases results in a smaller scope of work for each phase, and the end deliverable of each phase can be reviewed and improved if necessary before moving to the next phase. Overall risk is thus reduced. Although the iterative method is an improvement over the traditional Waterfall method, you are more likely to face an Agile approach to software development rather than either a standard or an iterative Waterfall methodology in today's environment.

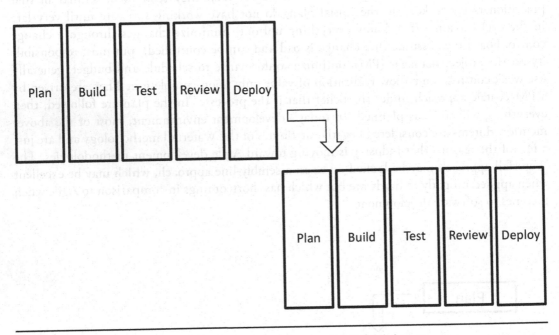

Figure 2.12   Iterative Waterfall software development methodology.

2.10.2 Agile Development

The Agile approach is based on both iterative and incremental development methods. Requirements and solutions evolve through collaboration among self-organizing, cross-functional teams, and a solution resulting from every iteration is reviewed and refined regularly throughout the process. The Agile method is a timeboxed iterative approach that facilitates a rapid and flexible response to change, which in turn encourages evolutionary development and delivery while promoting adaptive planning, development, teamwork, collaboration, and process adaptability throughout the life cycle of the project. Tasks are broken down into small increments that require minimal planning. These iterations have short time frames called "timeboxes," which can last from one to four weeks. Multiple iterations may be required to release a product or new features. A cross-functional team is responsible for all software development functions in each iteration, including planning, requirements analysis, design, coding, unit testing, and acceptance testing. An Agile project is typically cross-functional, and self-organizing teams operate independently from any corporate hierarchy or other corporate roles of individual team members, who themselves decide how to meet each iteration's requirements. This allows the project to adapt to changes quickly and minimizes overall risk. The goal is to have an available release at the end of the iteration, and a working product is demonstrated to stakeholders at the end of each iteration.

2.10.2.1 Scrum

Scrum (see Figure 2.13) is an iterative and incremental Agile software development method for managing software projects and product or application development. Scrum adopts an empirical approach, accepting that the problem cannot be fully understood or defined and focusing instead on maximizing the team's ability to deliver quickly and to respond to emerging requirements. This is accomplished through the use of co-located, self-organizing teams in which all disciplines can be represented. In contrast to traditional planned or predictive methodologies, this concept facilitates the ability to handle churn resulting from customers that change the requirements during project development. The basic unit of development for Scrum is called a "sprint," and a sprint can last from one week to one month. Each sprint is timeboxed so that finished portions of a product are completed on time. A prioritized list of requirements is

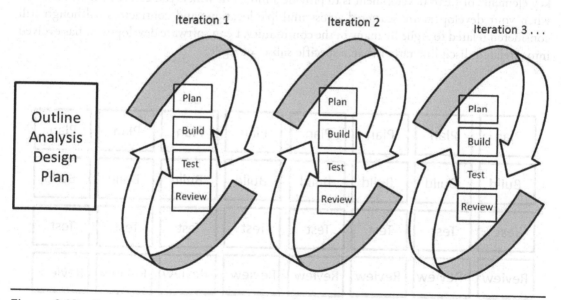

Figure 2.13 Scrum software development methodology.

derived from the product backlog, and if they are not completed during the sprint, they are left out and returned to the product backlog. The team demonstrates the software after each sprint is completed. Generally accepted value-added attributes of Scrum include its use of adaptive planning; that it requires feedback from working software early during the first sprint (typically two weeks) and often; that it stresses the maximization of good change, such as focusing on maximizing learning throughout the project; that it puts most responsibility on small, dedicated, tight-thinking, adaptive teams that plan and re-plan their own work; that it has strong and frequent controls; that it optimizes business value, time to market, and quality; and that it supports realization of value earlier, potentially after every sprint.

2.10.2.2 Lean Development

In our experience, for those of you who have recently moved from or are in the process of moving from a Waterfall methodology for software development, Scrum is the most likely variant of Agile that you will encounter. Lean (see Figure 2.14) is another methodology that is gaining popularity and is thus worth mentioning. Unfortunately, there are many definitions of Lean, and it is a methodology that is evolving in many directions. Although Lean is similar to Scrum in that it focuses on features rather than groups of features, it takes this idea one step further in that, in its simplest form, you select, plan, develop, test, and deploy one feature before you select, plan, develop, test, and deploy the next feature. The objective is to further isolate risk to the level of an individual feature. This isolation has the advantage of focusing on eliminating "waste" when possible and doing nothing unless it is absolutely necessary or relevant. Lean development can be summarized by seven principles based on Lean manufacturing principle concepts: (1) eliminate waste, (2) amplify learning, (3) decide as late as possible, (4) deliver as fast as possible, (5) empower the team, (6) build integrity in, and (7) see the whole. One of the key elements of Lean development is to provide a model in which you can see the whole, even when your developers are scattered across multiple locations and contractors. Although still considered related to Agile by many in the community, Lean software development has evolved into a related discipline rather than a specific subset of Agile.

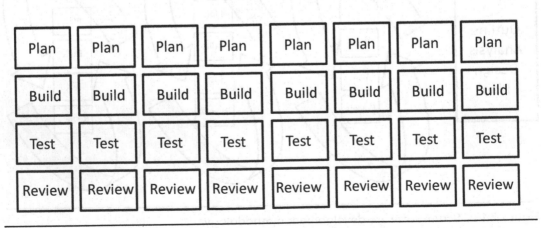

Figure 2.14   Lean software development methodology.

2.11 Summary

In this chapter we described the importance and applicability of the SDL and its relation and inclusion into the SDLC. Throughout the discussion, we highlighted the models, methodologies, tools, human talent, and metrics for managing and overcoming the challenges of making software secure. Our SDL process encompasses a series of security-focused activities and best practices at each of the phases of our SDL. These activities and best practices include the development of threat models during software design; the use of static analysis code-scanning tools during implementation; and the conduct of code reviews, security testing, and metrics. Lastly, we discussed our model for mapping the SDL to the SDLC and the various popular software methodologies to which we will apply the elements and best practices of our SDL in Chapter 9. In the next chapter, we will start the process of walking through each step of our SDL model and show that incremental implementation of the elements of the SDL will yield incremental improvements in an overall holistic approach to software security.

Chapter Quick-Check

1. The paradigm of Building Security In begins with the:
   a. Analysis phase
   b. Design phase
   c. Specification phase
   d. Development phase

2. The objectives of an SDL are to achieve all of the following except:
   a. To reduce the number of security vulnerabilities in software
   b. To reduce the severity of security vulnerabilities in software
   c. To eliminate threats to the software
   d. To document a complete understanding of the vulnerabilities in software

3. The fundamental approach to security in which an object has only the necessary rights and privileges to perform its task with no additional permissions is a description of:
   a. Layered security
   b. Least privilege
   c. Role-based security
   d. Clark-Wilson model

4. Which of the following statements best describes BSIMM?
   a. BSIMM is used to measure the maturity of a software assurance program by looking for evidence of security best practices in the SDLC.
   b. BSIMM is used to measure the maturity of a software assurance program by looking for evidence of security procedures in the SDLC.
   c. BSIMM is used to measure the maturity of a software assurance program by looking for evidence of security activities in the SDLC.
   d. BSIMM is used to measure the maturity of a software assurance program by looking for evidence of security requirements in the SDLC.

Exercises

1. What attributes of applications should be used to determine what level of attention to security the application should appropriately have? Since no two applications are the same, how can one prioritize one over the other to make sure that scarce resources are not being wasted?

2. Any organization that handles or processes credit card data must comply with the standards established by the Payment Card Industry (PCI) group that represents the international credit card issuers (Visa, MasterCard, American Express, etc.). Within the Data Security Standard (DSS), Section 6 is specific to securing applications and software that process payment card data. What are these requirements? How do they affect how a security development lifecycle is designed and implemented? In complying with PCI-DSS, what other industry secure development standards are also met?

3. The stakes for high-quality and secure software are high and getting higher as autonomous vehicles replace traditional vehicles and as machine learning and artificial intelligence (AI) find their way into making decisions about our daily lives. What types of guidance can you find on the Web to help management and development teams understand these stakes and prepare them to meet the responsibilities of software written that makes choices related to life and limb?

References

1. Microsoft Corporation. (2021). "About the Microsoft SDL." Retrieved from https://www.microsoft.com/en-us/securityengineering/sdl/about#:~:text=The%20Microsoft%20Security%20Development%20Lifecycle%20%28SDL%29%20was%20an,the%20software%20development%20process%20at%20Microsoft%20in%202004

2. bssim.com. (2021). "SSDL Touchpoints." Retrieved from https://www.bsimm.com/framework/software-security-development-lifecycle.html

3. owasp.org. (2021). "OWASP Code Review Guide." Retrieved from https://owasp.org/www-project-code-review-guide/

4. Cisco Systems. (2021). "Cisco Secure Development Lifecycle (CSDL)." Retrieved from https://www.cisco.com/c/dam/en_us/about/doing_business/trust-center/docs/cisco-secure-development-lifecycle.pdf

5. Microsoft Corporation. (2008). "Microsoft Security Development Lifecycle (SDL) Optimization Model." Retrieved from https://studylib.net/doc/7039753/introduction-to-the-sdl-optimization-model

6. Ibid.

7. bssim.com. (2021). "About BSIMM." Retrieved from https://www.bsimm.com/about.html

8. owasp.org. (2021). "OWASP SAMM." Retrieved from https://owasp.org/www-project-samm/

9. bssim.com. (2021). "BSIMM Framework." Retrieved from https://www.bsimm.com/framework.html

10. bssim.com. (2021). "BSIMM 12." Retrieved from https://www.bsimm.com/download.html

11. owasp.org. (2021). "OWASP SAMM." Retrieved from https://owasp.org/www-project-samm/

12. ISO. (2013). "ISO/IEC 27034-1:201: Information Technology—Security Techniques—Application Security—Part 1: Overview and Concepts." Retrieved from http://www.iso.org/iso/catalogue_detail.htm?csnumber=44378

13. Pickel, J. (May 2013). "ISO/IEC 27034—Why, What, and How." PowerPoint presentation at the 2013 Microsoft Software Development Conference, delivered on February 25, 2013, San Francisco, CA.

14. Ashord, W. (2013, May 13). "Microsoft Declares Conformance with ISO 27034." Computer Weekly.com. Retrieved from http://www.computerweekly.com/news/2240184149/Microsoft-declares-conformance-with-ISO-27034-1

15. SAFECode. (2021). "About SAFECode." Retrieved from https://safecode.org/about-safecode/

16. SAFECode. (2018). "Fundamental Practices for Secure Software Development, 3rd ed., Fundamental Practices for Secure Software Development: Essential Elements of a Secure Development Lifecycle Program—March 2018." Retrieved from https://safecode.org/wp-content/uploads/2018/03/SAFECode_Fundamental_Practices_for_Secure_Software_Development_March_2018.pdf

17. Software Engineering Institute. (2021). "Secure Development Research." Retrieved from https://www.sei.cmu.edu/our-work/secure-development/index.cfm

18. mitre.org. (2021). "About CWE." Retrieved from https://cwe.mitre.org/about/index.html

19. U.S. Department of Homeland Security. (2021). "Software Assurance." Retrieved from https://www.cisa.gov/uscert/sites/default/files/publications/infosheet_SoftwareAssurance.pdf

20. U.S. National Institute of Standards and Technology. (2012). "Introduction to SAMATE." Retrieved from http://samate.nist.gov/index.php/Introduction_to_SAMATE.html

21. U.S. National Institute of Standards and Technology. (2008). NIST Special Publication 800-64, Revision 2: "Security Considerations in the System Development Life Cycle," October 2008. Retrieved from http://csrc.nist.gov/publications/nistpubs/800-64-Rev2/SP800-64-Revision2.pdf

22. U.S. National Institute of Standards and Technology. (2012). "National Vulnerability Database, Version 2.2." Retrieved from http://nvd.nist.gov

23. U.S. National Institute of Standards and Technology. (2021). "CVSS Version 2: Common Vulnerability Scoring System Calculator." Retrieved from http://nvd.nist.gov/cvss.cfm?version=2

24. cve.org. (2021). Common Vulnerabilities and Exposures (CVE) homepage. Retrieved from https://www.cve.org

25. cve.org. (2021). Frequently Asked Questions (FAQs). Retrieved from https://www.cve.org/ResourcesSupport/FAQs

26. SANS Institute. (2012). "Twenty Critical Security Controls for Effective Cyber Defense: Consensus Audit Guidelines." Retrieved from http://www.sans.org/critical-security-controls

27. The MITRE Corporation. (2012). "CVE-Compatible Products and Services." Retrieved from http://cve.mitre.org/compatible/compatible.html

28. The MITRE Corporation. (2012). "CVE Frequently Asked Questions." Retrieved from http://cve.mitre.org/about/faqs.html

29. U.S. Department of Defense Cyber Security and Information Systems Information Analysis Center (CSIAC). (2012). CSIAC webpage. Retrieved from https://www.thecsiac.com/group/csiac

30. Goertzel, K., et al. (2008). "Enhancing the Development Life Cycle to Produce Secure Software: A Reference Guidebook on Software Assurance, Version 2," October 2008. Retrieved from https://www.academia.edu/1383839/Enhancing_the_Development_Life_Cycle_to_Produce_Secure_Software_A_Reference_Guidebook_on_Software_Assurance

31. Goertzel, K., et al. (2008). "Software Security Assurance: State-of-the-Art Report (SOAR)," July 31, 2008. Retrieved from http://iac.dtic.mil/iatac/download/security.pdf

32. Cert.org. (2013). Carnegie Mellon cert.org webpage. Retrieved from http://www.cert.org

33. SecurityFocus. (2013). Bugtraq website. Retrieved from http://www.securityfocus.com/archive/1

34. SecurityFocus. (2013). Security website. Retrieved from http://www.securityfocus.com

35. National Institute of Standards and Technology. (2013). National Vulnerability Database webpage. Retrieved from http://web.nvd.nist.gov/view/vuln/search

36. Denning, P. J. (1976, December). "Fault Tolerant Operating Systems." *ACM Computing Surveys*, vol. 8, no. 4, pp. 359–389. DOI: 10.1145/356678.356680.
37. Saltzer, J., and Schroeder, M. (1975, September). "The Protection of Information in Computer Systems." *Proceedings of the IEEE*, vol. 63, no. 9, pp. 1278–1308. DOI: 10.1109/PROC.1975.9939.
38. Microsoft Corporation. (2012). "Elevation of Privilege (EOP) Card Game." Retrieved from http://www.microsoft.com/security/sdl/adopt/eop.aspx
39. Microsoft Corporation. (2012). "Microsoft Security Development Lifecycle (SDL), Version 3.2." Retrieved from http://www.microsoft.com/en-us/download/details.aspx?id=24308
40. Quotationsbook.com. (2012). Lord Kelvin quote. Retrieved from http://quotationsbook.com/quote/46180
41. Noopur, D. (2013, July). "Secure Software Development Life Cycle Processes." Retrieved from https://www.cisa.gov/uscert/bsi/articles/knowledge/sdlc-process/secure-software-development-life-cycle-processes
42. Ibid.

Chapter 3

Security Assessment (A1): SDL Activities and Best Practices

CHAPTER OVERVIEW

In Chapter 3, we introduce the first phase of our security development lifecycle (SDL). This phase (A1) is called Security Assessment. We will describe different activities within this phase, why it is important, and then walk the reader through key success factors, deliverables, and metrics from this phase.

CHAPTER TAKE-AWAYS

- Explore the practices that compose the Security Assessment (Phase A1) of the security development lifecycle (SDL).
- Document the key success factors for completion of Phase A1.
- Create initial, draft deliverables for Phase A1 for the case study in Appendix A.
- Prepare an initial Privacy Impact Assessment (PIA) plan for the case study in Appendix A.

3.1 Software Security Team Is Looped in Early

Security Assessment (A1) is the first phase of our SDL (see Figure 3.1). This is the phase in which the project team identifies the product risk profile and the needed SDL activities; in some SDLs, it is called the discovery phase. An initial project outline for security milestones and controls is developed and integrated into the development project schedule to allow proper planning as changes occur. Throughout this phase, four principal questions should be addressed to determine what is required to ensure the security of the software:

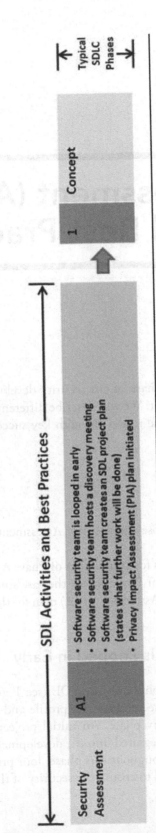

Figure 3.1 Security Assessment (A1): SDL activities and best practices.

1. How critical is the software to meeting the customers' mission?
2. What security objectives are required by the software (e.g., confidentiality, integrity, and availability [CIA], as described in Chapter 1)?
3. What regulations and policies are applicable in determining what is to be protected?
4. What threats are possible in the environment in which the software will be operating?

During the initial kick-off meeting, all key stakeholders should discuss, identify, and have a common understanding of the security and privacy implications, considerations, and requirements. The initial set of key security milestones, including time frames or development triggers that signal a security step is approaching, is also outlined in these discussions to enable the developers to plan to build security requirements and associated constraints into the project. It also reminds project leaders that many decisions being made have security implications that should be weighed appropriately as the project continues. These discussions should also include the identification of all sources of security requirements, including relevant laws, regulations, and standards.

Privacy, often neglected as part of the SDL in the past, is assessed at this phase as well. The Privacy Impact Assessment (PIA) process evaluates issues and privacy impact rating related to the privacy of personally identifiable information (PII) in the software and will be initiated during this stage of the development process.

Software development life cycles (SDLCs) typically have formalized kick-off meetings, and it is important that the software security team is included to ensure that security is a key element of the SDLC and is built into the process. An in-person or live web conference meeting will give attendees and stakeholders an important opportunity to gauge understanding and awareness. Bringing the security team into the development process early is the most cost-effective way to enable risk identification, planning, and mitigation. Early identification and mitigation of security vulnerabilities and misconfigurations will result in a lower cost of security control implementation and vulnerability mitigation, provide awareness of potential engineering challenges caused by mandatory security controls, and identify shared security services and reuse of security strategies and tools to reduce development costs while improving security posture through proven methods and techniques. The early involvement of the security team will enable the developers to plan security requirements and associated constraints into the project. It also reminds project leaders that many decisions being made have security implications that should be weighed appropriately as the project continues. Early planning and awareness will result in cost and time saving through proper risk management planning. Security discussions should be performed as part of, not separate from, the development project to ensure solid understandings among project personnel of business decisions and their risk implications to the overall development project.[1]

3.2 Software Security Hosts a Discovery Meeting

The discovery meeting is essentially an SDL kick-off meeting where the key SDLC stakeholders get on the same page at the beginning of the process so that security is built in rather than bolted on post-release. Security planning in the discovery meeting should include preparations for the entire system life cycle, including the identification of key security milestones and deliverables, as well as tools and technologies. Special consideration should be given to items that may need to be procured, such as software security testing and assessment tools and the potential use of third-party software security architects or engineers, if staff augmentation is needed or the customer requires third-party attestation. Other resource impacts such as active testing, accreditation, and required training must be considered as well. A series of milestones or security meetings should be planned to discuss each of the security considerations throughout the system development. The outcomes of the discovery meeting are typically in terms of decisions that are made for future activities, which are followed later in the SDL by actual security or privacy activities. A project schedule should integrate security activities to ensure proper planning of any future decisions associated with schedules and resources. All meeting participants and stakeholders should walk away from this meeting with a common understanding of the security implications, considerations, and requirements for the software.

The following four questions should be addressed in this phase to determine the security controls that will be required for the software being developed:

1. How critical is the system to meeting the organization's mission?
2. What are the security objectives required by the software in terms of confidentiality, integrity, and availability (CIA)?
3. What regulations and policies are applicable in determining what is to be protected?
4. What threats are possible in the environment where the system will be operating?

Key tasks during the discovery meeting include the following:

- Develop an initial project outline for security milestones, which will be integrated into the development project schedule and will allow proper planning as changes occur.
- Identify the sources for the security requirements, such as relevant laws, regulations, standards, and customer requirements.
- Identify any required certification and/or accreditation requirements and the resources required for them.
- Identify any third-party or open-source software that will be required.
- Identify the common security controls that will be used for the software being developed, including those that will be needed if the software is to be used in a SaaS/cloud environment or as part of a larger solution using multiple software products.
- Identify any API security requirements.
- Identify and define the required security reporting metrics in both tactical and strategic (business) terms.
- Develop an initial framework of key security milestones, including time frames or development triggers that will signal a security step is approaching.
- Define the security responsibilities of the core software security team, the software security champions, developers, privacy team, and any other stakeholders required to support security during the SDL/SDLC process.
- Identify and document the software security design, architecture, and security coding practices to be used.
- Identify security testing and assessment techniques that will be used.
- Lay out a pre-privacy impact assessment process, including the determination of information categorization and identification of known special handling requirements to

transmit, store, or create information, such as personally identifiable information, and preliminary identification of any privacy requirements.

- When possible, project artifacts such as meeting minutes, briefings, and role identifications should be standardized and provided to developers for proper level-of-effort planning. This should be an ongoing process throughout the SDL.

3.3 Software Security Team Creates an SDL Project Plan

This can actually be considered initial project planning because the formal plan will be finalized as an outcome of the design phase, which will be covered in the next chapter. At this stage, the SDL project plan should outline security milestones based on the information gained during the discovery phase in 3.1 and integrate them into the overall SDLC schedule to allow proper planning as changes occur. As in the discovery phase, activities may be more in terms of decisions translated into milestones that will be followed by security activities. This project plan integrates the common understanding of security expectations identified in the discovery phase reflecting the initial schedule of security and privacy activities or decisions.

3.4 Privacy Impact Assessment (PIA) Plan Initiated

There are a number of methods available that can be used to ensure privacy protection and for management. In the past, however, privacy tools have generally been applied in an ad hoc way, or in a piecemeal fashion to address immediate issues. As with security, these issues are typically addressed post-release. Just as with security, treating privacy as a secondary consideration or as an issue for future exploration during system design does not provide an effective level of privacy protection. Addressing components of privacy issues and not through a holistic design and implementation leads to further potential privacy issues. Privacy must be a fundamental design consideration that is integrated into every phase of the SDLC.

There are a growing number of privacy regulatory requirements on a variety of levels—state, federal, and international—resulting in a patchwork of compliance requirements that have serious penalties for noncompliance. The cloud adds to the complexity of boundaries and requirements. Rather than devote an entire chapter to recent and upcoming privacy requirements and the potential ramifications of each, we will discuss the best practices needed to adequately cover a majority of what you will face in terms of privacy, regulatory, and policy compliance. Software programs are designed to integrate with the user's computer and, therefore, may be able to access and store personal information. Software developers must adhere to the guidelines and privacy policies that relate to the operating systems and platforms for which their software is designed. The bottom line is that when customers entrust your company with sensitive information, every employee is obligated to protect that information. As with security, privacy violations have significant implications for the trust customers have in you, which in turn will affect your company's reputation and the potential revenue from the software you develop.

Before you can begin developing a PIA, you will need to evaluate what regulatory legislation or policies are applicable to the software you are developing. In some models, this is called the data sensitivity assessment. Since most developers do not have a background in law, and regulators generally do not have a background in software development, understanding the issues surrounding regulatory compliance can be difficult and frustrating. It is often very difficult for developers to understand fully the language and requirements described by legislation, and it is often not easy to pin down explicit software requirements. To successfully translate regulations into requirements, it will be necessary to engage with your corporate legal counsel and any external legal privacy experts who may be on retainer. If you happen to have a chief privacy officer (CPO), this person can be an ideal partner who can offer you the resources and training you will need to meet the challenge of building privacy into the SDL and ultimately the SDLC.

Microsoft®'s "Privacy Guidelines for Developing Software Products and Services"[2] and NIST Special Publication 800-64 Revision 2: "Security Considerations in the System Development Life Cycle"[3] are among the most popular references for developing a PIA in your SDL: You can use either in its entirety or as a template to develop your own. Unfortunately, Microsoft's "Privacy Guidelines for Developing Software Products and Services" is no longer available; however, its content is still relevant and of value. The key elements that you need from that document are included in the remainder of this section and are also covered in Chapter 5. No matter what methodology you use, the following should be included in your PIA:

- **Summary of the Legislation:** Explains the act from a developer's point of view, telling you what you need to know in order to understand its implications on your application development.
- **Required Process Steps:** Explains in more depth which requirements are relevant to software developers. Generally speaking, this section describes what types of data are considered sensitive and how they need to be protected.
- **Technologies and Techniques:** Explains strategies and techniques for meeting the legislative requirements. These are separated into five main categories: Confidentiality, Integrity, Availability, Auditing and Logging, and Authentication.
- **Additional Resources:** Provides links where you can gather more information on the legislation in question.[4]

The primary task of the PIA process is the determination of need in the system, along with an initial definition of the problem to be solved. The PIA created at this phase is only a preliminary version for initial system specifications and requirements and is designed to guide developers in assessing privacy through the early stages of development. For simplicity, we have included only the privacy design principles requirements analysis and part of the initial PIA analysis. At its core, this stage of the PIA is the planning, documentation, and assessment of preliminary requirements for PII and personal information used by the software and includes or accesses the following:

- **Education of stakeholders.** All stakeholders should be educated on the "four C's" of privacy design (comprehension, consciousness, control, and consent) at the Security Assessment (A1) discovery and kick-off meeting. The architects and developers should be asking whether they need to collect the data and have a valid business need to do so, and whether the customer will support the software's business purpose for collecting their PII.
- **Additional software interaction.** External system processes, other systems interacting with the new software and their use of PII, personal information, and system users.

- **Collection of PII.** The purposes and requirements for the collection of PII.
- **PII storage retention.** Proposed personal information retention periods and reasons for the lengths of those periods.
- **Access.** Determine what entities will have access to the PII and personal information and the preliminary design for the separation of duty/tasks/roles/data in the software.
- **Privacy management tools.** Identification of privacy management tools and system processes that may be needed to manage personal information in the software and the solution it may be part of. This is particularly important if the software is going to be a component of an SaaS- or cloud-based solution.
- **Security safeguards.** The setting of requirements for security safeguards that will be used to protect PII and personal information.
- **Integrity of the data.** Determine that PII and personal information is kept up to date and accurate.
- **Assess whether there are any conflicts between security and privacy requirements.** If so, they need to be addressed and resolved at this stage of the development process. This step includes the categorization of the level of privacy and security protection that the software will require.
- **Apply the principle of least privilege.** Essentially, this entails limiting access to "need to know." Access to user data should be limited to those who have a legitimate business purpose for accessing the data. In addition, nonusers, such as administrators or database managers, should only be given access to the smallest amount of user data needed to achieve the specific business purpose. This must include third parties that have access to the data or to which it is transferred: They should only be given the specific data they need to fulfill their business purpose. Data protection provisions, including retention and destruction requirements, are typically required of third parties through contract agreements.
- **Websites and web services.** All externally facing websites must have a link to a privacy statement on every page. This includes pop-ups that collect PII. Whenever possible, the same privacy statement should be used for all sites within a domain.
- **The use of cookies.** PII and identifiers that facilitate tracking may be stored in cookies as small files that are stored on a user's computer. They are designed to hold a modest amount of data specific to a particular client and website and can be accessed either by the web server or the client computer. Privacy guidelines for cookie usage apply to locally stored text files that allow a server-side connection to store and retrieve information, including HTTP cookies (e.g., web cookies) and Flash cookies (e.g., Flash Shared Objects). Persistent cookies must not be used where a session cookie would satisfy the purpose. Persistent cookies should expire within the shortest time frame that achieves the business purpose. PII stored in a persistent cookie must be encrypted.
- **IP addresses.** The customer's IP address is always sent with the data as part of the communication protocol when it is transferred over the network. As of the date of this writing, there is still a lot of debate and discussion as to whether or not an IP address is PII. The fact that privacy regulators are even discussing this is a warning sign that we may need to consider the possibility that this information will fall into the category of PII in the foreseeable future. Storing an IP address with PII should be avoided if anonymity is required in order to avoid correlation between the two. If possible, the IP address should be stripped from the payload to reduce its sensitivity by limiting the number of digits. The IP address can also be discarded after translating it to a less-precise location.

- **Customer privacy notification.** Software that collects user data and transfers it must provide and give notice to the customer. These are also called disclosure notices and must inform users of the type of information that software will collect and how it will be used. Depending on the type of software, an opt-out clause may be required to allow users the ability to withhold certain types of personal information if they so choose. The type of notice and consent required depends on the type of user data being collected and how it will be used. Customers must also be presented with a choice of whether they want to share this information or not. All notices must be written in clear, easy-to-read language. There are two types of notification—prominent and discoverable. A "Prominent Notice" is one that is designed to catch the customer's attention and invites customers to inspect the current privacy settings, learn more about their options, and make choices. A "Discoverable Notice" is one the customer has to find. This can be done by selecting a privacy statement link from a help menu in a software product or by locating and reading a privacy statement on a website. This notification typically includes the type of data that will be stored, how it will be used, with whom it will be shared, how it is protected, available user controls (including the update process, if the PII is stored and reusable), and the company's contact information. If you are developing a product to be used by another company or as an original equipment manufacturer (OEM), the customer company typically has specific privacy statements that third-party software developers are required to include. Other companies may require that software that is designed to work with their products contain a privacy statement that informs users that their information will not be sold to other companies or displayed publicly. Software developers must inform users of the software's method of safeguarding users' personal information in the privacy policy and notification. As we will discuss later in the book, this can be done via a valid SSL certificate, or by using other security and encryption methods. As with other privacy-related areas, regulatory and other requirements are dynamic, and you should consult your privacy expert or legal counsel for the latest guidance for your software.
- **Children's privacy.** Care must be taken to consider children's privacy, since they may lack the discretion to determine when disclosing their PII may put them at risk. This has become particularly important with the advent of collaboration and sharing features found in social software. Parental controls are typically added to products, websites, and web services to help protect the privacy of children. Special efforts must be made to ensure that parents retain control over whether their children can reveal PII. There are numerous privacy requirements for those offering websites and web services that target children and/or collect the age of their customers. There are numerous existing and forthcoming state, local, and international requirements for this area. Make sure you consult your privacy expert and/or corporate counsel (or equivalent) if you have software that will fall into this area.
- **Third parties.** Two types of third parties must be considered when assessing your privacy requirements. One type of third party is authorized to act on the company's behalf and uses data in accordance with the company's privacy practices. An independent third party follows its own privacy practices and uses customer information for its own purposes, which require a contract specifying data protection requirements. This requires a software provision for the customer to provide opt-in consent. The customer must provide opt-in consent before PII is shared with an independent third party. Only a

Discoverable Notice is required if PII is transferred via a third party authorized to act on the company's behalf.

- **User controls.** User controls give users the ability to manage and control the privacy of their data and change their settings. These controls should be intuitive and easy to find. The data may reside on a computer, within a web service, or on a mobile device. A webpage is used as the privacy site for web services. Privacy controls for mobile devices can be on the device itself or via a computer-based user interface or a website that links to the device.

- **Privacy controls required for software used on shared computers.** It is common for software used in home or small office/home office (SOHO) environments to be shared by multiple users. Software designed for use in these environments that also collects or stores PII must provide controls over which users have access to the data. These controls may include strict computer/file/document access control and file permissions or encryption. Controls must also be a default setting and not opt-in. Shared folders must be clearly marked or highlighted.

- **Collaboration, sharing, and social software privacy features.** This is an area with very complex challenges in that content can be shared among a community and, in some cases, linked community members and shared friends or contacts. Software that supports these types of applications should provide controls and notifications to help prevent inadvertent sharing of PII with unintended audiences.

- **Security.** Security, of course, is the topic of this book, and a critical element of both privacy and quality. The security requirements will depend on the type of user data collected and whether it will be stored locally, transferred, and/or stored remotely. The end goal for security controls and measures is to protect PII from loss, misuse, unauthorized access, disclosure, alteration, and destruction. The controls and measures include not only software controls such as access controls and encryption in transfer and storage but also physical security, disaster recovery, and auditing. Compensating controls may be needed when standard protection is not possible due to business needs, such as the use of PII as a unique identifier or an IP address or e-mail address used for routing.

- **Privacy Impact Ratings.** The Privacy Impact Rating (P1, P2, or P3) is a practice used in the Microsoft SDL. It measures the sensitivity of the data your software will process from a privacy point of view. Early awareness of all the required steps for deploying a project with high privacy risk may help you decide whether the costs are worth the business value gained. General definitions of privacy impact are as follows:
  - **P1 High Privacy Risk.** The feature, product, or service stores or transfers PII or error reports, monitors the user with an ongoing transfer of anonymous data, changes settings or file type associations, or installs software.
  - **P2 Moderate Privacy Risk.** The sole behavior that affects privacy in the feature, product, or service is a one-time, user-initiated, anonymous data transfer (e.g., the user clicks a link and goes out to a website).
  - **P3 Low Privacy Risk.** No behaviors exist within the feature, product, or service that affect privacy. No anonymous or personal data is transferred, no PII is stored on the machine, no settings are changed on the user's behalf, and no software is installed.[5]

The risk assessment questionnaire and risk ranking system developed by Microsoft can be a great tool in assessing the risk and prioritizing the work to remediate those risks in the SDL.

In summary, the purpose of the PIA is to provide details on where and to what degree privacy information is collected, stored, or created within the software that you are developing. The PIA should continue to be reviewed and updated as major decisions occur or the proposed use of the software and scope change significantly.

3.5 Security Assessment (A1) Key Success Factors and Metrics

3.5.1 Key Success Factors

Setting success criteria for any SDL phase will make it more effective and will help in performing postmortem to understand what worked and what didn't. Table 3.1 outlines success criteria suggested by the authors. However, each environment is different, and security teams are in the best position to understand success criteria within their own environment.

Table 3.1 Key Success Factors

Key Success Factor	Description
1. Accuracy of planned SDL activities	All SDL activities are accurately identified.
2. Product risk profile	Management understands the true cost of developing the product.
3. Accuracy of threat profile	Mitigating steps and countermeasures are in place for the product to be successful in its environment.
4. Coverage of relevant regulations, certifications, and compliance frameworks	All applicable legal and compliance aspects are covered.
5. Coverage of security objectives needed for software	"Must have" security objectives are met.

Success Factor 1: Accuracy of Planned SDL Activities

The Security Assessment (A1) phase is the first phase of our SDL and, therefore, is mostly discovery in nature. It sets the tone and direction of future SDL activities. During this phase, a rough outline of needed SDL activities is decided, as well as what emphasis should be placed on each SDL activity (code review, threat modeling, etc.). Though one can always course correct identified SDL activities and their importance later, a key measure of success of this phase is how many revisions are made to initial requirements and the direction of the SDL. Though this is not measurable at the start, once the SDL cycle is complete, one should go back to the initial planning documents to identify its deviations and why those variances happened. It should help in estimating future SDL activities more accurately.

Success Factor 2: Product Risk Profile

Another key success factor is a product risk profile. A baseline product risk profile can be prepared based on software, its importance to customers (including its use in their environment), data processed through the software, relevant regulations, and target market/countries. The profile should include risk arising out of customer expectations and use of the product, regulatory compliance, and security changes needed to cater to different markets. This will also help articulate actual costs to management.

Success Factor 3: Accuracy of Threat Profile

Too often, the software is developed without a complete understanding of its intended use or the environment in which it will operate. Though a product may be designed for specific uses, customers often add enhancements and use them in ways that were not intended. Another example is APIs exposed to the public. In most cases, the number of APIs exposed increases over time (often after the software is released). However, the threat profile from exposure APIs is not always considered or done correctly. In other cases, the software depends on open-source (or closed-source) software that was not considered in defining the threat profile for the product. Thus, one of the critical success factors to take away from this phase is the accuracy of the threat profile. The profile should cover perceived use cases, research on customer integrations, and security exposure through dependency on other products or software.

Success Factor 4: Coverage of Relevant Regulations, Certifications, and Compliance Frameworks

One key criterion for the success of this phase is whether all key regulations, compliance frameworks, and certifications for the product (or libraries) have been identified. This success factor depends on understanding product objectives and customer uses. One may think that specific regulations will not be applicable because their use cases are not considered valid. Customers, however, often have a different take on this. A cloud product that a customer uses to interact with other customers might not need to comply with HIPAA from one viewpoint. However, for a customer, it is crucial that this product, if not compliant with HIPAA, at least does not create issues that may result in noncompliance.

Compliance frameworks are another thing to watch out for. Depending on how the product is used (in-house or in the cloud), different permutations are expected by customers. If customers require ISO® 27001 certification and use your product in a cloud environment, they will expect a demonstrable and verifiable operational and product security posture. If customers are paying for your service using credit cards, not only they but your environment may fall under the regulations applicable to the payment card industry. Though we are focusing on product security here, operational security is equally important.

Finally, while covering regulations, compliance frameworks, and certifications, security and development teams fail to look closely at dependencies. For example, if the product needs to comply with the Federal Information Processing Standards (FIPS), how will using an open-source library affect compliance? If the product needs to obtain certification A, will dependent software make or break this certification? These questions need to be carefully considered to prevent future firefighting.

Success Factor 5: Coverage of Security Objectives Needed for Software

Finally, one should look at how many of the security objectives were met at the conclusion of this phase. If some objectives were not met, why not? One may start with a laundry list of security objectives, but they often compete with other product features and product management may shoot them down. An example might be logging. If one of the critical security objectives is to detect and respond to threats as they happen, logging and real-time visibility is crucial to the effort. However, the feasibility of logging relevant events (securely) may compete with other product requirements (operational efficiency, features). One could insist on logging events securely by encrypting them and transporting them safely to a central repository. However, depending on resources and other competing demands, such logging efforts might not make it to the final list.

Before closing out the phase, it is good to see whether any security objectives were not met in their entirety; if not, were these important to have, or were they just "nice to have." This knowledge should help future product SDL cycles. Having too many "nice to haves" may undermine the credibility of the security team.

3.5.2 Deliverables

In each of our SDL phases, we will outline a key set of deliverables for that phase. The idea is to make sure that all required activities have a tangible documented outcome. Often, we see only verbal or nonofficial documents created and kept by a project management team. In our opinion, formal documentation should be created and kept in a central repository with appropriate sign-offs and versioning.

Key deliverables for Phase A1 are listed in Table 3.2 and discussed below.

Table 3.2 Deliverables for Phase A1

Deliverable	Goal
Product risk profile	Estimate actual cost of the product.
SDL project outline	Map SDL activities to the development schedule.
Applicable laws and regulations	Obtain formal sign-off from stakeholders on applicable laws.
Threat profile	Guide SDL activities to mitigate threats.
Certification requirements	List requirements for product and operations certifications.
List of third-party software	Identify dependence on third-party software.
Metrics template	Establish cadence for regular reporting to executives.

- **Product risk profile.** The product risk profile helps management see the actual cost of the product from different perspectives, including selling it in different markets and liabilities that might be incurred if it is a SaaS/cloud product.
- **SDL project outline (for security milestones and mapping to development schedule).** An essential outcome of this phase is an SDL project outline or plan. The SDL plan should include security milestones that will be met during each phase and mapped to the development plan/schedule. Reporting should be set up to keep track of progress on the project.
- **Applicable laws and regulations.** This deliverable is a comprehensive review of laws and regulations that may be applicable to the product. The legal department should be heavily involved in preparing this documentation and, for laws/regulations that are not applicable, clearly articulate our understanding as to why those were not applicable.

- **Threat profile.** This deliverable articulates our assumptions about the environment in which the product will operate and potential threats in that environment. This will be helpful in later stages to focus our SDL activities to ensure the product is as secure as possible under the threat profile developed by the team. It will also be useful for post-mortem in case we missed a threat/scenario in the SDL phases.
- **Certification requirements.** This deliverable should clearly articulate certifications needed for the product (e.g., FIPS) and resulting requirements. In the case of SaaS/cloud software, it should identify operational controls that will be needed for the software to be certified by various frameworks.
- **List of third-party software.** The purpose of this list is to identify all third-party components to be used with our software and thereby incorporate them in our threat profile. It should also help us to finalize the list of changes/requirements required for certifications.
- **Metrics template.** This deliverable is a template on metrics that we plan to report to management on a periodic basis.

3.5.3 Metrics

In the SDL model we propose, we outline metrics that should be measured in each and every phase. First, however, we would like to point out a few things we have learned in our professional careers.

We should decide what to measure upfront and stick to those decisions as much as possible. Although we understand we may have to modify metrics as we go along, we should resist the temptation to overhaul metrics frequently. The metrics template should be put together with its audience in mind. However, there is a tendency among executives to ask for a slightly different set of metrics as the project moves along. We should educate and make executives aware of why the metrics were chosen and their importance to the SDL process. Often, that should take care of conflicting suggestions on metrics. In a nutshell, identify a set of appropriate metrics for your audience and stick to it. In the long term, metrics will guide your overall progress so that whatever set of metrics you choose consistently, it will serve you well.

Here are our suggestions for metrics for this phase:

- Time in weeks when the software security team was looped in
- Percent of stakeholders participating in the SDL activities
- Percent of SDL activities mapped to development activities
- Percent of security objectives met

3.6 Summary

We have described the importance of and best practices for addressing security and privacy at the very beginning of the SDLC process. By now, it should be clear that security and privacy are fundamental aspects of quality required to have a secure software development process and that the optimal time to define the requirements for these two areas is during the initial planning stage described in this chapter. Defining and establishing these requirements allows the team to identify key milestones and deliverables for the integration of security and privacy into the software in a manner that will minimize disruption to plans and schedules. Identification of the key stakeholders and security roles for the SDL/SDLC, assessment and specification of minimum security and privacy requirements for the software to run in its planned operational environment, the overall SDL plan, and an agreed-upon security vulnerability identification/remediation work item tracking system are the key elements of the Security Assessment (A1) phase described in this chapter. It should be clear that both security and privacy risk assessments are mandatory components of an SDL. These are key elements in defining functional aspects of the software that will require a deeper review later in the development process.

Toward the end of the chapter, we discussed key success factors and their importance, deliverables from this phase, and metrics that should be collected from this phase.

The best practices discussed in this chapter will serve as the groundwork and baseline for the future phases of our SDL model. The next phase, Architecture (A2), will be discussed in Chapter 4.

Chapter Quick-Check

1. The purpose for the discovery meeting with stakeholders early in the development life cycle is to:
   a. Discover who is on the development team
   b. Discover what budgets and resources are available to the initiative
   c. Discover how security can be built into the development process from the start
   d. Discover which platforms and languages will be used for development of the application

2. A Privacy Impact Assessment (PIA) is needed to:
   a. Identify laws and regulations related to the controls needed for the application
   b. Identify the data elements and their sensitivity for proper selection of security controls
   c. Identify communications and platform controls to apply to data in acquisition, processing, and storage
   d. None of the above
   e. All of the above

3. A threat profile developed in Phase A1 serves as input to which subsequent development activities?
   a. Requirements gathering
   b. Threat modeling
   c. Static analysis
   d. Post implementation sign-offs

Exercises

The following exercises are based on the case study discussed in Appendix A. These exercises are intended to give you some practice in applying the steps and producing deliverables for Phase A1 of the SDL.

1. Document the stakeholders and agenda for conducting an initial discovery meeting that will occur to determine the plans for redeveloping the Revvin' Engines E-commerce application and operating platform(s).
2. Map the SDL activities to the development activities that must be included in the project plan for replacing the E-commerce application and processes.
3. Determine the regulatory and industry standards that govern the development of E-commerce systems. Pay close attention to the payment aspects of the application and determine which regulations and requirements must be considered.
4. Create an initial threat profile that considers the incident, threat actors, privacy aspects, and possible threat vectors that plague E-commerce applications.

References

1. Kissel, R., et al. (2008). U.S. Department of Commerce, NIST Special Publication 800-64 Revision 2: "Security Considerations in the System Development Life Cycle." Retrieved from http://csrc.nist.gov/publications/nistpubs/800-64-Rev2/SP800-64-Revision2.pdf
2. Microsoft Corporation. (2006). "New Guidelines to Help Developers Protect Customers' Privacy." Retrieved from https://news.microsoft.com/2006/10/19/new-guidelines-to-help-developers-protect-customers-privacy/
3. Kissel, R., et al. (2008). U.S. Department of Commerce, NIST Special Publication 800-64 Revision 2: "Security Considerations in the System Development Life Cycle." Retrieved from http://csrc.nist.gov/publications/nistpubs/800-64-Rev2/SP800-64-Revision2.pdf
4. Security Innovation, Inc. (2006). "Regulatory Compliance Demystified: An Introduction to Compliance for Developers." Retrieved from http://msdn.microsoft.com/en-us/library/aa480484.aspx
5. Microsoft Corporation. (2012). "Appendix C: SDL Privacy Questionnaire." Retrieved from http://msdn.microsoft.com/en-us/library/windows/desktop/cc307393.aspx

Chapter 4

Architecture (A2): SDL Activities and Best Practices

CHAPTER OVERVIEW

During the second phase of the security development lifecycle (SDL), security considerations are brought into the software development life cycle (SDLC) to ensure that all threats, requirements, and potential constraints on functionality and integration are considered.

CHAPTER TAKE-AWAYS

- Explore the practices that compose the Architecture (Phase A2) of the security development lifecycle (SDL).
- Document the key success factors for completion of Phase A2.
- Create initial, draft deliverables for Phase A2 for the case study in Appendix A.
- Prepare a threat model for the case study in Appendix A.

Figure 4.1 illustrates the Architecture (A2) phase of the SDL in preparation for planning future SDL activities. At this stage of the SDL, security is looked at more in terms of business risks, with inputs from the software security group and discussions with key stakeholders in the SDLC. Business requirements are defined in the security terms of confidentiality, integrity, and availability, and needed privacy controls are discussed for creation, transmission, and personally identifiable information (PII). SDL policy and other security or privacy compliance requirements are also identified at this stage of the SDL. This ensures that security and privacy discussions are performed as part of, rather than separate from, the SDLC, so that there are solid understandings among project personnel about business decisions and their risk implications for the overall development project. A cost analysis for development and support costs required for security and privacy consistent with business needs is also done as part of the

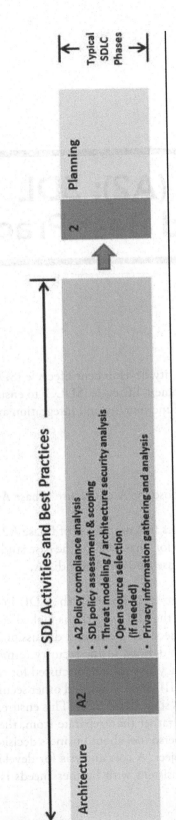

Figure 4.1 Architecture (A2): SDL activities and best practices.

requirements analysis. As discussed previously, the planning and awareness of security, privacy, and risk management early in the SDLC through the proper used of an SDL will result in significant cost and time savings.

Perhaps the most important, complex, and difficult part of the SDL starts during this phase of the SDL. As discussed previously, threat modeling and architectural security analysis typically fall into the domain of the senior software security architects and require the most experience and expertise of any of the tasks within the SDL. Fortunately, tools are currently available and in the process of being developed that can assist in this phase and help leverage and scale a skill set that is typically a limited resource in a software security group.

Additional security training that may be needed for key developers to understand the current threats and potential exploitations of their products, as well as training for secure design and coding techniques specific to the software being developed and for the systems with which the software will be interacting, are identified at this stage of the SDL. This enables the developers to work more efficiently with the software security architects and others from the software security group to create more secure designs and empower them to address key issues early in the development processes.

4.1 A2 Policy Compliance Analysis

The purpose of a software security policy is to define what needs to be protected and how it will be protected, including reviewing and incorporating policies from outside the SDL that may impact the development process. These might include policies governing software or applications developed or applied anywhere in the organization. During this phase, any policy that exists outside the domain of the SDL policy is reviewed. Corporate security and privacy policies will likely instruct designers and developers on what the security and privacy features need to be and how they must be implemented. Other policies may include those that govern the use of third-party and open-source software or the protections and control of source code and other intellectual property within and outside the organization. Assuming the software security group is separate from the centralized information security group, it is important that both groups collaborate on all policies and guidelines related to the development and post-release security support and response of software from that organization. It is also important to collaborate with the privacy function of the company, whether it is part of a centralized group or outside legal counsel.

4.2 SDL Policy Assessment and Scoping

The SDL also provides an invaluable guide for software developers setting a security standard for their organization and should offer a roadmap for implementation without disrupting the core business of producing quality software applications. Unless the senior leadership of the development organization and the management team support this model, the SDL will likely fail. It must be driven by a policy that is signed off, promulgated, and provides support by the software development management team and ideally by the CEO. An organization should have a documented and repeatable SDL policy and guideline that supports the SDLC, including its business needs, and as a complement to the engineering and development culture that it supports. The culture and maturity of the organization are very important to consider in the development of the SDL policy so that you ensure it will be both feasible and practical to implement. The management style, complexity of people, process, and technology needs, including the overall architecture of the product, will help determine how granular or objective in focus the guidelines will be. The amount of outsourced development, if any, will need to be assessed as part of this process as well. An internal development team will require more detailed procedures, whereas an outsourced function will require more contractual objects, service levels, and detailed deliverables. The vulnerabilities and risk of using outsourced development resources will be covered later in the book.

4.3 Threat Modeling/Architecture Security Analysis

4.3.1 Threat Modeling

As discussed previously, threat modeling requires a special set of skills, experience, and mindsets: The people on the team who do this must be able to think like an adversary. A senior software security architect or one of the more seasoned software security champions typically runs this aspect. The developers and team members who are pulled into this process must know not only how to develop or build software but also how to deconstruct or take apart the software and its architecture while thinking like an adversary.

Microsoft® first documented its threat modeling methodology in 1999, and its method has evolved into an industry standard since that time.[1] This was not the first time anyone threat modeled at Microsoft, of course, but rather the first time the methodology was formalized or considered as an abstracted engineering activity. The threat risk modeling process has five steps, enumerated below and shown graphically in Figure 4.2. They are as follows:

1. Identify security objectives.
2. Survey the application.
3. Decompose it.
4. Identify threats.
5. Identify vulnerabilities.

Following these five steps will help you understand what assets you need to protect, from whom you need to protect them, how you can protect them, what is the implementation priority, and what risk you will have to live with if a few of the threats are not included in the implementation scope.

The focus of threat modeling should not be simply on the software product itself but also include the context of the business and the user. The implementation priorities can be limited to the software product itself after the threat modeling, analysis, and architectural security risk analysis are completed. Besides the cost savings achieved by building security in early in the process, another advantage is to take into account the business and user needs and requirements so you can balance out and make security decisions that are cost-efficient and relevant to the competitiveness of the product in addition to facilitating expected and required security and privacy controls.

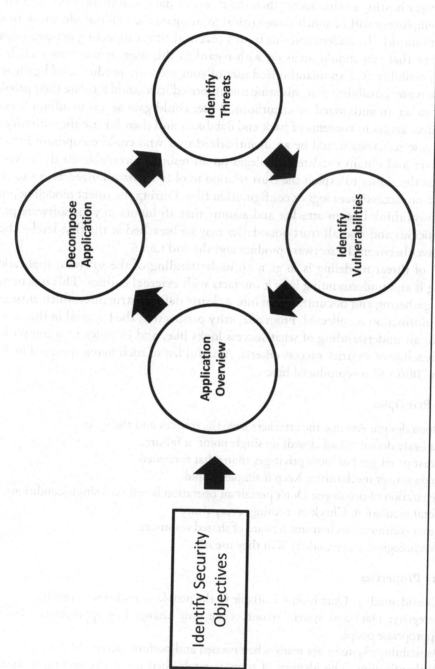

Figure 4.2 The five steps of threat modeling.

The user context influences not only the scope of threats and vulnerabilities, it may also strongly affect priorities for implementation. For example, if you are storing customers' credit card data in your hosting environment, then the threat of data stealing by your internal support staff or employees will be much more critical to mitigate then an outside attack from an unknown community. To understand this from a practical threat modeling perspective, some of the scenarios that you should focus on with regard to this user-centric view include considering any possibility that an unauthorized user of your software product could gain access, whether there is any possibility that this same unauthorized user could escalate their privileges, and whether either an authorized or unauthorized user could gain access to admin functions or provide direct access to contents of back-end databases and then misuse the authority. One of the worst-case scenarios would be an unauthorized user who could compromise the web/front-end server and obtain escalated privileges on all resources available on the server; this would provide the ability to exploit the trust relation to obtain unauthorized access to critical information from access/event logs or configuration files. During the threat modeling process, you must always think like an attacker and assume that all inputs to your software product could be malicious and that all trust boundaries may be breached at the first level—the first interaction layer between the software product and the end user.[2]

The goal of threat modeling is to gain an understanding of the software application by decomposing it and understanding how it interacts with external entities. This is achieved by information gathering and documentation into a clearly defined structure, which ensures that the correct information is collected. From a security perspective, the key goal in threat modeling is to gain an understanding of what success looks like, and in order to accomplish that, you need a baseline of security success criteria. A useful list of such items appeared in *MSDN Magazine* in 2006 and is reproduced here:

Design Principles

- Open design: Assume the attackers have the sources and the specs.
- Fail-safe defaults: Fail closed; no single point of failure.
- Least privilege: No more privileges than what is needed.
- Economy of mechanism: Keep it simple, stupid.
- Separation of privileges: Don't permit an operation based on a single condition.
- Total mediation: Check everything, every time.
- Least common mechanism: Beware of shared resources.
- Psychological acceptability: Will they use it?

Security Properties

- Confidentiality: Data is only available to the people intended to access it.
- Integrity: Data and system resources are only changed in appropriate ways by appropriate people.
- Availability: Systems are ready when needed and perform acceptably.
- Authentication: The identity of users is established (or you're willing to accept anonymous users).
- Authorization: Users are explicitly allowed or denied access to resources.
- Nonrepudiation: Users can't perform an action and later deny performing it.[3]

The key steps involved in threat modeling are as follows:[4]

1. Break down your product architecture using data flow diagrams
2. Use STRIDE threat categories to identify what threats are applicable to each element of the data flow diagram.
3. Map all threats with relevant vulnerabilities as applicable in the context of the usage scenario.
4. Rank threats. Assign a risk rating to each threat and vulnerability to understand the impact; this will help define the priority for fixing. Use DREAD or other methodologies.
5. Define the mitigation plan/countermeasures for each of the vulnerabilities identified.
6. Fix the vulnerabilities that are not acceptable to the business in order of priority as decided in the preceding steps.

4.3.2 Data Flow Diagrams

The first step of the threat modeling process is to develop a visual representation of the threat flows in the form of a diagram typically drawn during a whiteboard session. It is important to provide a structure for this process. Providing structure helps avoid mistakes. Without a good diagram, you likely won't have a good threat model. It is important to understand, first, that this exercise is about data flow and not code flow. This is a mistake often made by developers on the team because they live, breath, and eat code development and are not typically focused on the data security of the code they are developing. It should be no surprise that the diagram produced in this stage of the threat modeling process is called a data flow diagram or DFD. The focus of the DFD is on how data moves through the software solution and what happens to the data as it moves, giving us a better understanding of how the software works and its underlying architecture by providing a visual representation of how the software processes data. The visual representation is hierarchical in structure, so it allows you to decompose the software architecture into subsystems and then lower-level subsystems. At a high level, this allows you to clarify the scope of the application being modeled; at the lower levels, it allows you to focus on the specific processes involved when processing specific data.

Before you start developing your DFD, it is always a good idea to understand the element images you are going to use. The basic elements and symbols that are typically used in DFDs are shown in Figure 4.3. You build the DFD by connecting these various elements as data flows and applying boundaries between the elements where appropriate.

Our first example of the use of a DFD is a data flow diagram for threat modeling of a web application, as shown in Figure 4.4. This data flow diagram represents the process by which customers and remote employees access corporate marketing data from a corporate website. The first and most obvious security control differentiates between file access by an employee of the company versus file access by a customer. The employee data might contain company IP information authorized only for company employees and, depending on their role, very sensitive competitive marketing and pricing data authorized only for employees who have a "need to know."

Element Type	Type Description	Element Symbol
External Element	An element outside your control and external to your software application but may be called to or interact with the software being modeled via an entry point.	▭
Process	This represents a task that handles data within the software. This task may process or perform a task based on the data.	 ○
Multiple Processes	This is used to represent a collection of sub-processes for the data and typically indicates that another DFD will be involved in which case its sub-processes are broken down and extended into an additional DFD.	 ◎
Data Store	This represents where data is stored but not modified.	‖
Data Flow	This represents the movement of the data within the software and its direction of movement is represented by the arrow.	 ⌒→
Trust Boundary	A trust boundary occurs when one component doesn't trust the component on the other side of the boundary. Trust boundaries always exist between elements running at different privilege levels. There can also be trust boundaries between different components running at the same privilege level.	 ⌒ (dashed)

Figure 4.3 DFD element types.

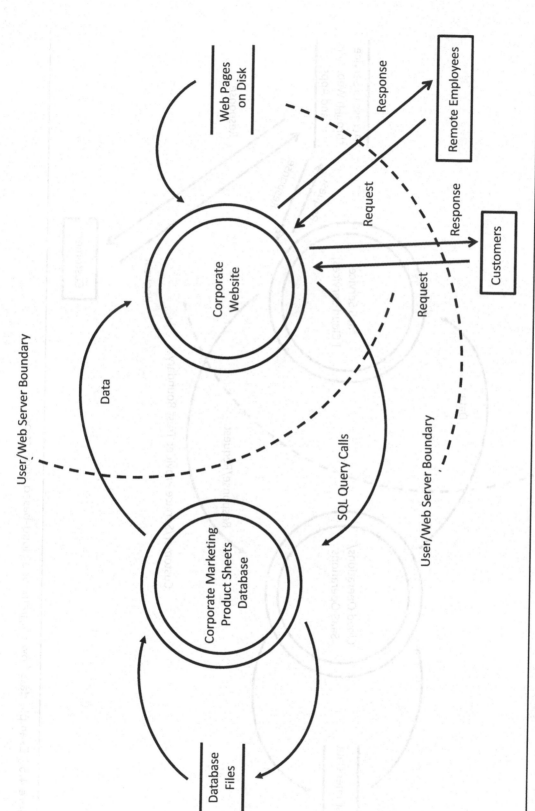

Figure 4.4 Example data flow diagram for application threat modeling.

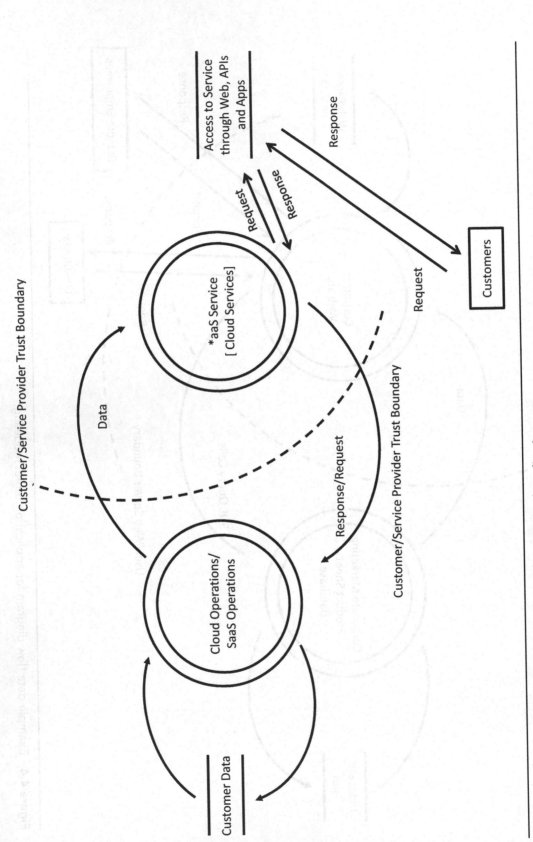

Figure 4.5 Example data flow diagram for a cloud-based application.

The DFD in Figure 4.4 is for illustrative purposes only and does not represent the best way to develop an application. Examining the flow diagram more closely, we notice the following:

- There is no segmentation between data for employees and customers.
- There does not seem to be two-factor authentication for remote employees (e.g., VPN) before they access data on the site.
- Tiered structure that should be part of web applications is not developed fully (or at least not part of this DFD). This might simplify the diagram, but it may also hide some use cases and flows.

The DFD in Figure 4.5 is an example of *aaS-based services provided to customers. Instead of a traditional web application, this DFD shows an example of how customers access services through a cloud provider. The most obvious security control is protecting customer data through cloud operations. Customers can access service in multiple ways—through API calls, web applications, or custom application development.

Examining the flow diagram more closely, we notice the following:

- There is no distinction between application access through an API or the web.
- Cloud operations is a high-level abstraction for more detailed cloud operations architecture.
- The DFD does not tell us anything about segmentation between different customers.
- It also does not show how secure the data is—that is, is it encrypted, are web servers talking only to database servers in a cluster or is communication any-any?

Getting the DFD right is key to getting the threat model right. Spend enough time on yours, making sure all the pieces of your system are represented. Each of the elements (processes, data stores, data flows, and interactors) has a set of threats to which it is susceptible, as you can see in Figure 4.6. This chart, along with your DFD, gives you a framework for investigating how your system might fail.[5]

	Data Flow	Data Store	Process	External
Spoofing			✓	✓
Tampering	✓		✓	
Repudiate		✓*	✓	✓
Information Disclosure	✓	✓	✓	
Denial of Service	✓	✓	✓	
Elevate Privilege			✓	

Figure 4.6 Threats affecting elements. (*For data stores that are logs, there is concern about repudiation issues, and attacks on the data store to delete the logs. A set of questions to make these threats more concrete and accessible should be used to make this assessment more complete.[6])

The DFD process requires not only that you think like an attacker but possibly like multiple attackers, particularly if your software product is going to be operating in the cloud or an SaaS environment. Once the DFD is completed, you should have an accurate overview of how data is processed by the software, including how it moves and what happens to it within the application and others that may be associated with it. The high levels of the DFD clarify the scope of the application, and the lower levels clarify processes involved when specific data is being processed.

4.3.3 Architectural Threat Analysis and Ranking of Threats

4.3.3.1 Threat Determination

The first step in determining threats is to adopt a methodology by which you can categorize them. This provides the ability to systematically identify sets of threat categories within the software application in a structured and repeatable manner. STRIDE is a method of threat categorization that was popularized by Microsoft a number of years ago and will be used in this chapter as an example of a threat determination tool, but it is certainly not the only methodology that can be used. Each letter in the acronym STRIDE helps classify attacker goals:

- **Spoofing**
- **Tampering**
- **Repudiation**
- **Information disclosure**
- **Denial of service**
- **Elevation of privilege**[7]

The first step in STRIDE is to decompose your system into relevant components, then analyze each component for susceptibility to the threats, and, finally, mitigate the threats. The process is then repeated until you are comfortable with any remaining threats. The system is then considered secure, since you have now broken your software application and system down into individual components and mitigated the threats to each. Of course, this methodology has its flaws in that the individual components of the software and system can be part of a larger system, and you are only as secure as your weakest link. Individual components of a software product and system may not be susceptible to a threat in isolation, but they may be, once they are part of a larger system. This is particularly true for software products that were not designed to be used on the Internet, in the cloud, or in an SaaS environment.

General threats and the security controls they may affect within each of the STRIDE categories include the following:

- Spoofing: A threat action that is designed to illegally access and use another user's credentials, such as username and password—*Authentication*
- Tampering: Threat action aimed to maliciously change/modify persistent data, such as persistent data in a database, and the alteration of data in transit between two computers over an open network, such as the Internet—*Integrity*
- Repudiation: Threat action aimed to perform illegal operations in a system that lacks the ability to trace the prohibited operations—*Nonrepudiation*

- Information disclosure: Threat action to read a file that one was not granted access to, or to read data in transit—*Confidentiality*
- Denial of service: Threat aimed to deny access to valid users, such as by making a web server temporarily unavailable or unusable—*Availability*
- Elevation of privilege: Threat aimed to gain privileged access to resources for gaining unauthorized access to information or to compromise a system—*Authorization*[8]

4.3.3.2 Threat Analysis

After you have completed the DFD, you should identify the design and implementation approaches for input validation, authentication, authorization, configuration management, and the other areas where applications are most susceptible to vulnerabilities, creating what is called a security profile.

A practical example of the kind of questions that are typically asked in analyzing each aspect of the design and implementation of your software application is the following.[9] We divide these into broad categories of input validation, authentication, authorization, configuration management, sensitive data, session management, cryptography, exception management, parameter manipulation, and audit and logging.

Input Validation

The rationale behind this is that all user input should be considered untrusted and should be validated before being used in software. Below are relevant questions to ask for input validation:

1. Is all input data validated?
2. Could an attacker inject commands or malicious data into the application?
3. Is data validated as it is passed between separate trust boundaries (by the recipient entry point)?
4. Can data in the database be trusted?
5. Would you prefer whitelisting or blacklisting of user input?

Authentication

All user (and software/API) interactions with the overall system should be thought through and validated through authentication. None of the services and functionality should be available without validating if the user/system/API/component is legitimate. Whether it can use the functionality takes us into authorization. Typical questions to ask for authentication are as follows:

1. Are credentials secured if they are passed over the network?
2. Are strong account policies used?
3. Are strong passwords enforced?
4. Are you using certificates? Are there any wild card certificates in use?
5. Are password verifiers (using one-way hashes) used for user passwords?
6. How do system components authenticate to each other (e.g., how does a service authenticate to a database)?

7. During the boot process for the service/application, how do system components authenticate to each other?
8. Are keys used for authentication instead of passwords?

Authorization

Many times, we would like to restrict users/systems/API/components from accessing certain functionality in a software system. Authorization enables us to do just that—that is, prevent certain operations to certain agents. Questions typically related to authorization are as follows:

1. What gatekeepers are used at the entry points of the application?
2. How is authorization enforced at the database?
3. Is a defense-in-depth strategy used?
4. Do you fail securely and only allow access upon successful confirmation of credentials?

Configuration Management

Configuration management enables us to harden software, systems, services, and devices and lock them down, thus reducing risk to the environment. Components of configuration management include hardening standards and guidelines, reviewing application dependencies on services, looking at user and administrator interfaces, security change management, and so on. Questions are along the following lines:

1. What administration interfaces does the application support?
2. How are they secured?
3. How is remote administration secured?
4. What configuration stores are used and how are they secured?
5. Have hardening standards been developed for the software stack (OS, DB, application)?
6. Does the software system provide a way to detect variances from approved security configuration changes?
7. Do all groups (IT, QA, Engineering, Operations) only use approved (golden master or hardened) software images for different components such as OS, DB, web, and application servers?
8. Are approved images used across the entire life cycle, from development to deployment?

Sensitive Data

This aspect deals with awareness around the type of data handled by the application and systems. In many cases, we have found that developers and operations teams are not aware or educated enough on the types of data their application will handle (either by design or mistake) and if the protection is enough for the data elements.

1. What sensitive data is handled by the application?
2. What regulatory/compliance requirements are applicable to data/data elements?
3. How is it secured over the network and in persistent stores? Is this good enough, given legal/regulatory requirements?

4. What type of encryption is used and how are encryption keys secured?
5. Are sensitive data elements present in logs, source code, or configuration (e.g., XML) files?

Session Management

Securely establishing and mainlining the integrity of session is one of the key components of today's applications—specifically, web applications. Once the user is authenticated, a session is established. This can result in multiple scenarios wherein a session can be abused. Session management focuses on preventing such abuses. Questions asked for this aspect are typically along the following lines:

1. How are session cookies generated?
2. How are they secured to prevent session hijacking?
3. How is persistent session state secured?
4. Where is session information stored? On the server or the client side?
5. How is session state secured as it crosses the network?
6. How does the application authenticate with the session store?
7. Are credentials passed over the wire, and are they maintained by the application? If so, how are they secured?
8. How are multiple sessions from a user/component handled?

Cryptography

Everyone uses cryptography. Cryptography tends to provide a sense of security for most developers and users. However, proper use of cryptography is not that common in our experience. Using cryptography to solve the wrong problem can often cause frustration and even exposure. When dealing with cryptography, it is best to stick with well-tested, publicly available algorithms and libraries. Questions on cryptography can include the following:

1. What is the problem cryptography is going to solve (confidentiality, integrity, or both)?
2. What algorithms and cryptographic techniques are used?
3. Are there any proprietary or in-house algorithms used?
4. How long are encryption keys and how are they secured?
5. Does the application put its own encryption into action?
6. How often are keys recycled? Are certificates checked for their validity? Are certificates checked against revocation lists?

Parameter Manipulation

Application often passes parameters to communicate with the other side. Parameters range from (not so important) iterators, variable names, and values to session tokens. Man-in-the-middle (MITM) attacks and deliberate parameter tampering makes it important for us to devise a mechanism to detect if parameters received are indeed safe and can be used as designed. Imperative here is on the receiver side—like input validation, do not blindly trust parameters.

1. Does the application detect tampered parameters?
2. Does the application rely on only client-side validation, or is there server-side validation as well?

3. Does it validate all parameters in form fields, view state, cookie data, and HTTP headers?
4. Are parameters directly used in database queries?
5. Are parameters directly reflected back to the browser?

Exception Management

Gracefully handling error conditions and exceptions is critical to software applications. Often, developers miss such conditions or handle them incorrectly. Side effects from improper error handling/exception management range from denial of service or information leakage. Sample questions to probe this aspect are as follows:

1. How does the application handle error conditions?
2. Is there a default catch for exceptions?
3. Are exceptions ever allowed to propagate back to the client?
4. Are generic error messages used that do not contain exploitable information?
5. Do exceptions log any sensitive information to logs?
6. Are built-in capabilities from programming languages used for this purpose, or do developers rely on in-house modules?

Auditing and Logging

Audit and logging are critical for security, operations, debugging, compliance, and legal reasons. Operations and debugging are often the drivers for audit/logging though security requirements are considered integral today. Below are sample questions that can be asked to understand audit and logging.

1. Does your application audit activity across all tiers on all servers?
2. How are log files secured?
3. Does the application log any sensitive information (e.g., credentials, data elements, session tokens)?
4. Are log files transported securely (e.g., TCP/TLS)?
5. Is the retention period clearly defined for log files? Does it align with regulatory and legal requirements?
6. How often are logs rotated?
7. Are trigger levels defined for certain types of events?

Now that you have a visual representation of the threat and have answered questions as above, the next step is to identify the threats that may affect your software application. This is also where you bring together elements of the software security group and the development team for a whiteboard meeting to brainstorm cost-effective and practical solutions to the vulnerabilities that have been identified in threat modeling. The goals of the attacker are addressed in relation to the threats and questions during the STRIDE assessment. This is done from a somewhat higher architectural and multifunctional perspective given the makeup of the brainstorming team. It is also common practice to use any available categorized threat list and apply it to any of the vulnerabilities identified earlier.

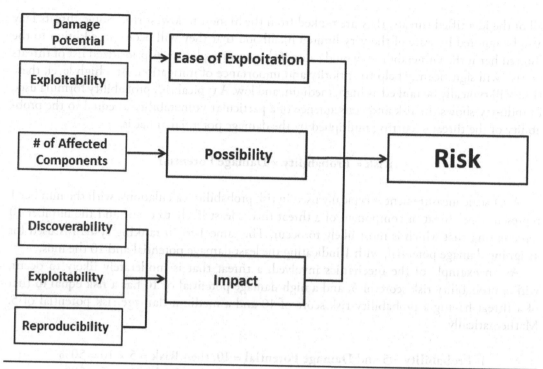

Figure 4.7   Risk assessment process.

The use of attack trees and attack patterns is a traditional approach to threat assessment that can help you identify additional potential threats. Although attack patterns represent commonly known attacks, their combination with attack trees can be used for a greater depth of analysis highlighting areas you may have missed in your initial analysis or through the use of categorized lists of known threats. Since attack trees are in a hierarchical, structured, and flow diagram style, they give a great visual representation of attacks and help focus efforts on potential additional approaches to avoiding or mitigating such attacks. They are also useful for the creation of test plans and the assessment of security costs. Since the primary focus of attack patterns, attacker techniques, and STRIDE is on the goals of the attacker, using them in combination with attack trees helps bring a holistic approach to this process, especially when used in face-to-face brainstorming sessions.

Before you move on to the next stage of the threat modeling and architectural risk assessment process and start assigning values to the risk, it is important to be sure you have addressed risk with regard to the ease of exploitation, possibility, and impact. A visual representation of what knowledge you must have before moving on to the next step is given in Figure 4.7. If you don't have the information required to address an area of risk, you will need to go back through the process and fill in the gaps in your knowledge and understanding.

4.3.3.3 Ranking the Threats

During the final stage of the threat modeling and architecture security analysis, the threats are ranked from a risk perspective. Given that it may not be economically feasible to mitigate all of the identified threats, they are ranked from the highest to lowest risk. Some threats may also be ignored because of the very limited likelihood that they will occur, in addition to the limited harm the vulnerabilities would cause if they were exploited. A prioritized list of threats by risk will significantly help the priority and importance of mitigation. At a high level, these risks will typically be ranked as high, medium, and low. A typical risk probability formula used in industry shows the risk and consequence of a particular vulnerability as equal to the probability of the threat occurring multiplied by the damage potential. That is,

Risk = Probability × Damage Potential

A 10-scale measurement is typically used in risk probability calculations, with the number 1 representing a threat or component of a threat that is least likely to occur and the number 10 representing that which is most likely to occur. The same 1-to-10 ranking system is used for assigning damage potential, with 1 indicating the least damage potential and 10 the most.

As an example of the mechanics involved, a threat that is moderately likely to occur, with a probability risk score of 5, and a high damage potential of 10 has a risk equal to that of a threat having a probability risk score of 10 and a medium damage risk potential of 5. Mathematically,

If **Probability** = 5 and **Damage Potential** = 10, then **Risk** = 5 × 10 = 50%
If **Probability** = 10 and **Damage Potential** = 5, then **Risk** = 10 × 5 = 50%

As you can see from this example, 100 can be divided into three ranges of numbers to indicate a high, medium, or low risk rating. Obviously, your level of priority to fix the vulnerabilities will start with the highest priority of risk, which likely means that immediate mitigation is required. Then you would tackle vulnerabilities of medium risk, which should be done shortly thereafter but with less priority. The priority of low risks, as noted previously, will depend on the level of effort, exposure, and financial or legal risk also associated with the risk.

4.3.3.4 DREAD

Although many different risk models can be used when assessing vulnerabilities during the software development process, the DREAD model used by Microsoft is one the most popular. The acronym DREAD stands for **D**amage potential, **R**eproducibility, **E**xploitability, **A**ffected users, and **D**iscoverability. Answers to questions used to establish a risk rating for each of these elements produces a number from 0 to 10; the higher the number, the more serious is the risk. These numbers are used as a classification scheme for quantifying, comparing, and prioritizing the amount of risk presented by each evaluated threat and calculating the overall risk in numeric form so that threats can be ranked and sorted with any other risks found in the software application.

The DREAD algorithm, shown below, is used to compute a risk value, which is an average of all five categories:

Risk_DREAD = (<u>D</u>AMAGE + <u>R</u>EPRODUCIBILITY + <u>E</u>XPLOITABILITY + <u>A</u>FFECTED USERS + <u>D</u>ISCOVERABILITY)/5[10]

Here are some examples of how you arrive at the risk rating for a given threat by asking questions to quantify the DREAD categories:[11]

Damage Potential

- If a threat exploit occurs, how much damage will be caused?
  - 0 = nothing
  - 5 = individual user data is compromised or affected
  - 10 = complete system or data destruction

Reproducibility

- How easy is it to reproduce the threat exploit?
  - 0 = very hard or impossible, even for administrators of the application
  - 5 = one or two steps required; may need to be an authorized user
  - 10 = just a web browser, and the address bar is sufficient, without authentication

Exploitability

- What is needed to exploit this threat?
  - 0 = advanced programming and networking knowledge, with custom or advanced attack tools
  - 5 = malware exists on the Internet, or an exploit is easily performed using available attack tools
  - 10 = just a web browser

Affected Users

- How many users will be affected?
  - 0 = none
  - 5 = some users, but not all
  - 10 = all users

Discoverability

- How easy is it to discover this threat?
  - 0 = very hard to impossible; requires source code or administrative access
  - 5 = can figure it out by guessing or by monitoring network traces
  - 9 = details of faults like this are already in the public domain and can be easily discovered using a search engine
  - 10 = the information is visible in the web browser address bar or in a form

The next step is to classify your threat ratings as low (value = 1), medium (value = 2), or high (value = 3) for each category of DREAD based on your answers. Answers that would indicate a low, medium, or high risk for each DREAD category are shown below:[12]

Damage Potential

Low (value = 1): Leaking trivial information.
Medium (value = 2): Leaking sensitive information.
High (value = 3): The attacker can subvert the security system; get full trust authorization; run as administrator; upload content.

Reproducibility

Low (value = 1): The attack is very difficult to reproduce, even with knowledge of the security hole.

Medium (value = 2): The attack can be reproduced, but only with a timing window and a particular race situation.

High (value = 3): The attack can be reproduced every time and does not require a timing window.

Exploitability

Low (value = 1): The attack requires an extremely skilled person and in-depth knowledge every time to exploit.

Medium (value = 2): A skilled programmer could make the attack, and then repeat the steps.

High (value = 3): A novice programmer could make the attack in a short time.

Affected Users

Low (value = 1): Very small percentage of users, obscure feature; affects anonymous users.

Medium (value = 2): Some users, nondefault configuration.

High (value = 3): All users, default configuration, key customers.

Discoverability

Low (value = 1): The bug is obscure, and it is unlikely that users will work out damage potential.

Medium (value = 2): The vulnerability is in a seldom-used part of the product, and only a few users should come across it. It would take some thinking to see malicious use.

High (value = 3): Published information explains the attack. The vulnerability is found in the most commonly used feature and is very noticeable.

DREAD Category	Low Risk (1)	Medium Risk (2)	High Risk (3)	Subtotal Risk Scores
Damage Potential (D)				
Reproducibility (R)				
Exploitability (E)				
Affected Users (A)				
Discoverability (D)				Total Risk Score

Figure 4.8 DREAD threat rating table.

These numbers can then be put into a matrix similar to the one shown in Figure 4.8. After you count and sum the values for a given threat, the result will fall in the range of 5 to 15. Threats with overall ratings of 12 to 15 are typically considered high risk, those with ratings from 8 to 11 as medium risk, and those with ratings from 5 to 7 as low risk.

4.3.3.5 Web Application Security Frame

The Web Application Security Frame, also called the Application Security Frame (ASF), uses categories to organize common security vulnerabilities focused on web software applications. If you use these categories when you review your application design to create a threat model, you can systematically reveal the threats and vulnerabilities specific to your application architecture. There are nine frame categories; sample questions used in the process are listed below.

Web Application Security Frame Categories and Assessment Questions[13]

- **Input and Data Validation**
  How do you know that the input your application receives is valid and safe? Input validation refers to how your application filters, scrubs, or rejects input before additional processing. Consider constraining input through entry points and encoding output through exit points. Do you trust data from sources such as databases and file shares?

- **Authentication**
  Who are you? Authentication is the process whereby an entity proves the identity of another entity, typically through credentials, such as a user name and password.

- **Authorization**
  What can you do? Authorization is how your application provides access controls for resources and operations.

- **Configuration Management**
  Who does your application run as? Which databases does it connect to? How is your application administered? How are these settings secured? Configuration management refers to how your application handles these operational issues.

- **Sensitive Data**
  How does your application handle sensitive data? Sensitive data refers to how your application handles any data that must be protected either in memory, over the network, or in persistent stores.

- **Session Management**
  How does your application handle and protect user sessions? A session refers to a series of related interactions between a user and your web application.

- **Cryptography**
  How are you keeping secrets (confidentiality)? How are you tamper-proofing your data or libraries (integrity)? How are you providing seeds for random values that must be cryptographically strong? Cryptography refers to how your application enforces confidentiality and integrity.

- **Exception Management**
  When a method call in your application fails, what does your application do? How much do you reveal? Do you return friendly error information to end users? Do you pass valuable exception information back to the caller? Does your application fail gracefully?

- **Auditing and Logging**
  Who did what and when? Auditing and logging refer to how your application records security-related events.

4.3.3.6 The Generic Risk Model

Microsoft threat modeling processes such as STRIDE and DREAD may not be appropriate for your application, and you may want to use other threat risk models or modify the Microsoft processes for your own use, adopting the most appropriate threat modeling methodologies for your own organization. Using qualitative values such as high, medium, and low can also help avoid the ranking becoming too subjective, as with the numbering system used in DREAD.

These examples help in the calculation of the overall risk values by assigning qualitative values such as high, medium, and low to likelihood and impact factors. Here, too, using qualitative values rather than numeric ones, as in the DREAD model, helps avoid the ranking becoming overly subjective.

An example of a more subjective model is the Generic Risk Model, which takes into consideration the likelihood (e.g., the probability of an attack) and the impact (e.g., damage potential) and is represented mathematically as[14]

$$\text{Risk} = \text{Likelihood} \times \text{Impact}$$

The likelihood or probability is defined by the ease of exploitation, which depends mainly on the type of threat and the system characteristics, and by the possibility to realize a threat, which is determined by the existence of an appropriate countermeasure. The following is a set of considerations for determining ease of exploitation:

1. Can an attacker exploit this remotely?
2. Does the attacker need to be authenticated?
3. Can the exploit be automated?

The impact depends mainly on the damage potential and the extent of the impact, such as the number of components that are affected by a threat. Examples to determine the damage potential are as follows:

1. Can an attacker completely take over and manipulate the system?
2. Can an attacker gain administration access to the system?
3. Can an attacker crash the system?
4. Can the attacker obtain access to sensitive information such as secrets, PII?

Examples to determine the number of components that are affected by a threat include:

1. How many data sources and systems can be impacted?
2. How "deep" into the infrastructure can the threat agent go?

4.3.3.7 Trike

An alternative threat modeling methodology to STRIDE and DREAD is Trike. Trike is a unified conceptual framework for security auditing from a risk management perspective through the generation of threat models in a reliable, repeatable manner.[15] Trike uses a threat modeling framework that is similar to the Microsoft threat modeling methodologies. However, Trike differs in that it uses a risk-based approach with distinct implementation, threat, and risk models, instead of using the STRIDE/DREAD aggregated threat model (attacks, threats, and weaknesses).[16]

Trike is distinguished from other threat modeling methodologies by the high levels of automation possible within the system, the defensive perspective of the system, and the degree of formalism present in the methodology.[17] The latest version of the Trike tool can be downloaded at the SourceForge® website at http://sourceforge.net/projects/trike/files/trike.

A security auditing team can use it to describe the security characteristics of a system from its high-level architecture to its low-level implementation details. The goal of Trike is to automate the repetitive parts of threat modeling. Trike automatically generates threats (and some attacks) based on a description of the system, but this requires that the user describe the system to Trike and check whether these threats and attacks apply.[18] A key element of Trike is the empowerment, involvement, and communications with the key stakeholders with complete progress and task status transparency so that they know the level of risk and can evaluate acceptance of the risk throughout the software development process.

4.3.3.8 Process for Attack Simulation and Threat Analysis (PASTA)

In 2011, a new application threat modeling methodology developed by Marco Morana and Tony Uceda Velez was presented. PASTA is a seven-step process that is applicable to most application development methodologies and is platform-agnostic. It not only aligns business objectives with technical requirements but also takes into account compliance requirements, business impact analysis, and a dynamic approach to threat management, enumeration, and scoring. The process begins with a clear definition of business objectives, security and compliance requirements, and business impact analysis. Similar to the Microsoft process, the application is decomposed into components, with use case diagrams and DFDs to illustrate the threat model with which threat and vulnerability analysis can be performed. The next step involves use of threat trees, abuse cases, scoring systems, and enumerations for further reference in analysis. Following this, the threat model is viewed from an attacker perspective by attack modeling in attack trees and attack surface analysis. In the final step, risk and business impact can be qualified and quantified, and necessary countermeasures identified. This process combines the best of various threat modeling approaches, with the attack trees serving as an attacker-centric means of viewing a threat, as well as, in combination with risk and impact analysis, helping to create an asset-centric means of planning a mitigation strategy. The threat trees, with mapping of threats to existing vulnerabilities, work in favor of easy and scalable threat management. Beyond the technical aspects, the risk and business impact analysis take threat modeling beyond just a software development exercise to involve participation of key decision makers in the vulnerability management process. What differentiates this methodology from Trike is that it focuses on involving risk management steps in the final stage of the process. This ensures that it is not limited to a specific risk estimation formula.[19]

The seven-step PASTA Threat Modeling Methodology is as follows:[20]

1. Define Objectives
   - Identify business objectives.
   - Identify security and compliance requirements.
   - Business impact analysis.

2. Define Technical Scope
   - Capture the boundaries of the technical environment.
   - Capture infrastructure, application, and software dependencies.

3. Application Decomposition
   - Identify uses cases and define application entry points and trust levels.
   - Indentify actors, assets, services, roles, and data sources.
   - Data flow diagramming and trust boundaries.

4. Threat Analysis
   - Probabilistic attack scenarios analysis.
   - Regression analysis on security events.
   - Threat intelligence correlation and analytics.

5. Vulnerability and Weakness Analysis
   - Queries of existing vulnerability reports and issues tracking.
   - Threat to existing vulnerability mapping using threat trees.
   - Design flaw analysis using use and abuse cases.
   - Scorings (CVSS/CWSS) and enumerations (CWE™/CVE®).

6. Attack Modeling
   - Attack surface analysis.
   - Attack tree development and attack library management.
   - Attack to vulnerability and exploits analysis using attack trees.

7. Risk and Impact Analysis
   - Qualify and quantify business impact.
   - Countermeasure identification and residual risk analysis.
   - ID risk mitigation strategies.

There is threat-modeling tool called ThreatModeler® that supports the PASTA methodology. ThreatModeler is a threat modeling product that brings a mind mapping approach to threat modeling. It allows companies to scale their threat modeling initiative across thousands of applications easily and effortlessly. ThreatModeler automatically generates threats and classifies them under various risk categories. It provides a centralized threat management platform in which organizations can define threats related to network, host, applications, mobile, web services, etc., and associate attributes such as technical impacts, business impacts, and threat agents to better understand a threat and prioritize mitigation strategies.[21,22]

Although its original focus was on banking malware threats, PASTA certainly has applicability across all software applications and will fit well into most SDLCs. It will be interesting to see how widely it is accepted in industry over the next few years.

4.3.3.9 CVSS

Another risk assessment methodology that is very popular and is used extensively by corporate product security incident response teams (PSIRTs) and internal software security groups to classify externally discovered software vulnerabilities is the U.S. government's Common Vulnerability Scoring System (CVSS). The National Infrastructure Advisory Council (NIAC) commissioned CVSS to support the global Vulnerability Disclosure Framework. CVSS is currently maintained by the Forum of Incident Response and Security Teams (FIRST),[23] and was a joint effort involving many companies, including CERT®/CC, Cisco Systems, DHS/MITRE®, eBay®, IBM® Internet Security Systems (ISS®), Microsoft, Qualys,® and Symantec®. The CVSS model is designed to provide end users with an overall composite score representing the severity and risk of a vulnerability. It is derived from metrics and formulas. The metrics are in three distinct categories that can be quantitatively or qualitatively measured. Base metrics contain qualities that are intrinsic to any given vulnerability; these qualities do not change over time or in different environments. Temporal metrics contain characteristics of a vulnerability that evolve over the lifetime of the vulnerability. Environmental metrics contain characteristics of a vulnerability that are related to an implementation in a specific user's environment. Scoring is the process of combining all metric values according to specific formulas and based on a series of measurements called metrics based on expert assessment, which is described below:[24]

- Base scoring is computed by the vendor or originator with the intention of being published, and, once set, is not expected to change. Base scoring is also computed from confidentiality, integrity, and availability. This is the foundation that is modified by the temporal and environmental metrics. The base score has the largest bearing on the final score and represents vulnerability severity.
- Temporal scoring is also computed by vendors and coordinators for publication and modifies the base score. It allows for the introduction of mitigating factors to reduce the score of a vulnerability and is designed to be reevaluated at specific intervals as a vulnerability ages. The temporal score represents vulnerability urgency at specific points in time.
- Environment scoring is optionally computed by end-user organizations and adjusts the combined base-temporal score. This adjusted combined score should be considered the final score and represents a moment in time, tailored to a specific environment. User organizations should use this score to prioritize responses within their own environments.

A useful tool is the Common Vulnerability Scoring System Version 3.1 Calculator, which can be found at https://www.first.org/cvss/calculator/3.1.

The CVSS has become an industry standard for assessing the severity of computer system security vulnerabilities. It establishes a measure of how much concern vulnerability should warrant compared to other vulnerabilities so that mitigation efforts can be prioritized. As of the writing of this book, the current version of CVSS is version 3.1.

The CVSS is typically used by an internal software security group to respond to a security researcher or other source that has notified you that your software product has a vulnerability. This provides the ability to keep your severity ratings normalized, consistent, and accurate. The scores are also used in the communication to the customers acknowledging that there is a vulnerability in the product that they have purchased, the severity of the vulnerability, and what your company is doing to mitigate that vulnerability, including any patch releases for the vulnerability. In turn, a security researcher will likely use the CVSS ranking system to provide a risk rating to the company within whose software product they have found a vulnerability, so that the vendor has a good idea of the severity of the vulnerability that is being disclosed and the details of what to verify with its product development team.

It should be noted that the CVSS is not a threat modeling methodology and is not used to find or reduce the attack surface or to help specify risks within a piece of code. It is, rather, a risk scoring system and it adds complexities that don't exist in STRIDE and DREAD. It is used to calculate risks that are identified post-product release in addition to environmental factors.

4.3.3.10 OCTAVE®

Operationally Critical Threat, Asset, and Vulnerability Evaluation (OCTAVE) is a very complex risk methodology approach originating from Carnegie Mellon University's Software Engineering Institute (SEI) in collaboration with the SEI Computer Emergency Response Team (CERT). OCTAVE focuses on organizational risk, not technical risk. It comprises a suite of tools, techniques, and methods for risk-based information security strategic assessment and planning. There are three OCTAVE methods: (1) the original OCTAVE method, which forms the basis for the OCTAVE body of knowledge; (2) OCTAVE-S, for smaller organizations; and (3) OCTAVE-Allegro, a streamlined approach for information security assessment and assurance. All of the methods have specific catalogs of practices, profiles, and worksheets to document the modeling outcomes. OCTAVE methods are founded on the OCTAVE criteria—a standard approach for a risk-driven and practice-based information security evaluation. The OCTAVE criteria establish the fundamental principles and attributes of risk management that are used by the OCTAVE methods.[25]

OCTAVE is a valuable structured approach to documenting and measuring overall IT security risk, particularly as it relates to corporate IT and business risk management and when documenting risks surrounding complete systems becomes necessary. Although a software security professional may be involved in a portion of the assessment as a software or process for building software security into the development process may be within its scope, it is not valuable for modeling, defining, and ranking specific risks and vulnerabilities within the SDL process. As with CVSS scoring, OCTAVE does not include threat risk modeling and is used primarily to enumerate risk. It is also much more complex than most other risk assessment and scoring methodologies in that it consists of 18 volumes with many worksheets to work through. The comprehensive version of OCTAVE (unlike OCTAVE-S for small organizations) defines "likelihood" assuming that the threat will always occur, which is not applicable to many large organizations. For these reasons, it is not likely to be an approach that is used throughout the software development life cycle.

4.3.3.11 AS/NZS ISO® 31000:2009

The Australian/New Zealand Standard AS/NZS 4360, first issued in 1999 and revised in 2004, was the world's first formal standard for documenting and managing risk and is still one of the few formal standards for managing it.[26] AS/NZS ISO 31000:2009 is a newer standard, published November 20, 2009, for managing risk and supersedes AS/NZS 4360:2004.[27]

ISO 31000:2009 provides principles and generic guidelines on risk management and can be used by any public, private, or community enterprise, association, group, or individual. It is not specific to any industry or sector. It can be applied throughout the life of an organization, and to a wide range of activities, including strategies and decisions, operations, processes, functions, projects, products, services, and assets. It can also be applied to any type of risk, whatever its nature, whether having positive or negative consequences. Although ISO 31000:2009 provides generic guidelines, it is not intended to promote uniformity of risk management across organizations. The design and implementation of risk management plans and frameworks will need to take into account the varying needs of a specific organization; its particular objectives, context, structure, operations, processes, functions, projects, products, services, or assets; and specific practices employed. It is intended that ISO 31000:2009 be utilized to harmonize risk management processes in existing and future standards. It provides a common approach in support of standards dealing with specific risks and/or sectors and does not replace those standards.[28]

ISO 31000:2009 does not define the methodology to perform a structured threat risk modeling exercise or a structured approach to specify software application security risks, and it works best in evaluating business or systemic risks rather than for technical risks. As with OCTAVE, this methodology is likely to be used by a centralized corporate risk management team. Software security professionals may be involved in a portion of the assessment because their software or process for building software security into the development process may be in scope, but it is not likely that this methodology will be used in the SDL as a primary risk methodology because it is not valuable for modeling, defining, and ranking specific risks and vulnerabilities within the SDLC process.

4.3.4 Risk Mitigation

Before you move onto the risk mitigation phase you will need to make a master list of high-risk vulnerabilities during the threat modeling process, including STRIDE or an equivalent. This will give you a priority list from which to work as you follow through your mitigation plan.

There are four ways you can plan mitigation and address threats:[29]

1. Redesign the process to eliminate the threat.
2. Apply a standard mitigation as per general recommendations.
3. Invent a new mitigation strategy (risky and time-consuming).
4. Accept vulnerabilities with low risk and high effort to fix them.

Vulnerability threats that have no countermeasures in STRIDE or Application Security Frame (ASF) are categorized, and countermeasured for specific threats that are identified for each of the categories they fall into.

STRIDE Threat & Mitigation Techniques List[30]

Spoofing identity

- Appropriate authentication
- Protect secret data
- Don't store secrets

Tampering with data

- Appropriate authorization
- Hashes
- MACs
- Digital signatures
- Tamper-resistant protocols

Repudiation

- Digital signatures
- Timestamps
- Audit trails

Information disclosure

- Authorization
- Privacy-enhanced protocols
- Encryption
- Protect secrets
- Don't store secrets

Denial of service

- Appropriate authentication
- Appropriate authorization
- Filtering
- Throttling
- Quality of service

Elevation of privilege

- Run with least privilege

ASF Threat and Countermeasures List[31]

Authentication

1. Credentials and authentication tokens are protected with encryption in storage and transit.
2. Protocols are resistant to brute force, dictionary, and replay attacks.
3. Strong password policies are enforced.
4. Trusted server authentication is used instead of SQL authentication.
5. Passwords are stored with salted hashes.
6. Password resets do not reveal password hints and valid usernames.

Authorization

1. Strong ACLs are used for enforcing authorized access to resources.
2. Role-based access controls are used to restrict access to specific operations.

3. The system follows the principle of least privilege for user and service accounts.
4. Privilege separation is correctly configured within the presentation, business, and data access layers.

Configuration management

1. Least privileged processes are used and service accounts with no administration capability.
2. Auditing and logging of all administration activities is enabled.
3. Access to configuration files and administrator interfaces is restricted to administrators.

Data protection in storage and transit

1. Standard encryption algorithms and correct key sizes are used.
2. Hashed message authentication codes (HMACs) are used to protect data integrity.
3. Secrets (e.g., keys, confidential data) are cryptographically protected, both in transport and in storage.
4. Built-in secure storage is used for protecting keys.
5. No credentials and sensitive data are sent in clear text over the wire.

Data validation/parameter validation

1. Data type, format, length, and range checks are enforced.
2. All data sent from the client is validated.
3. No security decision is based on parameters—for example, URL parameters—that can be manipulated.
4. Input filtering via white list validation is used.
5. Output encoding is used.

Error handling and exception management

1. All exceptions are handled in a structured manner.
2. Privileges are restored to the appropriate level in case of errors and exceptions.
3. Error messages are scrubbed so that no sensitive information is revealed to the attacker.

User and session management

1. No sensitive information is stored in clear text in the cookies.
2. The contents of the authentication cookies is encrypted.
3. Cookies are configured to expire.
4. Sessions are resistant to replay attacks.
5. Secure communication channels are used to protect authentication cookies.
6. User is forced to re-authenticate when performing critical functions.
7. Sessions are expired at logout.

Auditing and logging

1. Sensitive information (e.g., passwords, PII) is not logged.
2. Access controls (e.g., ACLs) are enforced on log files to prevent unauthorized access.
3. Integrity controls (e.g., signatures) are enforced on log files to provide nonrepudiation.

4. Log files provide for audit trail for sensitive operations and logging of key events.
5. Auditing and logging is enabled across the tiers on multiple servers.

After you have identified the software threats and associated mitigation strategies and ranked the risks, it is possible to identify a mitigation threat profile for each threat that has been identified through the threat modeling/architecture security analysis process. The following criteria are used to categorize your final list from this process:

- **Fully mitigated threats:** Threats that have appropriate countermeasures in place and do not expose vulnerability or cause impact.
- **Partially mitigated threats:** Threats partially mitigated by one or more countermeasures, which represent vulnerabilities that can only partially be exploited and cause a limited impact.
- **Nonmitigated threats:** Threats that have no countermeasures and represent vulnerabilities that can be fully exploited and cause an impact.[32]

Now that you have categorized your threats in one of the three categories above, you have a choice to make concerning what strategy you are going to pursue. Your choices of action will likely fall under one of the following five options:

1. Do nothing: for example, hope for the best.
2. Inform about the risk: for example, warn your user population about the risk.
3. Mitigate the risk: for example, by putting countermeasures in place.
4. Accept the risk: for example, after evaluating the impact of the exploitation (business impact).
5. Transfer the risk: for example, through contractual agreements and insurance.[33]

Your decision as to which of the strategies listed above will be used will depend on several factors:

- The impact an exploitation of a threat can have
- The likelihood of its occurrence
- The costs for transferring (i.e., costs for insurance) or avoiding (i.e., costs or losses due to redesign) it[34]

Risk in this sense is an identified threatening situation due to the potential presence of an actor, motivation, and vulnerability with a significant probability and business impact. The

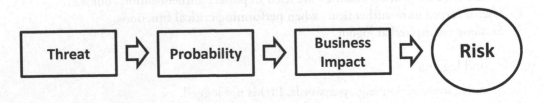

Figure 4.9   Elements of risk.

risk of a threat is not the issue, but rather an identified risk that has been ranked in severity with a significant business consequence as the result of the outcome of a threat. The probability of the threat is considered separately because it is affected by the motivation of the actor and the specifics and external factors affecting the vulnerability. Business impact is also a key element of risk that is affected by both the type of actor, which can be state, industrial, or criminal, and the specifics of the vulnerability. This can be visualized as shown in Figure 4.9.

In this section, we have shown some of the options and standard methodologies that can be used to assess your threats, rank your risk, and develop a risk mitigation plan. The process we have described is visualized in Figure 4.10.

The bottom line is that risk assessment is about business risk and results in trade-offs as it relates to security risk to the software, the system it interacts with, and the overall business risk management strategy. It is important for security professionals to know this, and that is why we have included two popular overall business risk assessment methodologies that focus on information security risk, specifically, OCTAVE and AS/NZS ISO 31000:2009. As with the ecosystem the software is part of, the risk assessment methodology used for secure software development will also have points of intersection with the overall business risk management methodology, and those areas need to be taken into account as part of the software risk analysis.

Ultimately, this will be a business decision. This is why one decision may be to fix vulnerabilities only where the cost to fix is less than the potential business impact that might result from exploitation of the vulnerability, or why another decision may be made to accept the risk when the loss of some security controls (e.g., confidentiality, integrity, and availability) risks only a small degradation of the service, not a loss of a critical business function.[35]

4.4 Open-Source Selection

There has been an increasing trend in the software industry over the last few years to draw on the strengths of both open-source and proprietary software to deliver the highest value at the lowest cost. The blend of both is called "mixed source" and is becoming a dominant practice in industry. Understanding and managing the licensing of your software assets will be critical as open source becomes an ever-greater part of the software development landscape, but this is beyond the scope of our discussion and will be handled by others on the software development team.

There is an ongoing debate as to whether open-source software increases software security or is detrimental to it, but the bottom line is that you are importing software into your software application or solution that your company did not develop or have security oversight over. This will require an extensive review, typically called a third-party security assessment, which will be conducted by your software security architect, a third party, or a combination of both. Although it may be tempting to rely on tools and a cursory review of the open-source development processes, without the proper training and experience, it is easy to misinterpret results and difficult to create an actionable remediation strategy. That is why senior software security architects or a third-party equivalent must be involved in this review process. They have years of code security auditing experience, routinely review and mitigate highly complex and advanced software security and architectural challenges, know how to identify

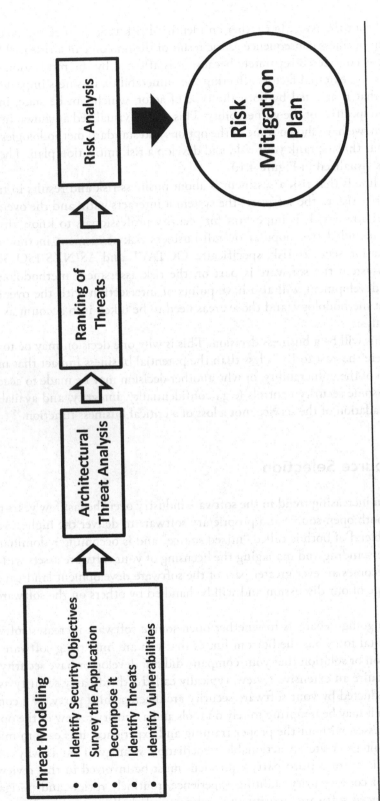

Figure 4.10 A holistic approach for software security risk assessment.

and examine vulnerable points in design, and can uncover flaws that may result in a security compromise. Without the proper training and experience, it is easy to misinterpret results and difficult to create any necessary actionable remediation strategy. Essentially, the review of any open-source software or component used in your software product will require both tool assessment and follow-on threat modeling as well as risk assessment conducted by a seasoned software security architect.

4.5 Privacy Information Gathering and Analysis

It is important to consider if the system will transmit, store, or create information that may be considered privacy information early in the SDLC. The gathering of information and identification and development of a plan for implementing proper safeguards and security controls, including processes to address privacy information incident handling and reporting requirements, are determined at this stage. This stage of the SDL is where the information gathering and analysis for the Privacy Impact Assessment (PIA) begins. The analysis phase determines how PII will be handled to ensure that it conforms to applicable legal, regulatory, and policy requirements regarding privacy and what the risks and effects are of collecting, maintaining, and disseminating privacy information in identifiable form in the software and overall system being developed or one that it potentially interfaces with in a cloud or SaaS environment, and it examines and evaluates protections and alternative processes for handling information to mitigate potential privacy risks.

4.6 Key Success Factors and Metrics

4.6.1 Key Success Factors

The success of this second phase of the SDL depends on how well the SDLC identifies the threats, requirements, and constraints in functionality and integration and mitigates the risk. Key success factors for this second phase are listed in Table 4.1.

Table 4.1 Key Success Factors

Key Success Factor	Description
1. Identification of business requirements and risks	Mapping of business requirements and risks defined in terms of CIA
2. Effective threat modeling	Identifying threats for the software
3. Effective architectural threat analysis	Analysis of threats to the software and probability of threat materializing
4. Effective risk mitigation strategy	Risk acceptance, tolerance, and mitigation plan per business requirements
5. Accuracy of DFDs	Data flow diagrams used during threat modeling

Success Factor 1: Identification of Business Requirements and Risks

During this phase, key stakeholders, including the software security group, help write out business risks and requirements. Business requirements are defined through the CIA pillars of information security. A successful SDL cycle must identify and capture all requirements to the best extent possible.

Success Factor 2: Effective Threat Modeling

Though it is a complex and challenging task, the entire risk mitigation plan rests on threat modeling. Any gaps in a threat model will result in ineffective secure development and deployment controls.

Success Factor 3: Effective Architectural Threat Analysis

Architectural threat analysis enables the identification of threats and ranks them in order of priority. All threat vectors resulting in the risk must be identified and prioritized.

Success Factor 4: Effective Risk Mitigation Strategy

A key outcome from threat modeling and analysis is risk acceptance and a mitigation plan. Business appetite for risk acceptance and tolerance must be thoroughly vetted, including legal and finance.

Success Factor 5: Accuracy of DFDs

DFDs are used during threat modeling to identify various components/elements of interest. DFDs should be as detailed as possible. Any assumptions should be reviewed carefully. Specifically, trust boundaries (client/server, private/public infrastructure, tiered architecture) should be properly documented and reviewed.

4.6.2 Deliverables

Table 4.2 lists deliverables for this phase of the SDL.

Table 4.2 Deliverables for Phase A2

Deliverable	Goal
Business requirements	Software requirements, including CIA
Threat modeling artifacts	Data flow diagrams, elements, threat listing
Architecture threat analysis	Prioritization of threats and risks based on threat analysis
Risk mitigation plan	Plan to mitigate, accept, or tolerate risk
Policy compliance analysis	Analysis of adherence to company policies

Business Requirements

A formal business requirement is an artifact that lists software requirements and business risks mapped to the three pillars of information security: confidentiality, integrity, and availability.

Threat Modeling Artifacts

Key artifacts include DFDs, technical threat modeling reports, high-level executive threat modeling reports, threat lists, and recommendations for threat analysis.

Architecture Threat Analysis

The key artifact from this step of the SDL is an artifact that outlines the risks of threat materializing. Another one that should be required from this step is threat ranking/priority.

Risk Mitigation Plan

The risk mitigation plan outlines risks (and threats) to be mitigated, accepted, or tolerated. For each of these categories, it also outlines steps on mitigation risks. Finally, this report should be presented to the business for sign-off before actual work on the project begins.

Policy Compliance Analysis

This artifact is a report on compliance with different security and nonsecurity policies within the company—for example, how software or its components comply with information security policy, data governance policy, data retention, cryptography policy, etc.

4.6.3 Metrics

The following metrics should be collected and recorded for this second phase of the SDL cycle:

- List of business threats, technical threats (mapped to business threats), and threat actors
- Number of security objectives unmet after this phase
- Percent compliance with company policies (existing)
- Number of entry points for software (using DFDs)
- Percent of risk (and threats) accepted, mitigated, and tolerated
- Percent of initial software requirements redefined
- Number of planned software architectural changes (major and minor) in a product
- Number of software architectural changes needed based on security requirements

4.7 Summary

The primary goal of the Architecture (A2) phase of our DSL model is to identify the overall requirements and structure for the software from a security perspective. The key elements of this phase are threat modeling, documentation of elements of the software attack surface from an architectural perspective; definition of security architecture and design guidelines;

continued security, SDL, and privacy policy and requirements compliance reviews; and software product security release requirements.

These best practices result in the definition of the software's overall structure from a security perspective. They identify those components whose correct functioning is essential to security. They also identify the appropriate security design techniques applicable for the software product architecture, including the application of least privilege, and minimize the attack surface of the software product and any supporting infrastructure. Although a higher layer may depend on the services of lower layers, the lower layers are forbidden from depending on higher layers. Although the security architecture identifies an overall perspective on security design, the specifics of individual elements of the architecture will be detailed in individual design specifications.

The identification and measurement of the individual elements of the attack surface provides the development and software security team with an ongoing metric for default security and enables them to detect instances in which the software has been made susceptible to attack. During this phase, all exceptions to reducing the attack surface must be reviewed because the goal is to maximize security as a default for a software product that is being developed. Threat modeling uses a structured approach at a component-by-component level, identifying the assets that the software must manage and the interfaces by which those assets can be accessed. The likelihood of harm being done to any of the assets identified during threat modeling is estimated as a measure of risk. Countermeasures or compensating controls to mitigate the risk are also identified. Where appropriate and feasible, tools should be used that can capture the threat models in machine-readable form for storage and updating. Specific pre-ship software security criteria are also identified at this stage of the SDL.

Toward the end of the chapter, we discussed key success factors and their importance, deliverables, and metrics that should be collected from this phase.

Chapter Quick-Check

1. Threats are identified using a process described by this mnemonic:
   a. THREATEXPOSE
   b. STRIDE
   c. DREAD
   d. CAPEC

2. Risk is calculated for each identified threat to prioritize findings and needs for remediation using which technique?
   a. RISKCOMPUTE
   b. DANGER
   c. DREAD
   d. THREATORDER

3. Which of the following is not a mitigation method for threats identified in threat modeling?
   a. Redesign to eliminate vulnerability
   b. Apply a standard mitigation

    c. Change the security requirements to eliminate the threat

    d. Accept the vulnerability

4. The preferred security mitigation to use during threat modeling is:

    a. A custom control created specifically for the threat

    b. Encryption from an approved library to prevent information disclosure

    c. Acceptance of the vulnerability

    d. Standard enterprise-level security controls in common use

Exercises

1. For a replacement application, you'll need to start with a drawing. If you have already thought out what the architecture should be for the project, you can use that diagram. If you have ideas on system flows, you can create a dataflow diagram like the ones shown in Figures 4.4 and 4.5 in this chapter. Mark up the diagram with the sensitivity of the data elements in the flows, the protection of those flows with network security protocols (e.g., TLS), and what database security controls are present (row-level encryption, etc.). At this point, you'll have the basis to conduct a simple threat modeling exercise:

    a. Look for all the assets being managed by the application and determine if any of the classes of threats using STRIDE apply. If they do, document them as a possible threat.

    b. Continue this process until you've considered all the STRIDE classes of threats and documented them. Five to eight identified threats are sufficient for this step.

    c. Once you think that you've identified the threats to the would-be system, you can move into the risk assessment step using DREAD.

    d. Estimate the rankings for each DREAD category, sum up the rankings, and divide by 5.

    e. Continue this for each threat you identified, and once you're done, you should have a prioritized list of threats that need further analysis and countermeasure development to remediate design defects or errors.

2. Once you've completed the threat modeling exercise activities, document the metrics you've collected to close out Phase A2 of the SDL.

References

1. Kohnfelder, L., and Garg, P. (1999). "The Threats to Our Products." Retrieved from https://www.coursehero.com/file/107921084/The-Threats-To-Our-Productsdocx/

2. cisodesk.com. (2012). "SiteXposure: Threat Modeling Process—Overview." Retrieved from http://www.cisodesk.com/web-application-security/threat-modeling-overview

3. Hernan, S., et al. (2006). "Threat Modeling: Uncover Security Design Flaws Using the STRIDE Approach." Retrieved from http://msdn.microsoft.com/en-us/magazine/cc163519.aspx#S3

4. cisodesk.com. (2012). "SiteXposure: Threat Modeling—Practice." Retrieved from http://www.cisodesk.com/web-application-security/threat-modeling-in-practice

5. Hernan, S., et al. (2006). "Threat Modeling: Uncover Security Design Flaws Using the STRIDE Approach." *MSDN Magazine*. Retrieved from http://msdn.microsoft.com/en-us/magazine/cc163 519.aspx#S3

6. Shostack, A. (2008). "Experiences Threat Modeling at Microsoft." Retrieved from http://www .homeport.org/~adam/modsec08/Shostack-ModSec08-Experiences-Threat-Modeling-At-Micro soft.pdf

7. microsoft.com (2009). "The STRIDE Threat Model." Retrieved from http://msdn.microsoft.com /en-us/library/ee823878(v=cs.20).aspx

8. OWASP. (2012). "Application Threat Modeling." Retrieved from https://www.owasp.org/index .php/Application_Threat_Modeling#Data_Flow_Diagrams

9. Meier, J., et al. (2003, June). "Microsoft Corporation MSDN Library Doc: Improving Web Application Security: Threats and Countermeasures." Retrieved from http://msdn.microsoft.com/en-us /library/ff648644.aspx

10. Conklin, C. (2021). "Threat Modeling Process." Retrieved from https://owasp.org/www-community/Threat_Modeling_Process

11. Ibid.

12. Meier, J., et al. (2003, June). "Microsoft Corporation MSDN Library Doc: Improving Web Application Security: Threats and Countermeasures." Retrieved from http://msdn.microsoft.com/en-us /library/ff648644.aspx

13. Microsoft MSDN. (2012). "Cheat Sheet: Web Application Security Frame—Web Application Security Frame Categories." Retrieved from http://msdn.microsoft.com/en-us/library/ff649461.aspx

14. Conklin, C. (2021). "Threat Modeling Process." Retrieved from https://owasp.org/www-community/Threat_Modeling_Process

15. Saitta, P., Larcom, B., and Eddington, M. (2005). "Trike v.1 Methodology Document." (Draft). Retrieved from http://octotrike.org/papers/Trike_v1_Methodology_Document-draft.pdf

16. Jagannathan, V. (2021). "Threat Modeling: Architecting & Designing with Security in Mind." Retrieved from https://owasp.org/www-pdf-archive/AdvancedThreatModeling.pdf

17. Saitta, P., Larcom, B., and Eddington, M. (2005). "Trike v.1 Methodology Document." (Draft). Retrieved from http://octotrike.org/papers/Trike_v1_Methodology_Document-draft.pdf

18. U.S. Department of Homeland Security—US CERT. (2009). "Requirements and Analysis for Secure Software—Software Assurance Pocket Guide Series: Development, Volume IV Version 1.0," October 5, 2009. Retrieved from https://www.yumpu.com/en/document/view/43001070 /requirements-and-analysis-for-secure-software-build-security-in-

19. MyAppSecurity. (2012). "Comparison of Threat Modeling Methodologies: P.A.S.T.A (Process for Attack Simulation and Threat Analysis)." Retrieved from http://www.myappsecurity.com/threat -modeling/comparison-threat-modeling-methodologies

20. Morana, M., and Ucedavelez, T. (2011). "OWASP Threat Modeling of Banking Malware-Based Attacks Presentation," AppSec EU, June 10, 2011, Trinity College, Dublin, Ireland. Retrieved from https://www.owasp.org/images/5/5f/Marco_Morana_and_Tony_UV_-_Threat_Modeling_of _Banking_Malware.pdf

21. Morana, M. (2011). "Writing Secure Software Blog: Attack Simulation and Threat Analysis of Banking Malware-Based Attacks," June 10, 2011. Retrieved from http://securesoftware.blogspot .com/2011/06/attack-simulation-and-threat-analysis.html

22. threatmodeler.com. (2021). "ThreatModeler." Retrieved from https://threatmodeler.com

23. FiRST. (2021). FiRST Homepage. Retrieved from http://www.first.org

24. FiRST. (2021). "Common Vulnerability Scoring System version 3.1: Specification Document." Retrieved from https://www.first.org/cvss/specification-document

25. Caralli et al. (2007). "Introducing OCTAVE Allegro: Improving the Information Security Risk Assessment Process." Retrieved from https://resources.sei.cmu.edu/library/asset-view.cfm?assetID =8419

26. STANDARDS Australia–New Zealand. (2009). "AS/NZS ISO 31000:2009 Risk Management—Principles and Guidelines." Retrieved from https://www.isa.org.jm/files/files/documents/asnzs _31000_2009.pdf

27. Ibid.

28. ISO. (2012). "ISO 31000:2009—Risk Management—Principles and Guidelines." Retrieved from http://www.iso.org/iso/catalogue_detail?csnumber=43170

29. Cisodesk. (2012). "Threat Modeling—Practice Guide." Retrieved from http://www.cisodesk.com /web-application-security/threat-modeling-in-practice

30. OWASP. (2012). "Application Threat Modeling: STRIDE Threat & Mitigation Techniques List." Retrieved from https://www.owasp.org/index.php/Application_Threat_Modeling

31. Conklin, C. (2021). "Threat Modeling Process." Retrieved from https://owasp.org/www-community/Threat_Modeling_Process

32. Ibid.

33. Ibid.

34. OWASP. (2021). "OWASP Risk Rating Methodology." Retrieved from https://owasp.org/www -community/OWASP_Risk_Rating_Methodology

35. Ibid.

Chapter 5

Design and Development (A3): SDL Activities and Best Practices

CHAPTER OVERVIEW

This chapter covers the design and development (A3) phase when the end user of your software is foremost in your mind. During this phase, you will do an analysis of policy compliance; create the test plan documentation; update your threat model, if necessary; conduct a design security analysis and review; and do a privacy implementation assessment so you can make informed decisions about how to deploy your software securely and establish development best practices to detect and remove security and privacy issues early in the development cycle.

CHAPTER TAKE-AWAYS

- Explore the practices that compose the Architecture (Phase A3) of the security development lifecycle (SDL).
- Document the key success factors for completion of Phase A3.
- Create initial, draft deliverables for Phase A3 for the case study in Appendix A.
- Prepare a testing plan for the case study in Appendix A.

Figure 5.1 illustrates the steps and activities found in Phase A3 of the SDL.

In Phase A3, you'll perform a static analysis during both the design and development (A3) and the ship (A4) phases of your SDL. We will provide a detailed description of a static analysis in the next chapter. You will build the plan for how you will take your project through the rest of the SDL process, from implementation, to verification, to release. During the design and development (A3) phase, you establish best practices for this phase using functional and design specifications.

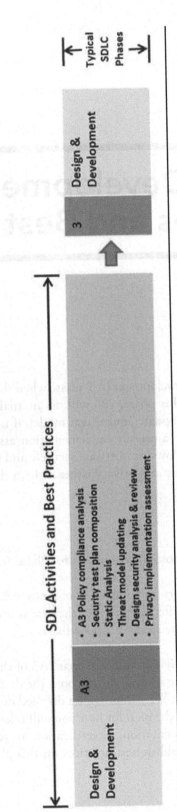

Figure 5.1 Design and Development (A3): SDL activities and best practices.

5.1 A3 Policy Compliance Analysis

A3 policy compliance analysis is a continuation of the A2 policy compliance review described in Chapter 4. During this phase, any policy that exists outside the domain of the SDL policy is reviewed. These might include policies from outside the development organization that set security and privacy requirements and guidelines to be adhered to when developing software or applications. Corporate security and privacy policies will likely instruct designers and developers on what the security and privacy features need to be and how they must be implemented. Other policies might focus on third-party and open-source software used as part of a software product, or on the protection and control of source code and other intellectual property within and outside the organization. Assuming the software security group is separate from the centralized information security group, it is important that both groups collaborate on all policies and guidelines related to the development and post-release security support and response of software from that organization. It is also important to collaborate with the privacy function of your company, whether it is a centralized group or outside legal counsel.

5.2 Security Test Plan Composition

Testing activities validate the secure implementation of a product, which reduces the likelihood of security bugs being released and discovered by customers and/or malicious users. Software assurance and competency from a security perspective is demonstrated by security testing and the use of artifacts, reports, and tools. The goal is not to test for insecurity but rather to validate the robustness and security of the software products before making the product available to customers. These security testing methods do find security bugs, especially in products that may not have undergone critical secure development process changes. The results of security testing and evaluation may also uncover deficiencies in the security controls used to protect the software that is under development. A detailed plan of action and milestone schedule are required to document the corrective measures planned to increase the effectiveness of the security controls and provide the requisite security for the software prior to its release.

As with the risk analysis methodologies discussed in Chapter 4, a holistic approach is necessary for security testing to be effective. Security testing confirms that the software complies with security requirements through design and code analysis and software behavior investigation. In other words, security testing is conducted to demonstrate that the software functions as specified by the requirements, and every software requirement must be tested using at least one relevant test case. The number of requirements tested versus the total number of requirements can be traced from test cases to functional requirements; then the ratio of requirements tested to the total number of requirements will become a test requirement metric.

Another element of security testing is to identify software weaknesses so that security violations and noncompliance with security requirements that could cause the software to fail or be out of compliance with any of software security requirements are avoided. As discussed in the risk analysis ranking section, due to resource limitations, security test plan efforts typically focus only on software requirement items that are considered to be critical. A master test plan is used to outline the entire test process and is augmented by detailed test plans for individual test stages and individual modules.

Although traditional requirements-based testing is important for the correctness and adequacy of security functions implemented by software, no amount of testing can fully demonstrate that software is free from vulnerabilities; any such testing can only provide a small-scale view of what is needed to verify the security of the software. Even the most robustly specified security requirements are not likely to address all possible conditions under which the software may be forced to operate in the real world, including the behavior of software under anomalous and hostile conditions.

Generally, the shortcomings of requirements-based over risk-based software security testing can be summarized as follows:

- The changing nature of threats to the software you have in development may result in new attack methodologies, both pre- and post-release.
- Your software may change its position as a functional component of an SaaS- or cloud-based solution, which changes the attack surface, thus requiring new security fixes or mitigations.
- In today's competitive and rapidly changing environment, the design assumptions on which the requirements were based may be obsolete by the time the software is ready for testing.
- Other factors change frequently and likely more rapidly than your specification can keep up.
- If the software is going to use components acquired from a third party, the original architecture may not account for future versions that were not planned for in the initial implementation.
- The original design assumptions may not account for vulnerability susceptibilities due to design changes or new external attacker capabilities or exploits that may occur during the time taken to develop later versions of the software.

This list highlights why software risk-based security testing as described in this section should always augment traditional requirements-based testing.

As mentioned previously and used as a continuing theme throughout this book, problems found early in the software life cycle by "building security in" are significantly easier and less costly to correct than problems discovered post-implementation or, worse, post-deployment. This is why it is imperative that a disciplined approach to security reviews and tests begin early in the software development life cycle (SDLC) process and continue post-release until the software reaches end of life.

Software security testing takes the perspective that the tester is the attacker. Test scenarios should be based on misuse and abuse possibilities developed through the methodologies and threat modeling described in Chapter 4 and should incorporate both known attack patterns as well as anomalous interactions that seek to invalidate assumptions made by and about the software and its environment. Comprehensive test scenarios, test cases, and test oracles should be derived. Be sure that all that misuse cases developed in the previous stage are executed and thoroughly tested. The testing of each development iteration, use case, and misuse case will identify major design flaws early in the SDL and should catch up to 95 percent of defects well before the last phase.[1]

The test environment should duplicate as closely as possible the anticipated execution environment in which the software will be deployed, and it should be kept entirely separate from the development environment. It should also provide for strict configuration management control to prevent tampering or corruption of test data, testing tools, and the integrated test environment, as well as the test plan itself and both the raw and finalized test results. It is also important to ensure that each tool set and test technique is appropriate for the individual software vulnerabilities that are being tested.

Testing for both functionality and security requires execution of the code and validation/verification of the results. It is also not always automated, because human intervention by experienced software security architects is typically needed. Because of the complexities and interactions of software ecosystems such as SaaS or cloud environments, the knowledge of such experts is required so that a wider range of scenarios can be tested.

As mentioned previously, the test plan lays out what needs to be tested for functionality, protected for security, and how the application will react to specific attacks. The test plan is a joint effort by the project management, development, and security teams, among others, to specify the logistics of the test plan, including who will execute the testing and when testing will begin and end.

The following are common steps that can be used to implement a test plan regardless of the strategy, framework, or standard being used:

- **Define test scripts.** Scripts are very detailed, logical steps of instructions that tell a person or tool what to do during the testing. Functional testing scripts are step-by-step instructions that depict a specific scenario or situation that the use case will encounter as well as the expected results. Secure testing scripts are scripts created specifically to test the security of the application. The basis for these scripts comes from the threat models that were generated during the design phase. Misuse cases define what needs to be protected (assets) and what types of attacks can gain access to those assets. Secure test scripts define the acts of carrying out those attacks.
- **Define the user community.** Defining the user community helps testers identify acceptable levels of failures and risk.
- **Identify the showstoppers.** Defining the must-haves and the "what-if-available" scenarios should be in the use case. If not, a revisit to the requirements might be necessary so that these specifications can be documented.
- **Identify internal resources.** Internal resources come from the company's organization, including developers, analysts, software tools, and sometimes project managers.
- **Identify external resources.** External resources are tools or people who are hired on a temporary basis to come into a project, test the application, and report findings. External resources are best suited for security testing because they typically come highly trained in secure programming techniques and they are far removed from the code and any internal politics. If external resources are needed, the test plan needs to answer the following questions: (1) What are they going to test? (2) To whom will they report? and (3) With whom will they be working?[2]

Assessing the security properties and behaviors of software as it intersects with external entities such as human users, the environment, and other software and as its own components interact with each other is a primary objective of security testing. As such, it should verify that software exhibits the following properties and behaviors:

- Its behavior is predictable and secure.
- It exposes no vulnerabilities or weaknesses.
- Its error- and exception-handling routines enable it to maintain a secure state when confronted by attack patterns or intentional faults.
- It satisfies all of its specified and implicit nonfunctional security requirements.
- It does not violate any specified and implicit nonfunctional security requirements.
- It does not violate any specified security constraints.
- As much of its runtime interpretable source code and byte code as possible has been obscured or obfuscated to deter reverse engineering.[3,4]

A security test plan should be included in the overall software test plan and should define all security-related testing activities, including the following:

- Security test cases or scenarios (based on abuse cases)
- Test data, including attack patterns
- Test oracle (if one is to be used)
- Test tools (white box, black box, static, and dynamic)
- Analysis to be performed to interpret, correlate, and synthesize the results from the various tests and outputs from the various tools[5,6]

Software security testing techniques can be categorized as white box, gray box, or black box:

- **White box.** Testing from an internal perspective, that is, with full knowledge of the software internals; the source code, architecture and design documents, and configuration files are available for analysis.
- **Gray box.** Analyzing the source code for the purpose of designing the test cases, but using black-box testing techniques; both the source code and executable binary are available for analysis.
- **Black box.** Testing the software from an external perspective, that is, with no prior knowledge of the software; only binary executable or intermediate byte code is available for analysis.[7,8]

The commonly used security testing techniques can be categorized using the above as follows:

- **Source-code analysis (white box).** Source-code security analyzers examine source code to detect and report software weaknesses that can lead to security vulnerabilities. The principal advantage that source-code security analyzers have over the other types of static analysis tools is the availability of the source code. The source code contains more information than code that must be reverse engineered from byte code or binary. Therefore, it is easier to discover software weaknesses that can lead to security vulnerabilities. Additionally, if the source code is available in its original form, it will be easier to fix any security vulnerabilities that are found.
- **Property-based (white box).** Property-based testing is a formal analysis technique developed by the University of California—Davis. Property-based testing validates that the software's implemented functionality satisfies its specifications. It does this by examining

security-relevant properties revealed by the source code, such as the absence of insecure state changes. Then these security-relevant properties in the code are compared against the software's specification to determine if the security assumptions have been met.

- **Source-code fault injection (white box, gray box).** Fault injection is a technique used to improve code coverage by testing all code paths, especially error-handling code paths that may not be exercised during functional testing. In fault injection testing, errors are injected into the software to simulate unintentional attacks on the software through its environment, and attacks on the environment itself. In source-code fault injection, the tester decides when environment faults should be triggered. The tester then "instruments" the source code by non-intrusively inserting changes into the program that reflect the changed environment data that would result from those faults. The instrumental source code is then compiled and executed, and the tester observes the ways in which the executing software's state changes when the instrumental portions of code are executed. This allows the tester to observe the secure and nonsecure state changes in the software resulting from changes in its environment. The tester can also analyze the ways in which the software's state change results from a fault propagating through the source code. This type of analysis is typically referred to as fault propagation analysis and involves two techniques of source-code fault injection: extended propagation analysis and interface propagation analysis.

- **Dynamic code analysis (gray box).** Dynamic code analysis examines the code as it executes in a running application, with the tester tracing the external interfaces in the source code to the corresponding interactions in the executing code, so that any vulnerabilities or anomalies that arise in the executing interfaces are simultaneously located in the source code, where they can be fixed. Unlike static analysis, dynamic analysis enables the tester to exercise the software in ways that expose vulnerabilities introduced by interactions with users and changes in the configuration or behavior of environmental components. Because the software is not fully linked and deployed in its actual target environment, the testing tool essentially simulates these interactions and their associated inputs and environment conditions.

- **Binary fault injection (gray box, black box).** Binary fault injection is a runtime analysis technique whereby an executing application is monitored as faults are injected. By monitoring system call traces, a tester can identify the names of system calls, the parameters to each call, and the call's return code. This allows the tester to discover the names and types of resources being accessed by the calling software, how the resources are being used, and the success or failure of each access attempt. In binary fault analysis, faults are injected into the environment resources that surround the application.

- **Fuzz testing (black box).** Fuzzing is a technique that is used to detect faults and security-related bugs in software by providing random inputs (fuzz) to a program. As opposed to static analysis, where source code is reviewed line by line for bugs, fuzzing conducts dynamic analysis by generating a variety of valid and invalid inputs to a program and monitoring the results. In some instances, the result might be the program crashing.

- **Binary code analysis (black box).** Binary code scanners analyze machine code to model a language-neutral representation of the program's behaviors, control and data flows, call trees, and external function calls. Such a model may then be traversed by an automated vulnerability scanner in order to locate vulnerabilities caused by common coding errors and simple back doors. A source code emitter can use the model to generate a human-readable source code representation of the program's behavior, enabling manual code review for design-level security weaknesses and subtle back doors that cannot be found by automated scanners.

- **Byte code analysis (black box).** Byte code scanners are used just like source-code security analyzers, but they detect vulnerabilities in the byte code. For example, the Java® language is compiled into a platform-independent byte code format that is executed in the runtime environment (Java Virtual Machine). Much of the information contained in the original Java source code is preserved in the compiled byte code, thus making de-compilation possible. Byte code scanners can be used in cases where the source code is not available for the software—for example, to evaluate the impact a third-party software component will have on the security posture of an application.

- **Black-box debugging (black box).** Debuggers for low-level programming languages such as C or ASM are software tools that enable the tester to monitor the execution of a program, start and stop a program, set breakpoints, and modify values. Debuggers are typically used to debug an application when the source code or the compiler symbols are available. The source-code and compiler symbols allow information, the values of internal variables, to be tracked to discover some aspect of internal program behavior. However, sometimes only the binary is available, and the binary was compiled from code with no compiler symbols or debug flags set. This is typical in commercial software, legacy software, and software that implements protective measures, such as code obfuscation, to prevent reverse engineering. In this case, traditional debugging is not possible. It should be noted that if the focus of debugging effort is on the software interaction with an external component, the binary may be all that is needed.

- **Vulnerability scanning (black box).** Automated vulnerability scanning of operating system and application-level software involves the use of commercial or open-source scanning tools that observe executing software systems for behaviors associated with attack patterns that target specific known vulnerabilities. Like virus scanners, vulnerability scanners rely on a repository of "signatures," in this case indicating recognizable vulnerabilities. Like automated code review tools, although many vulnerability scanners attempt to provide some mechanism for aggregating vulnerabilities, they are still unable to detect complex vulnerabilities or vulnerabilities exposed only as a result of unpredictable (combinations of) attack patterns. In addition to signature-based scanning, most vulnerability scanners attempt to simulate the reconnaissance attack patterns used by attackers to "probe" software for exposed, exploitable vulnerabilities.

- **Penetration testing (black box).** The portion of security testing in which the evaluators attempt to circumvent the security features of a system. The evaluators might be assumed to use all systems design and implementation documentation, which can include listings of system source code, manuals, and circuit diagrams. The evaluators work under the same conditions as are applied to ordinary users.[9–12]

The test plan organizes the security testing process and outlines which components of the software system are to be tested and what test procedure is to be used on each one. The outline is more than just a list of high-level tasks to be completed; it should also include which artifacts are to be tested, what methodologies are to be used, and a general description of the tests themselves, including prerequisites, setup, execution, and what to look for in the test results. The risk analysis described previously is typically used to prioritize the tests, since it is usually not possible, given time and budget constraints, to test every component of the software. Security test planning is an ongoing process, and the details of the test process are fleshed out as additional information becomes available.

The developing organization may modify software because problems have been uncovered and then send the software back to be retested. It is often more efficient that one component is tested while other components of the same system are still being developed than for it to be tested after development is complete. For larger projects, the test plan is typically broken down into test cycles. Given the examples above, test cycles may be created because of the need to retest software that was already tested once before; or test cycles may be created because the nature of the development effort requires that different modules be tested at different times.

Intercomponent dependencies, including those elements or software components in an SaaS or cloud environment that may interact with the software being developed, must be taken into account so that the potential need for retesting is minimized. A development organization typically has a very regimented development process, so the security team needs to be involved from the beginning of the SDLC process. The security team needs to specify early the order in which components should be tested, to ensure that each module is tested before other modules that might depend on it are developed and tested. The concept of "building security in" should be used not just to promote the security program; it must be strictly adhered to if the SDL is to be successful. This means that the security team needs to be included in the general test plan discussions to ensure that the elements of security are included in the validation of the test environment and the test data, and how the test cases define the test condition. The *test condition* is what is going to be tested to see how the software is actually going to respond. Test cases are created during the test-execution process and include information about the test pre-conditions and post-conditions, how it will be set up and terminated, and how the results will be evaluated.

Automation will be key to making the process run smoothly and, most importantly, repeatable, and it should be used wherever possible. As mentioned, previously, this will not always be possible, and the human element will be absolutely necessary, particularly the skills of senior software security architects. The test plan will be expected to provide as much guidance as possible to let the tester know precisely what they are looking for in each test and what the specific test preparations are.

Michael and Radosevich, of Cigital, listed the following typical elements of a security test plan that can be used as a guideline for developing your own plan in their 2005 white paper titled "Risk-Based and Functional Security Testing":

- Purpose
- Software Under Test Overview
  - Software and Components
  - Test Boundaries
  - Test Limitations
- Risk Analysis
  - Synopsis of Risk Analysis
- Test Strategy

- Assumptions
- Test Approach
- Items Not to Be Tested
- Test Requirements
  - Functionality Test Requirements
  - Security Test Requirements
  - Installation/Configuration Test Requirements
  - Stress and Load Test Requirements
  - User Documentation
  - Personnel Requirements
  - Facility and Hardware Requirements
- Test Environment
- Test Case Specifications
  - Unique Test Identifier
  - Requirement Traceability (what requirement number from requirement document does test case validate)
  - Input Specifications
  - Output Specifications/Expected Results
  - Environmental Needs
  - Special Procedural Requirements
  - Dependencies Among Test Cases
- Test Automation and Testware
  - Testware Architecture
  - Test Tools
  - Testware
- Test Execution
  - Test Entry Criteria
  - QA Acceptance Tests
  - Regression Testing
  - Test Procedures, Special Requirements, Procedure Steps
  - Test Schedule
  - Test Exit Criteria
- Test Management Plan
- Definitions and Acronyms[13]

5.3 Threat Model Updating

After working through the threat modeling process described in Chapter 4, it is important to know when you are done with the process. This will involve answering a few questions such as the following, whose answers will likely depend on competing business and security risk interests and may require some trade-offs:

1. Have you accounted for all the policies, laws, or regulations relevant to the software that you are developing, and accounted for and gained approval for the level of effort for each of these requirements?
2. Have all your stakeholders reviewed the security assessment and risks identified as a result of the threat modeling process? The appropriate architects, developers, testers,

program managers, and others who understand the software should have been asked to contribute to threat models and to review them. Broad input and reviews should have been solicited to ensure that the threat models are as comprehensive as possible. It is also important that all stakeholders agree on the threats and risks that have been identified. If this is not the case, implementing appropriate countermeasures may prove to be difficult.

3. Have you accounted for and have your stakeholders agreed to the availability of time and resources required as both a result of the threat modeling process and any resulting mitigation and testing?

4. Have you ranked your threats and risks according to consensus from stakeholders? If you were a buyer of this software, would you agree with this ranking?

5.4 Design Security Analysis and Review

In a 1974 paper, Saltzer and Schroeder of the University of Virginia addressed the protection of information stored in a computer system by focusing on hardware and software issues that are necessary to support information protection.[14] The paper presented the following 11 security design principles:

1. **Least privilege.** The principle of least privilege maintains that an individual, process, or other type of entity should be given the minimum privileges and resources for the minimum period of time required to complete a task. This approach eliminates the opportunity for unauthorized access to sensitive information.

2. **Separation of duties.** This principle requires that completion of a specified sensitive activity or access to sensitive objects is dependent on the satisfaction of multiple conditions. Separation of duties forces collusion among entities in order to compromise the system.

3. **Defense in depth.** This is the application of multiple layers of protection, such that a subsequent layer will provide protection if a previous layer is breached.

4. **Fail-safe.** This means that if a system fails, it should fail to a state where the security of the system and its data are not compromised. In the situation in which system recovery is not done automatically, the failed system should permit access only by the system administrator and not by users, until security controls are reestablished.

5. **Economy of mechanism.** This promotes simple and comprehensible design and implementation of protection mechanisms, so that unintended access paths do not exist or can be readily identified and eliminated.

6. **Complete mediation.** This is where every request by a subject to access an object in a computer system must undergo a valid and effective authorization procedure. This mediation must not be suspended or become capable of being bypassed, even when the information system is being initialized, undergoing shutdown, being restarted, or is in maintenance mode. Complete mediation entails: (a) identification of the entity making the access request; (b) verification that the request has not changed since its initiation; (c) application of the appropriate authorization procedures; and (d) reexamination of previously authorized requests by the same entity.

7. **Open design.** There has always been discussion of the merits and strength of security of designs that are kept secret versus designs that are open to scrutiny and evaluation by the community at large. For most purposes, an open-access control system design

that has been evaluated and tested by a large number of experts provides a more secure authentication method than one that has not been widely assessed.

8. **Least common mechanism.** This principle states that a minimum number of protective mechanisms should be common to multiple users, as shared access paths can be sources of unauthorized information exchange. Shared access paths that provide unintentional data transfers are known as covert channels. The least common mechanism promotes the least possible sharing of common security mechanisms.

9. **Psychological acceptability.** This refers to the ease of use and intuitiveness of the user interface that controls and interacts with the access control mechanisms. The user must be able to understand the user interface and use it without having to interpret complex instructions.

10. **Weakest link.** As in the old saying, "A chain is only as strong as its weakest link," the security of an information system is only as good as its weakest component. It is important to identify the weakest mechanisms in the security chain and layers of defense and improve them so that risks to the system are mitigated to an acceptable level.

11. **Leveraging existing components.** In many instances, the security mechanisms of an information system are not configured properly or used to their maximum capability. Reviewing the state and settings of the extant security mechanisms and ensuring that they are operating at their optimum design points will greatly improve the security posture of an information system. Another approach that can be used to increase system security by leveraging existing components is to partition a system into defended subunits. Then, if a security mechanism is penetrated for one subunit, it will not affect the other subunits and damage to the computing resources will be minimized.[15,16]

Designing good software isn't easy, and building security in makes it even more difficult. Although some software flaws may not matter from a user perspective, from a security perspective they may matter because an attacker may be able induce failures by setting up the highly specific conditions necessary to trigger a flaw. Something that may have had a low probability of happening randomly and dismissed as irrelevant may be significant if an attacker can take advantage of it. In the summary of Saltzer and Schroeder's design principles, the principles are stated clearly but they lack the success criteria for security. Fortunately, we have a general idea of what security looks like and can avoid failure in this area by incorporating the long-accepted properties of confidentiality, integrity, and availability into the design principles. There are, of course, different views of security—from that of a software developer, who may think of security primarily in terms of quality; to that of a network administrator, who may think of security in terms of firewalls, IDS/IPS systems, incident response, and system management; or even those of managers and academics, who may think of security mostly in terms of the classic design principles described above or in terms of various security models. All of these viewpoints are important in building secure systems and are relevant to modeling the overall threat to your software. You must stay focused on the ultimate prize when designing security in: the potential exploitation of the software you are developing.

Detailed design artifacts are used to build each software component needed to satisfy the use case requirements required to effectively design your software for security. A thorough analysis of each software artifact for possible vulnerabilities is conducted for every feature, property, and service that exists in every component. As a result of analyzing each software component for the use cases and in misuse case scenarios identified through the processes described in Chapter 4, developers will be able to design appropriate countermeasures up front and transparently, so that the entire team is able to see how software security is being handled in the application. As a result, the use case concepts can be converted to actual software requirement specifications. As the developers review the specific application software they are developing, they should also assess any vulnerabilities found in the associated ecosystem it will support, including its network, architecture, and supporting software. It is also important for the development security team to stay current with the latest vulnerabilities that may affect your specific software and associated ecosystem, both pre- and post-release, to prepare for new potential planes of attack previously unknown or discovered, both internally and externally. It will be much easier and less expensive to fix or develop a countermeasure to an identified risk as the software is being designed and developed than after it is released. Although the secure design of the code is critical and of upmost importance, mistakes will be made and new attack methodologies will be discovered and will continue to drive the need to research and assess new methods of attack and vulnerabilities long after the product has shipped and, likely, until it reaches end of life. This, of course, is why it is so important to minimize the attack surface through the methods described in Chapter 4, combined with good design principles to maximize the limitation of severity of any security flaws that may be missed in the code. The design as an organized framework will be a strategy breaking down the problem into smaller parts that are more easily solved. Threat modeling will be key to your success and process in this endeavor, as it will typically identify a secure design issue that might have gone unnoticed until much later. The data flow diagram results will be used next, along with the brainstorming of attacks and review of known checklists. Apply whatever combined methodology works best for you, conduct all the necessary research, and apply it early in your design to minimize any component failing late in the development process.

5.5 Privacy Implementation Assessment

The authors believe that the most concise, clear, and field-tested privacy implementation assessment processes, procedures, and guidelines for software development are available from Microsoft® and are contained in three primary documents:

1. Microsoft's "Privacy Guidelines for Developing Software Products and Services," Version 3.1; September 2008[17] As noted in Chapter 3, this document is no longer available online, but we include its pertinent elements as part of our privacy discussions.
2. Microsoft MSDN's "SDL–Process Guidance–Appendix C: SDL—Privacy Questionnaire."[18]
3. Microsoft's "Simplified Implementation of the Microsoft SDL."[19]

The process and guidance by which you determine your Privacy Impact Rating and estimate the work required to be compliant is described in Microsoft's "Privacy Guidelines for Developing Software Products and Services," Version 3.1; September 2008,[20] and their "SDL—Process Guidance—Appendix C: SDL Privacy Questionnaire."[21] The ratings (P1, P2, or P3) represent the degree of risk your software presents from a privacy perspective. You need to complete only the steps that apply to your rating, based on the following guidelines:

- **P1: High Privacy Risk.** The feature, product, or service stores or transfers personally identifiable information (PII), changes settings or file type associations, or installs software.
- **P2: Moderate Privacy Risk.** The sole behavior that affects privacy in the feature, product, or service is a one-time, user-initiated, anonymous data transfer (e.g., the user clicks on a link and the software goes out to a website).
- **P3: Low Privacy Risk.** No behaviors exist within the feature, product, or service that affect privacy. No anonymous or personal data is transferred, no PII is stored on the machine, no settings are changed on the user's behalf, and no software is installed.[22]

The questions are designed to help you complete the privacy aspects of the SDL, and you can complete some sections, such as the initial assessment and a detailed analysis, on your own. It is recommended that you complete other sections, such as the privacy review, together with your privacy advisor.[23]

One of the best ways to protect a customer's privacy is not to collect his or her user data in the first place. The questions that should constantly be asked by architects, developers, and administrators of data collection systems include:

- "Do I need to collect this data?"
- "Do I have a valid business purpose?"
- "Will customers support my business purpose?"[24]

The development organization must keep in mind that for customers to have control over their personal information, they need to know what personal information will be collected, with whom it will be shared, and how it will be used. In addition:

- Customers must provide consent before any personal information is transferred from their computer; and
- If customers' personal information is transferred over the Internet and stored remotely, they must be offered a mechanism for accessing and updating the information.[25]

As part of the design requirements activities, additional privacy actions include the creation of privacy design specifications, specification review, and specification of minimal cryptographic design requirements. Design specifications should describe privacy features that will be directly exposed to users, such as those that require user authentication to access specific data or user consent before use of a high-risk privacy feature. In addition, all design specifications should describe how to securely implement all functionality provided by a given feature or function. It is good practice to validate design specifications against the application's functional specification. The functional specification should include (1) an accurate and complete description of the intended use of a feature or function, and (2) a description of how to deploy the feature or function in a secure fashion.[26]

Security controls that help to protect PII data must consider all aspects of data protection, including, but not limited to, access controls, data encryption in transfer and storage, physical security, disaster recovery, and auditing. In many cases, the same security controls that are essential to protecting critical business data, including confidential and proprietary information, from compromise and loss are the same that will be used to protect personal information of customers and employees and should be leveraged whenever possible. This can only be determined after identifying, understanding, and classifying the PII data that the organization collects, stores, or transfers, according to the guidance described in this section.

5.6 Key Success Factors and Metrics

5.6.1 Key Success Factors

The success of this third phase of the SDL depends on a security test plan, design security analysis review, and privacy implementation assessment. It is during this phase that a plan for the rest of the SDL process, from implementation to testing, is built. Table 5.1 lists key success factors for this third phase.

Table 5.1 Key Success Factors

Key Success Factor	Description
1. Comprehensive security test plan	Mapping types of security testing required at different stages of SDLC
2. Effective threat modeling	Identifying threats to the software
3. Design security analysis	Analysis of threats to various software components
4. Privacy implementation assessment	Efforts required for the implementation of privacy-related controls based on assessment
5. Policy compliance review (updates)	Updates for policy compliance as related to Phase 3

Success Factor 1: Comprehensive Security Test Plan

During this phase, security architects and the assessment team define various aspects of the software that need to be tested and the types of testing that need to be scheduled and planned both before and after the release of the software. The security test plan should map code development phases to the type of testing. For example, with every check-in–associated static analysis, a comprehensive static analysis is a must after the final code commit. Once the software enters the pre-release cycle, vulnerability assessments, gray box testing, and binary testing should be scheduled. One of the most critical success factors of this phase and the overall SDL is that the security test plan can eliminate most security vulnerabilities before the product is deployed.

Success Factor 2: Effective Threat Modeling

If a new threat or attack vectors are identified during this phase, the threat model and artifacts need to be updated to make sure the risk mitigation plan is comprehensive.

Success Factor 3: Design Security Analysis

Along with the accuracy of security test plans, a software design review from a security viewpoint is perhaps the most crucial success factor during the first three phases of the SDL. It is essential to minimize the attack surface and improve design principles to reduce the severity of any security flaws that may be missed in the code.

Success Factor 4: Privacy Implementation Assessment

It is imperative that your estimate of work required in adhering to privacy policies and practices, both within the company and outside it, is as accurate as possible. This will enable significant cost savings down the road. For example, if privacy practices require that PII data be encrypted across the board, it is critical that this need be identified during the design phase. Once the software is in the execution and release stages, it is often cost-prohibitive. The authors have seen Fortune 500 companies where such decisions are taken during service pack release. By then, however, it is extremely difficult to fix the problem accurately. It is also very expensive. Another example of the problem is network segmentation. In a cloud/SaaS-based environment, this is an important decision to make. Often there will be multiple products hosted out from this shared environment. How to best protect one product from another is an important question for the design phase.

Success Factor 5: Policy Compliance Review (Updates)

If existing policies are updated, or additional policies are identified, it is a good idea to review compliance against the new set of requirements. An example of an updated policy might be the inclusion of any remaining privacy-related policies or forward-looking strategies.

5.6.2 Deliverables

Table 5.2 lists deliverables for this phase of the SDL.

Table 5.2 Deliverables for Phase A3

Deliverable	Goal
Updated threat modeling artifacts	Data flow diagrams, elements, threat listing
Design security review	Modifications to the design of software components based on security assessments
Security test plans	Plan to mitigate, accept, or tolerate risk
Updated policy compliance analysis	Analysis of adherence to company policies
Privacy implementation assessment results	Recommendations from privacy assessments

Updated Threat Modeling Artifacts

Updated data flow diagrams (DFDs), a technical threat modeling report, a high-level executive threat modeling report, threat lists, and recommendations for threat analysis based on any new requirements/inputs to attack vectors that need to be created.

Design Security Review

This is a formal specification that lists changes to software components and design based on a review from security architects and the assessments team.

Security Test Plans

This is a formal security test schedule that maps different stages of the SDL process to different types of security testing (static analysis, fuzzing, vulnerability assessments, binary testing, etc.)

Updated Policy Compliance Analysis

Policy compliance analysis artifacts (see Chapter 4) should be updated based on any new requirements or policies that might have come up during this phase of the SDL.

Privacy Implementation Assessment Results

This is a roadmap to implement recommendations from the privacy implementation assessment. It should be based on privacy risk (high, medium, or low).

5.6.3 Metrics

Since some of the success factors and deliverables are similar to those for Phase 2 of the SDL, the same metrics should be collected and recorded:

- Threats, probability, and severity
- Percent compliance with company policies (updated)
  - Percent of compliance in Phase 2 versus Phase 3
- Entry points for software (using DFDs)
- Percent of risk accepted versus mitigated
- Percent of initial software requirements redefined
- Percent of software architecture changes
- Percent of SDLC phases without corresponding software security testing
- Percent of software components with implementations related to privacy controls
- Number of lines of code
- Number of security defects found using static analysis tools
- Number of high-risk defects found using static analysis tools
- Defect density (security issues per 1000 lines of code)

Note that if too many controls related to privacy need to be implemented in the software components, you might want to review the design of the components.

5.7 Summary

During our discussion of design and development (Phase A3), we described the importance of an analysis of policy compliance; creation of the test plan documentation; updates to the threat modeling discussed in the last chapter, if necessary; completion of a design security analysis and review; and a privacy implementation assessment. Out of all of this, best practices are created from the functional and design specifications that have been created that will be used throughout the remainder of the SDL process. Toward the end of the chapter, we discussed key success factors, deliverables, and metrics for this phase.

Chapter Quick-Check

1. The use of standardized design functions for similar or repeated functionality is referred to as:
   a. Psychological acceptability
   b. Complete mediation
   c. Open design
   d. Economy of mechanism

2. Logging of errors and failure information should be designed to protect:
   a. Sensitive information
   b. Availability through resilient controls
   c. Separation of duties
   d. Fail-safe designs

3. Designing a system so all parties can easily understand design objectives and maintaining a simple design embrace the principle of:
   a. Single point of failure
   b. Least common mechanism
   c. Fail-safe
   d. Open design

4. The security principle of fail-safe is related to:
   a. Session management
   b. Exception management
   c. Complete mediation
   d. Single point of failure

Exercises

The following exercises are based on the case study discussed in Appendix A. These exercises are intended to give you some practice in applying the steps and producing deliverables for Phase A3 of the SDL.

1. Revisit your threat model and associated documentation for completeness, accuracy, and assurance that all regulatory- and industry-dictated security requirements are present
2. Prepare a comprehensive testing plan for the applications once you've changed your system design to remediate defects you discovered during threat modeling.
3. Prepare or update your policy compliance review document.
4. Conduct a privacy implementation assessment for assurance that all privacy-related requirements are present.

References

1. McConnell, S. (1996). *Rapid Development*. Redmond, WA: Microsoft Press.

2. Grembi, J. (2008). *Secure Software Development: A Security Programmer's Guide.* Boston: MA: Course Technology.

3. Krutz, R., and Fry, A. (2009). *The CSSLP Prep Guide: Mastering the Certified Secure Software Lifecycle Professional.* Indianapolis, IN: John Wiley & Sons.

4. Goertzel, K., et al. (2007). "Information Assurance Technology Analysis Center (ITAC)/Data and Analysis Center for Software (DACS): Software Security Assurance State-of-the-Art Report (SOAR)." Retrieved from https://apps.dtic.mil/sti/pdfs/ADA472363.pdf

5. Krutz, R., and Fry, A. (2009). *The CSSLP Prep Guide: Mastering the Certified Secure Software Lifecycle Professional.* Indianapolis, IN: John Wiley & Sons.

6. Goertzel, K., et al. (2007). "Information Assurance Technology Analysis Center (ITAC)/Data and Analysis Center for Software (DACS): Software Security Assurance State-of-the-Art Report (SOAR)." Retrieved from https://apps.dtic.mil/sti/pdfs/ADA472363.pdf

7. Krutz, R., and Fry, A. (2009). *The CSSLP Prep Guide: Mastering the Certified Secure Software Lifecycle Professional.* Indianapolis, IN: John Wiley & Sons.

8. Goertzel, K., et al. (2007). "Information Assurance Technology Analysis Center (ITAC)/Data and Analysis Center for Software (DACS): Software Security Assurance State-of-the-Art Report (SOAR)." Retrieved from https://apps.dtic.mil/sti/pdfs/ADA472363.pdf

9. Krutz, R., and Fry, A. (2009). *The CSSLP Prep Guide: Mastering the Certified Secure Software Lifecycle Professional.* Indianapolis, IN: John Wiley & Sons.

10. Goertzel, K., et al. (2007). "Information Assurance Technology Analysis Center (ITAC)/Data and Analysis Center for Software (DACS): Software Security Assurance State-of-the-Art Report (SOAR)." Retrieved from https://apps.dtic.mil/sti/pdfs/ADA472363.pdf

11. Fink, G., and Bishop, M. (1997). "Property-Based Testing: A New Approach to Testing for Assurance." *SIGSOFT Software Engineering Notes,* vol. 22, no. 4, pp. 74–80.

12. Goertzel, K., et al. (2008). "Enhancing the Development Life Cycle to Produce Secure Software. Version 2.0." U.S. Department of Defense Data and Analysis Center for Software, Rome, NY. Retrieved from https://www.researchgate.net/publication/233575692_Enhancing_the_Development_Life_Cycle_to_Produce_Secure_Software

13. Michael, C., and Radosevich, W. (2005). "Risk-Based and Functional Security Testing." Cigital white paper, U.S. Department of Homeland Security. Retrieved from https://us-cert.cisa.gov/bsi/articles/best-practices/security-testing/risk-based-and-functional-security-testing

14. Saltzer, J., and Schroeder, M. (1974). "The Protection of Information in Computer Systems." Fourth ACM Symposium on Operating Systems Principle, October 1974.

15. Ibid.

16. Grembi, J. (2008). *Secure Software Development: A Security Programmer's Guide.* Boston, MA: Course Technology.

17. Microsoft Corporation. (2006). "New Guidelines to Help Developers Protect Customers' Privacy." Retrieved from https://news.microsoft.com/2006/10/19/new-guidelines-to-help-developers-protect-customers-privacy/

18. Microsoft Corporation. (2012). MSDN, "SDL—Process Guidance—Appendix C: SDL Privacy Questionnaire." Retrieved from http://msdn.microsoft.com/en-us/library/cc307393.aspx

19. Microsoft Corporation. (2011). "Simplified Implementation of the Microsoft SDL." Retrieved from http://www.microsoft.com/en-us/download/details.aspx?id=12379

20. Microsoft Corporation (2006). "New Guidelines to Help Developers Protect Customers' Privacy." Retrieved from https://news.microsoft.com/2006/10/19/new-guidelines-to-help-developers-protect-customers-privacy/

21. Microsoft Corporation. (2012). MSDN, "SDL—Process Guidance—Appendix C: SDL Privacy Questionnaire." Retrieved from http://msdn.microsoft.com/en-us/library/cc307393.aspx

22. Microsoft Corporation. (2011). "Simplified Implementation of the Microsoft SDL." Retrieved from http://www.microsoft.com/en-us/download/details.aspx?id=12379

23. Microsoft Corporation. (2012). MSDN, "SDL—Process Guidance—Appendix C: SDL Privacy Questionnaire." Retrieved from http://msdn.microsoft.com/en-us/library/cc307393.aspx

24. Microsoft Corporation. (2006). "New Guidelines to Help Developers Protect Customers' Privacy." Retrieved from https://news.microsoft.com/2006/10/19/new-guidelines-to-help-developers-protect-customers-privacy/

25. Ibid.

26. Microsoft Corporation. (2011). "Simplified Implementation of the Microsoft SDL." Retrieved from http://www.microsoft.com/en-us/download/details.aspx?id=12379

Chapter 6

Design and Development (A4): SDL Activities and Best Practices

CHAPTER OVERVIEW

In this chapter, we will describe the activities for the design and development (A4) phase of our security development lifecycle (SDL). This phase can be mapped to the "readiness" phase in a typical software development life cycle (SDLC).

CHAPTER TAKE-AWAYS

- Explore the practices that compose the design and development (Phase A4) of the security development lifecycle (SDL).
- Document the key success factors for completion of Phase A4.
- Create initial, draft deliverables for Phase A4 for the case study in Appendix A.
- Prepare security testing reports for the case study in Appendix A.

Figure 6.1 illustrates the steps and activities found in Phase A4 of the SDL.

In Phase A4, we start with the continuation of policy compliance analysis for this phase and then move on to describe the elements of security test case execution. Building on the proper process for security testing that should have already been created, documented, and tested, the analysis will continue until necessary tuning is identified in order to accomplish the required security level. We then describe the use of automated tools, such as static, dynamic, and fuzz test tools, to help automate and enforce security practices efficiently and effectively at a low cost. Static analysis analyzes the source code prior to compiling, provides a scalable method of security code review, and helps ensure that secure coding policies are being followed. Dynamic analysis monitors application behavior and ensures that the software functionality works as

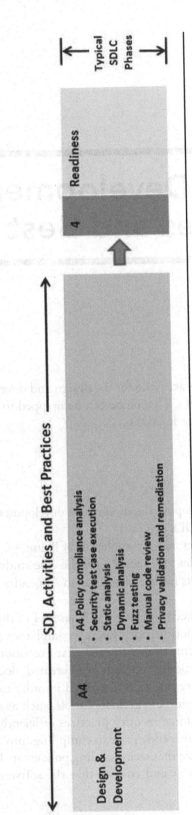

Figure 6.1 Design and Development (A4): SDL activities and best practices.

designed. Fuzz testing induces program failure by deliberately introducing malformed or random data to an application and can be used as an effective and low-cost way of finding potential security issues prior to release and potentially throughout the SDL process. Fuzz testing is a specialized form of dynamic analysis. By using the latest version of these automated tools, the latest known automated security analysis, vulnerabilities, and recommended protections will be identified. After these multiple automated tools have been used to quickly analyze the flaws and vulnerabilities in the software, the code is then reviewed manually, every issue validated, and the code inspected to overcome the limitations of automated tools and techniques. As part of this process, attack surface and threat model reviews will ensure that any new attack vectors that have been created by any design or implementation changes have been identified and mitigated. Finally, we discuss the need, value, and process for privacy validation and remediation to be conducted during this phase of the SDL.

6.1 A4 Policy Compliance Analysis

This is a continuation of the A3 policy compliance review described in the previous chapter. As you will see, we continue to perform policy compliance analysis during different phases and review it again and again. It is of paramount importance that you persist through this and not make an assumption that you have covered everything in previous iterations. You will be surprised how often things are missed during initial phases/iterations of this step.

During this phase, any policy that exists outside the domain of the SDL policy is reviewed (or reviewed again). This may include policies from outside the development organization that carry security and privacy requirements and guidelines to be adhered to when developing software or applications anywhere within the organization. Often, too, policies are updated during the development process, and new requirements are added. Thus, it is best to obtain a list of updated policies and make sure you have incorporated any additional requirements.

Corporate security and privacy policies will likely instruct designers and developers on what the security and privacy features need to be and how they must be implemented. Other policies may focus on the use of third-party and open-source software used as part of a software product or on the protections and control of source code and other intellectual property within and outside the organization. Assuming that the software security group is separate from the centralized information security group, it is important that the two groups collaborate on all policies and guidelines related to the development and post-release security support by the organization. It helps the information security group to fine-tune its policies not only for corporate security policies/practices but also for software development. It is also important to collaborate with the privacy function of your company, whether it be a centralized group or outside legal counsel. If the company identifies potential new markets, privacy policies and practices (for that particular market) may be updated.

6.2 Security Test Case Execution

Security testing is a time-consuming process that requires proper preparation, consistency, and coordination with all stakeholders, as well as a deep understanding of what you are actually testing. It starts early and continues throughout the SDLC process. The approach for security testing is different from other forms of testing in that its purpose is to identify various vulnerabilities in a software design that are exposed and due to improper design or coding issues. The premise of this book is to secure at the source, and testing at this level will prevent many of the vulnerabilities that are typically found only when the software is exposed at the network level. Security, especially at the design level, can help us identify potential security problems and their impact before they are part of a larger system and network and perhaps cost-prohibitive to fix. Software security is a dynamic risk management exercise in that you are balancing the costs of potential assurance remedies against the skills and resources of adversaries—and there are always intelligent adversaries who are focused on breaking and exploiting your software. Thus, the security test itself must assess the probability of occurrence of an event based on exploiting a vulnerability and the risk associated with each potential occurrence.

In a typical SDLC cycle, software goes through quality assurance (QA) testing that includes unit, performance, system, and regression testing. If the software passes through test criteria for this QA testing, it will be given a "Go" by the QA team. Basically, this means that the software has been tested for quality and is good to go. From the authors' point of view, QA testing is not complete unless all security tests have been performed and the security test acceptance criteria are all met. Software cannot be a quality product unless it has been comprehensively tested for security issues. Treating security testing as an add-on is a mistake that many companies still make. Once QA testing is complete, the software goes to the security team for security testing. In our opinion, routine security testing should be part of the QA cycle. The QA team should treat security testing just like any other testing and should create test cases and perform both manual and automated testing just as they would any other testing. The QA team, however, often does not have the skills to execute security test cases, which therefore often means that the QA team relies on the security team to perform *all* testing. This approach is not very effective and takes time away from the security team, which has to perform basic security tests instead of looking at advanced threats/corner cases. QA security testing is not meant to replace security testing by the security team. Instead, it should be looked upon as enabling the security team to focus on advanced testing. Below are a few examples of issues that QA security testing should look for:

- Plaintext passwords/weak passwords in configuration files
- Default accounts on the stack (web servers, database servers, operating systems)
- Sensitive information in log files
- Input validation (XSS, SQLi)
- Parameter tampering for web applications
- Insecure services used by the software team (e.g., Telnet)
- Security configurations for various services (e.g., NFS)

The QA team should focus not just on application but also on the stack on which the software will run. This means testing various configurations of operating systems and related services, web servers, etc., from a security point of view. Before QA gives the "Go" for a product, the entire stack (application, operation system, web servers, storage) should have been tested for basic security issues.

Security test case execution is carried out from two primary perspectives:

1. Security mechanisms are tested to ensure that their functionality is properly implemented; and
2. Security testing is conducted in relation to understanding and simulating the attacker's approach as identified during threat modeling and other associated risk-based analyses.

Typically, three specific test type categories are performed on a software product and its associated system(s):

1. **Benchmarks.** These tests are used to compare estimates to actual results.
2. **Scheduled tests.** These tests include mandatory requirements to validate the security of the software and associated system(s) being tested, which must be conducted regardless of whether security issues or vulnerabilities are detected or tuning is required.
3. **Exploratory tests.** Exploratory testing emphasizes the personal freedom and responsibility of the individual tester to continually optimize the quality of his or her work by treating test-related learning, test design, test execution, and test result interpretation as mutually supportive activities that run in parallel throughout the project.[1] The tester actively controls the design of the tests, and those tests are performed while testing to design new and better tests.

A successful security test execution plan assumes that:

- You have done a detailed risk analysis to evaluate the software and the system(s) with which it will be associated. This process was detailed in Chapter 5.
- Test assets have been developed as part of the risk management plan and the development of a security engineering/development test strategy.

Successful security test execution includes the following:

- Baseline and benchmark tests have been performed to ensure that obvious security issues have been identified early in the testing cycle.
- Automated test scripts have been validated as correct.
- Re-benchmarking testing has been conducted after tuning.
- A basis for future test comparison has been created.
- The results of the security test case execution have been analyzed.
  - *Test execution results have been evaluated.* Your seasoned software security architects have a key role here, as they apply their skills and experience to compare the evaluation to previous tests, finding and analyzing patterns (including identification of obvious or potential security issues and/or the effects of the tuning effort), and apply their past experiences to the evaluation. Since this evaluation is more an art than a science, the software security architects should also involve the testers and developers in the analysis after the architects' initial review and evaluation to optimize the results of the analysis toward driving tuning efforts.
  - *You have determined whether security test case execution acceptance criteria have been met.* This is a result of comparing the results from the most recent test, or suite of tests, to the acceptance criteria. If all of the results meet or exceed the security test execution criteria, then the test is complete; if not, the team should continue to evaluate the results.

    o *You have determined whether the security test case execution results are conclusive.* If the results do not meet the acceptance criteria, then the test is likely inconclusive because the test results are not reproducible and you are unable to determine what is causing the security issue in the software. If results are inconclusive, an exploratory test will be needed.

    o *You have determined whether tuning is required at this point.* At this stage, either a security issue has been detected or more tests are needed to validate compliance with additional acceptance criteria. Either the last test will be executed again to see whether the results are reproducible, or you will move on to tuning.

    o There are some tests where no security issues are found and no tuning is required, but the software must be tested because there it is mandatory to validate the security of the software and its associated system(s) against specifically known software security issues and vulnerabilities.

Successful security test case execution completion criteria include the following:

- The specific target security requirements and goals of the software that has been tested have been met.
- When a situation outside the control of the software security group or its equivalent cannot be resolved, the security testing may be deemed complete as a result of any one of the following situations, if the company stakeholders responsible for the development of the software accept the risk:
    o The situation preventing the software security group or its equivalent from achieving its security test case criteria is outside the group's control or contractual obligations.
    o The predetermined engagement end date is reached and company stakeholders responsible for the development of the software accept the risk of not meeting the security criteria. In many cases, this is accepted if a commitment to fix the vulnerability is scheduled for the next update of the product and/or patch release.
    o The software security group or its equivalent and all other stakeholders agree that the application performs acceptably, even though some security requirements or goals have not been achieved. As with the previous situation, this is typically not accepted unless the commitment to fix the vulnerability is scheduled for the next update of the product and/or patch release.

6.3 Code Review in the SDLC/SDL Process

Code review can be especially productive for identifying security vulnerabilities during software development. A properly conducted code review can do more for the security of your code than nearly any other activity. A code review allows you to find and fix a large number of security issues before the code is tested or shipped. There are four basic techniques for analyzing the security of a software application: automated scanning, manual penetration testing, static analysis, and manual code review. All of these methodologies, of course, have strengths, weaknesses, sweet spots, and blind spots. Collectively, these four types of security code reviews are likely the fastest and most accurate way to find and diagnose many security problems while being less expensive or time-consuming than they are warranted to be. If planned for and managed correctly, code reviews are very cost-effective, especially if they are built into the SDLC as part of the process, thereby avoiding the expensive process of handling, locating, and fixing security vulnerabilities during later stages of development or after software product release. Experienced and empowered security personnel who are knowledgeable about the four basic techniques of code review should be employed to ensure that the various techniques are mixed and matched as appropriate to create the most cost-effective and well-managed plan for identifying all potential and known significant security issues in the software being developed. The human element in the process will also help apply context to the security vulnerabilities found by the automated tools. This holistic approach will be able to find problems or potential issues, prove that they are exploitable, and verify them by examining the code. Another advantage of this approach is that it facilitates the experience and education of the development team in the use of security best practices, which will help prevent future security issues. The process can be broken down into four primary steps as shown graphically in Figure 6.2 and described below.

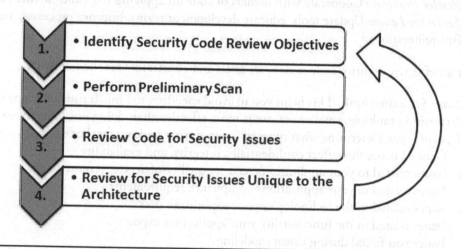

Figure 6.2   Four-step code review cycle.

1. Identify Security Code Review Objectives

During this step, goals and constraints are established for the review as the bases for an overall plan. As with most projects, if there is no basis for a plan, there will likely be a failed project. This is particularly the case when large amounts of code and/or complex SaaS/cloud applications are involved. A focused code review is an effective code review. This is why it is important to review the code with specific goals, time limits, and knowledge of the issues you want to uncover. This will significantly increase your chances for success while reducing the amount of time required for review. Having a plan will allow the reviewers to focus on reviewing the code each time there is a meaningful change rather than trying to find all of the security issues at once, or waiting until the end of the project and reviewing everything at one time. For efficiency, you should also identify any stated security objectives that are already known prior to review, so you can differentiate between vulnerability types that have elevated priority and others that may be out of scope based on your security objectives.

Security code review is most successful if it is planned and executed in the context of other security-related efforts such as threat modeling, as described in the previous chapter. Threat modeling helps to identify a critical area of code that then becomes a subject of detailed review, and its results can likewise be used to validate or question security assumptions specified in a threat model and help to understand the application's functionality, technical design, and existing security threats and countermeasures. A security code review should begin with a review of the threat models and design specifications, then move on to source code.

The ideal flow of activities for code review success is perhaps best described by the steps identified by Chmielewski et al. in *MSDN Magazine*:

(a) *Threat Modeling:* Understand code and data flows; identify high-risk areas and entry points.
(b) *Code Reviews:* Document all findings in an appropriate way, as well as the process itself.
(c) *Resolve Problems:* Cooperate with owners of code on applying fixes and further efforts.
(d) *Learn the Lesson:* Update tools, educate development teams, improve processes, and plan future iterations.[2]

For an effective security code review, set goals and constraints for the following.

- *Time:* Set a time limit. This helps you to avoid spending too much time on a single issue. Performing multiple, smaller reviews is more effective than doing one long review.
- *Types of issues:* Determine what types of issues you are looking for. For example, consider:
  o General issues that affect confidentially, integrity, and availability
  o Issues related to your application's security quality-of-service requirements
  o Issues related to your application's compliance requirements
  o Issues related to the technologies your application uses
  o Issues related to the functionality your application exposes
  o Issues you found during threat modeling
- *Out-of-scope items:* Identify what you will not be looking for. Explain why these things are out of scope.[3]

2. Perform Preliminary Scan

Static analysis is used to find an initial set of security issues and to improve your understanding of where you will be most likely to find security issues when you review the code more fully as well as to discover hot spots where additional security issues are likely to be found in later steps. This is typically done with automatic scans, manual scans, or a combination of both, depending on the review objectives and time limitations of the code review plan. Automated scans have an advantage in their ability to quickly identify "low-hanging fruit" across large sets of applications. The results from these scans are used in creating a prioritized list of potential security vulnerabilities and security mechanisms to review and investigate.

An automatic scan can be used to supplement a manual review, as an extra check to go through large volumes of code that would be cost- and/or time-prohibitive to do manually, to target areas to focus on for manual reviews, and to find security issues that may have been missed during a manual review. Automatic scanning tools are typically good at finding security issues that are a result of single lines of code and finding security issues that span multiple lines of code in a single function, and they may find problems that manual reviews will miss. Although automatic scanning can supplement a manual review, it should not be used to replace it because of the contextual problems and inability to find security issues over multiple functions, such as those found in SaaS/cloud applications. Another issue with automated tools is the number of false positives and negatives that are found, which may require significant efforts to tune down to a reasonable number. On the positive side, these types of results will force you to gain a better understanding of the code, including controls and data flow, by forcing you to review why a false positive is false. Another risk of using automated tools is the possible sense of security in believing there are no security issues in your software if no security issues are identified as a result of the scan. A significantly sized and complex software product should never be assumed to be free of security vulnerabilities. All possible steps should be taken to limit the number of coding errors and reduce their practical impact, but something is always missed. Automated security tools are able to identify more and more coding errors, but some vulnerabilities will still be missed and either not detected or hidden among large numbers of false positives. Manual source code analysis is not a replacement for these tools, but it helps maximize the identification of vulnerabilities when integrated with them. As mentioned throughout this book, it requires a holistic approach to security, including a human element, to ensure that both false positives are false and that the code is really free of security vulnerabilities in spite of being given what appears to be a clean bill of health by the automated tools. Using both methods together enables reviewers to identify more software security vulnerabilities both efficiently and cost-effectively. For these reasons, automated review combined with a manual review is the best approach.

To catch the simpler issues, available security tools should be run against the code before manual review begins. To avoid finding known issues, all previously identified security vulnerabilities should be fixed. A manual scan is then conducted to gain a better understanding of the code and to recognize patterns; the results of the scan will identify areas that merit further analysis as the reviewers analyze the code for security issues in Step 3 below. This effort, however, should be a small percentage of the total code review time and should focus on answering the following questions:

- *Input data validation:* Does the application have an input validation architecture? Is validation performed on the client, on the server, or both? Is there a centralized validation mechanism, or are validation routines spread throughout the code base?
- *Code that authenticates and authorizes users:* Does the application authenticate users? What roles are allowed, and how do they interact? Is there custom authentication or authorization code?
- *Error-handling code:* Is there a consistent error-handling architecture? Does the application catch and throw structured exceptions? Are there areas of the code with especially dense or sparse error handling?
- *Complex code:* Are there areas of the code that appear especially complex?
- *Cryptography:* Does the application use cryptography?
- *Interop:* Does the application use interop to call into native code?[4]

3. Review Code for Security Issues

The results from Step 2 are typically used to focus the analysis of the reviewer during Step 3.

4. Review for Security Issues Unique to the Architecture

This is where the software security architect or seasoned software security champion come into play. In some cases, a third party may be used if you don't have the expertise in-house. This allows experts to apply their knowledge of the business logic, use and abuse cases, and prior experience to identify vulnerabilities while reducing the likelihood of false positives and false negatives. Static analysis tools are incapable of finding application flaws and business logic vulnerabilities and require the context and application understanding of a human analyst to identify. Having seasoned security professionals involved throughout the SDLC process will balance the developers' tendency to overlook certain coding errors even though they wrote the specific fragments of code and usually understand them best. Seasoned security experts can also help in understanding the technological context of the code, including not only the specific technologies that are used in the software product but also operating-system and third-party dependencies as well as tools used in development. From a security perspective, these security experts can identify relationships between a product and other systems, applications, or services. In the context of security, it is possible for them to determine what components a product relies on, as well as what other software depends on the product, and how these relationships can be used to determine how a product affects the rest of the system and how it may be affected by it. Human errors are typically the cause of most security problems; given the current shortcomings of automated tools, humans should also be part of the solution. For example, a small coding error can result in a critical vulnerability that ends up compromising the security of an entire system or network or may result from a sequence of errors that occur during the course of the development cycle where a coding error is introduced and goes undetected during the testing phases, and available defense mechanisms do not stop a successful attack. This is just another example of why the human element is necessary in the process—to be able to assess these types of situations, which are currently beyond the capabilities of automated software security tools.

The basic design of a product may also contain flaws, and it should be noted that some coding errors, although they may affect product reliability, are not actual vulnerabilities. Remember that the ultimate goal of security code reviews is to find code vulnerabilities that are accessible by an attacker and that may allow the attacker to bypass a security boundary.

6.4 Security Analysis Tools

The final goal of the security code review process is to improve the overall security of the product and to provide output that can be used by the development team to make changes and/or mitigations that will achieve improved software product security compared to what existed at concept commit for the start of the SDLC/SDL process. In this section, we discuss the details of what functions and roles static analysis, dynamic analysis, fuzz testing, and manual code review have in this overall process. Before we begin, however, it is important to recognize that each approach has certain practical advantages and limitations.

Advantages of Static Code Analysis

1. Access to the actual instructions the software will be executing:
   - No need to guess or interpret behavior.
   - Full access to all of the software's possible behaviors.
2. Can find exact location of weaknesses in the code.
3. Can be conducted by trained software assurance developers who fully understand the code.
4. Allows quick turnaround for fixes.
5. Relatively fast if automated tools are used.
6. Automated tools can scan the entire code base.
7. Automated tools can provide mitigation recommendations, reducing research time.
8. Permits weaknesses to be found earlier in the development life cycle, reducing the cost to fix.[5,6]

Limitations of Static Code Analysis

1. Requires access to source code or at least binary code and typically needs access to enough software artifacts to execute a build.
2. Typically requires proficiency in running software builds.
3. Will not find issues related to operational deployment environments.
4. Time-consuming if conducted manually.
5. Automated tools do not support all programming languages.
6. Automated tools produce false positives and false negatives.
7. There are not enough trained personnel to thoroughly conduct static code analysis.
8. Automated tools can provide a false sense of security that everything is being addressed.
9. Automated tools are only as good as the rules they are using to scan with.
10. Does not find vulnerabilities introduced in the runtime environment.[7,8]

Advantages of Dynamic Code Analysis

1. Limited scope of what can be found:
   - Application must be footprinted to find the test area.
   - That can cause areas to be missed.
   - You can only test what you have found.
2. No access to actual instructions being executed:
   - The tool is exercising the application.
   - Pattern matching on requests and responses.
3. Requires only a running system to perform a test.
4. No requirement to have access to source code or binary code.
5. No need to understand how to write software or execute builds:
   - Tools tend to be more "fire and forget."
6. Tests a specific operational deployment:
   - Can find infrastructure, configuration, and patch errors that static analysis tools will miss.
7. Identifies vulnerabilities in a runtime environment.
8. Automated tools provide flexibility on what to scan for.

9. Allows for analysis of applications without access to the actual code.
10. Identifies vulnerabilities that might have been false negatives in the static code analysis.
11. Permits validation of static code analysis findings.
12. Can be conducted on any application.[9,10]

Limitations of Dynamic Code Analysis

1. Automated tools provide a false sense of security that everything is being addressed.
2. Automated tools produce false positives and false negatives.
3. Automated tools are only as good as the rules they are using to scan with.
4. As for static analysis, there are not enough trained personnel to thoroughly conduct dynamic code analysis.
5. It is more difficult to trace the vulnerability back to the exact location in the code, taking longer to fix the problem.[11,12]

If you have no access to source or binaries, are not a software developer, and don't understand software builds, or you are performing a "penetration test" or other test of an operational environment, you will likely choose to use a dynamic tool; otherwise, you will likely use a static analysis tool. Ideally, you should use both in combination to get adequate coverage.

Advantages of Fuzz Testing

1. The great advantage of fuzz testing is that the test design is extremely simple and free of preconceptions about system behavior.
2. The systematical/random approach allows this method to find bugs that would often be missed by human eyes. Plus, when the tested system is totally closed (e.g., a SIP phone), fuzzing is one of the only means of reviewing its quality.
3. Bugs found using fuzz testing are frequently severe, exploitable bugs that could be used by a real attacker. This has become even truer as fuzz testing has become more widely known because the same techniques and tools are now used by attackers to exploit deployed software. This is a major advantage over binary or source auditing—or even fuzzing's close cousin, fault injection—which often relies on artificial fault conditions that are difficult or impossible to exploit.

Limitations of Fuzz Testing

1. Fuzzers usually tend to find simple bugs; plus, the more a fuzzer is protocol-aware, the fewer weird errors it will find. This is why the exhaustive/random approach is still popular.
2. Another problem is that when you do some black-box testing, you usually attack a closed system, which increases the difficulty of evaluating the danger/impact of the found vulnerability (no debugging possibilities).
3. The main problem with fuzzing to find program faults is that it generally finds only very simple faults. The problem itself is exponential, and every fuzzer takes shortcuts to find something interesting in a timeframe that a human cares about. A primitive fuzzer may have poor code coverage; for example, if the input includes a checksum that

is not properly updated to match other random changes, only the checksum validation code will be verified. Code coverage tools are often used to estimate how "well" a fuzzer works, but these are only guidelines to fuzzer quality. Every fuzzer can be expected to find a different set of bugs.[13,14]

Advantages of Manual Source Code Review

1. Requires no supporting technology.
2. Can be applied to a variety of situations.
3. Flexible.
4. Promotes teamwork.
5. Early in the SDLC.

Limitations of Manual Source Code Review

1. Can be time-consuming.
2. Supporting material not always available.
3. Requires significant human thought and skill to be effective.[15]

6.4.1 Static Analysis

Static program analysis is the analysis of computer software that is performed without actually executing programs. It is used predominantly to perform analysis on a version of the source code; it is also performed on object code. In contrast, dynamic analysis is performed by actually executing the software programs. Static analysis is performed by an automated software tool and should not be confused with human analysis or software security architectural reviews, which involve manual human code reviews, including program understanding and comprehension. When static analysis tools are used properly, they have a distinct advantage over human static analysis in that the analysis can be performed much more frequently and with security knowledge superior to that of many software developers. It thus allows for expert software security architects or engineers to be brought in only when absolutely necessary.

Static analysis (see Figure 6.3) is also known as static application security testing (SAST). It identifies vulnerabilities during the development or QA phase of a project. SAST provides line-of-code-level detection that enables development teams to remediate vulnerabilities quickly.

The use of static analysis tools and your choice of an appropriate vendor for your environment is another technology factor that is key to success. Any technology that beneficially automates any portion of the software development process should be welcome, but this software has become "shelfware" in many organizations because the right people and/or the right process was not used in selecting the tool or tools. Not all tools are created equal in this space: Some are better at some languages than others, whereas others have great front-end GRC (governance, risk management, and compliance) and metric analysis capabilities. In some cases, you may have to use up to three different tools to be effective.

One of the challenges in using a static analysis tool is that false positives may be reported when analyzing an application that interacts with closed-source components or external systems because without the source code it is impossible to trace the flow of data in the external system

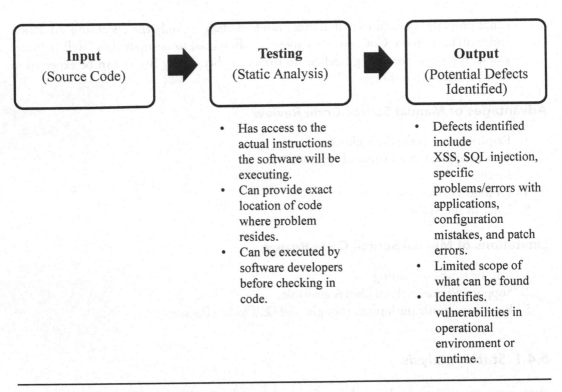

Figure 6.3 Static analysis flow diagram.

and hence ensure the integrity and security of the data. The use of static code analysis tools can also result in false negative results when vulnerabilities exist but the tool does not report them. This might occur if a new vulnerability is discovered in an external component or if the analysis tool has no knowledge of the runtime environment and whether it is configured securely. A static code analysis tool will often produce false positive results where the tool reports a possible vulnerability that in fact is not. This often occurs because the tool cannot be sure of the integrity and security of data as it flows through the application from input to output.[16]

Michael Howard, in his Security & Privacy 2006 IEEE® article titled "A Process for Performing Security Code Reviews,"[17] proposes the following heuristic as an aid to determining code review priority. The heuristic can be used as a guide for prioritizing static, dynamic, fuzzing, and manual code reviews.

- **Old code:** Older code may have more vulnerabilities than new code, because newer code often reflects a better understanding of security issues. All "legacy" code should be reviewed in depth.
- **Code that runs by default:** Attackers often go after installed code that runs by default. Such code should be reviewed earlier and more deeply than code that does not execute by default. Code running by default increases an application's attack surface.
- **Code that runs in elevated context:** Code that runs in elevated identities, for example, root in *nix, for example, also requires earlier and deeper review because code identity is another component of the attack surface.
- **Anonymously accessible code:** Code that anonymous users can access should be reviewed in greater depth than code that only valid users and administrators can access.

- **Code listening on a globally accessible network interface:** Code that listens by default on a network, especially uncontrolled networks such as the Internet, is open to substantial risk and must be reviewed in depth for security vulnerabilities.
- **Code written in C/C++/assembly language:** Because these languages have direct access to memory, buffer manipulation vulnerabilities within the code can lead to buffer overflows, which often lead to malicious code execution. Code written in these languages should be analyzed in depth for buffer overflow vulnerabilities.
- **Code with a history of vulnerabilities:** Code that has shown a number of security vulnerabilities in the past should be suspect, unless it can be demonstrated that those vulnerabilities have been effectively removed.
- **Code that handles sensitive data:** Code that handles sensitive data should be analyzed to ensure that weaknesses in the code do not disclose such data to untrusted users.
- **Complex code:** Complex code has a higher bug probability, is more difficult to understand, and may be likely to have more security vulnerabilities.
- **Code that changes frequently:** Frequently changing code often results in new bugs being introduced. Not all of these bugs will be security vulnerabilities, but compared with a stable set of code that is updated only infrequently, code that is less stable will probably have more vulnerabilities.

In Michael Howard's 2004 Microsoft® article titled "Mitigate Security Risks by Minimizing the Code You Expose to Untrusted Users,"[18] he also suggests a notional three-phase code analysis process that optimizes the use of static analysis tools:

Phase 1: Run all available code analysis tools.

- Multiple tools should be used to offset tool biases and minimize false positives and false negatives.
- Analysts should pay attention to every warning or error.
- Warnings from multiple tools may indicate that the code needs closer scrutiny (e.g., manual analysis). Code should be evaluated early, preferably with each build, and re-evaluated at every milestone.

Phase 2: Look for common vulnerability patterns.

- Analysts should make sure that code reviews cover the most common vulnerabilities and weaknesses, such as integer arithmetic issues, buffer overruns, SQL injection, and cross-site scripting (XSS).
- Sources for such common vulnerabilities and weaknesses include the Common Vulnerabilities and Exposures (CVE®) and Common Weaknesses Enumeration (CWE™) databases, maintained by the MITRE® Corporation and accessible at https://www.cve.org and http://cwe.mitre.org
- MITRE, in cooperation with the SANS Institute, also maintains a list of the "Top 25 Most Dangerous Programming Errors" that can lead to serious vulnerabilities (http://cwe .mitre.org/top25/index.html).
- Static code analysis tools and manual techniques should, at a minimum, address the "Top 25."

Phase 3: Dig deep into risky code.

- Analysts should also use manual analysis (e.g., code inspection) to more thoroughly evaluate any risky code that has been identified based on the attack surface, or based on the heuristics as discussed previously.
- Such code review should start at the entry point for each module under review and should trace data flow through the system, evaluating the data, how it is used, and whether security objectives might be compromised.

Below is an example of an issue that can be found through static analysis. Injection vulnerabilities are at the top of the OWASP® Top 10 2021 list.[19] These vulnerabilities occur when untrusted data is used directly for a query or as a result of construct commands without validation. There are different types of injection vulnerabilities—SQL, OS, and LDAP among them. SQL injection attacks are possible if user input is used directly to craft an SQL query.

Let's say that a user wants to review his account details. The application needs his user id or identifier to query account information from a back-end database. The application can pass this on through a URL parameter by doing something like this:

http://example.com/application/reviewaccount?account_id='1007'

In this case, the application is getting user `account _ id` `'1007'` and will use this id to pull information from the database. Let's say the backend query looks like this:

```
String insecureQuery = "SELECT * FROM accounts WHERE
accountID=' " + request.getParameter("account _ id") + " ' ";
```

If a malicious user changes the parameter value to ` or `1'='1`, the following string insecure query will have the value

```
SELECT * FROM accounts WHERE accountID=' " ` or `1'='1';
```

`1'='1'` will always be true, and thus this query can yield information about all accounts. This was not the intention of the developer, but by trusting user input to create a query, he or she has allowed a malicious user to execute arbitrary database commands.

Static analysis tools executed against code will identify that the query is built with user input and can result in SQL injection attacks.

6.4.2 Dynamic Analysis

Dynamic program analysis is the analysis of computer software that is performed by executing programs on a real or virtual processor in real time. The objective is to find security errors in a program while it is running, rather than by repeatedly examining the code offline. By debugging a program under all the scenarios for which it is designed, dynamic analysis eliminates the need to artificially create situations likely to produce errors. It has the distinct advantages of having the ability to identify vulnerabilities that might have been false negatives and to validate findings in the static code analysis.

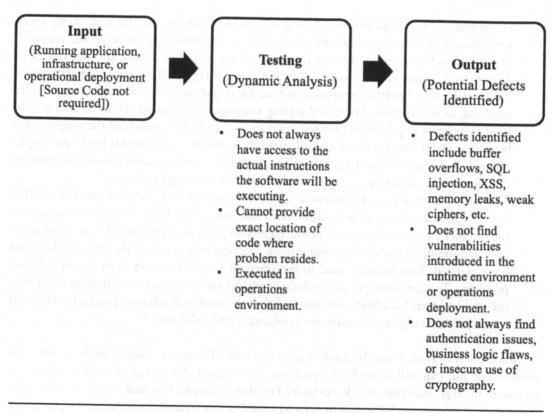

Input
(Running application, infrastructure, or operational deployment [Source Code not required])

Testing
(Dynamic Analysis)

Output
(Potential Defects Identified)

- Does not always have access to the actual instructions the software will be executing.
- Cannot provide exact location of code where problem resides.
- Executed in operations environment.

- Defects identified include buffer overflows, SQL injection, XSS, memory leaks, weak ciphers, etc.
- Does not find vulnerabilities introduced in the runtime environment or operations deployment.
- Does not always find authentication issues, business logic flaws, or insecure use of cryptography.

Figure 6.4   Dynamic analysis flow diagram.

Dynamic analysis (see Figure 6.4) is also known as dynamic application security testing (DAST). It identifies vulnerabilities within a production application. DAST tools are used to quickly assess a system's overall security and are used within both the SDL and SDLC. The same advantages and cautions about using static analysis tools apply to dynamic analysis tools.

The following explanation of how dynamic analysis is used throughout the SDLC is taken from the Peng and Wallace (1993) NIST Special Publication 500-209, "Software Error Analysis."[20]

- Commonly used dynamic analysis techniques for the design phase include sizing and timing analysis, prototyping, and simulation. Sizing and timing analysis is useful in analyzing real-time programs with response time requirements and constrained memory and execution space requirements. This type of analysis is especially useful for determining that allocations for hardware and software are made appropriately for the design architecture; it would be quite costly to learn in system testing that the performance problems are caused by the basic system design. An automated simulation may be appropriate for larger designs. Prototyping can be used as an aid in examining the design architecture in general or a specific set of functions. For large, complicated systems, prototyping can prevent inappropriate designs from resulting in costly, wasted implementations.[21]
- Dynamic analysis techniques help to determine the functional and computational correctness of the code. Regression analysis is used to re-evaluate requirements and design issues whenever any significant code change is made. This analysis ensures awareness of

the original system requirements. Sizing and timing analysis is performed during incremental code development, and analysis results are compared against predicted values.[22]

- Dynamic analysis in the test phase involves different types of testing and test strategies. Traditionally, there are four types of testing: unit, integration, system, and acceptance. Unit testing may be either structural or functional testing performed on software units, modules, or subroutines. Structural testing examines the logic of the units and may be used to support requirements for test coverage—that is, how much of the program has been executed. Functional testing evaluates how software requirements have been implemented. For functional testing, testers usually need no information about the design of the program because test cases are based on the software requirements.[23]

- The most commonly used dynamic analysis techniques for the final phase of the SDLC are regression analysis and test, simulation, and test certification. When any changes to the product are made during this phase, regression analysis is performed to verify that the basic requirements and design assumptions affecting other areas of the program have not been violated. Simulation is used to test operator procedures and to isolate installation problems. Test certification, particularly in critical software systems, is used to verify that the required tests have been executed and that the delivered software product is identical to the product subjected to software verification and validation.[24]

Static analysis finds issues by analyzing source code. Dynamic analysis tools do not need source code but can still identify the problem. During our discussion of static analysis, we reviewed an SQL injection attack example. For that example, the tool would identify that account_id is passed as a URL parameter and would try to tamper the value of the parameter and evaluate the response from the application.

6.4.3 Fuzz Testing

Fuzz testing (see Figure 6.5), or fuzzing, is a black-box software testing technique that can be automated or semiautomated and provides invalid, unexpected, or random data to the inputs of a computer software program. In other words, it finds implementation bugs or security flaws by using malformed/semi-malformed data injection in an automated fashion. Inputs to the software program are then monitored for exception returns such as crashes, failing built-in code assertions, and potential memory leaks. Fuzzing has become a key element in testing for software or computer system security problems. Fuzz testing has a distinct advantage over other tools in that the test design is extremely simple and free of preconceptions about system behavior.

Fuzzing is a key element of software security and must be embedded in the SDL. There are many vendors to choose from in this space, and some even develop their own tools. Fuzzing is used for both security and QA testing. Fuzzing has recently been recognized as both a key element and a major deficiency in many software development programs, so much so that it is now a U.S. Department of Defense (DoD) Information Assurance Certification and Accreditation Process (DIACAP) requirement.

Fuzzing is a form of attack simulation in which unexpected data is fed to the system through an open interface, and the behavior of the system is then monitored. If the system fails, for example, by crashing or by failing built-in code assertions, then there is a flaw in the

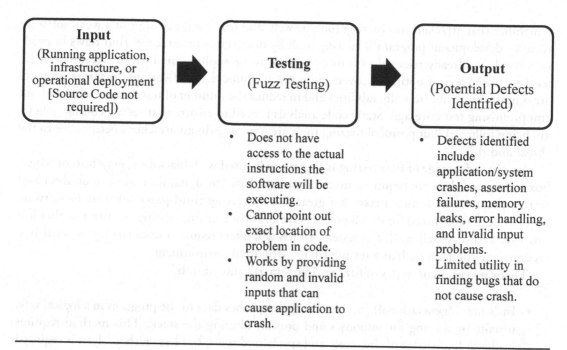

Input
(Running application, infrastructure, or operational deployment [Source Code not required])

Testing
(Fuzz Testing)

Output
(Potential Defects Identified)

- Does not have access to the actual instructions the software will be executing.
- Cannot point out exact location of problem in code.
- Works by providing random and invalid inputs that can cause application to crash.

- Defects identified include application/system crashes, assertion failures, memory leaks, error handling, and invalid input problems.
- Limited utility in finding bugs that do not cause crash.

Figure 6.5   Fuzz testing flow diagram.

software. Although all of the issues found by fuzzing tools are critical and exploitable, unlike static analysis tools, fuzzing can only find bugs that can be accessed through an open interface. Fuzzing tools must also be able to interoperate with the tested software so that they can access the deeper protocol layers and test the system more thoroughly by testing multiple layers.

Although static analysis has the benefit of full test coverage and is a good method for improving the general software quality level, it cannot easily provide test results that solve complex problems, and, as discussed previously, it also results in a large number of false positives, both of which require further analysis by a human and consume valuable and limited resources. There are no false positives in fuzz testing because every flaw discovered is a result of a simulated attack

Static analysis is performed on code that is not being executed, and it can only be performed offline. In contrast, fuzz testing must be executed against executable code, can be run against live software, and, therefore, can find vulnerabilities that may not be visible in the static code. Fuzz testing targets the problems attackers would also find and, therefore, is a good test for robustness while also streamlining the process by focusing only on the most critical interfaces that may be susceptible to attack. Because of its ability to test robustness, fuzz testing is typically used during the verification phase of the SDLC just before product release. As with static and dynamic analysis, fuzz testing can be used from the moment the first software components are ready and even after release—not just at some point in time during the SDLC process. This attribute, of course, can yield significant cost savings by finding and fixing vulnerabilities early in the SDLC.

Standard fuzz testing techniques are limited in their use of random mutation to create test cases, which will find only some of the software vulnerabilities. However, this testing still has value because these are the same vulnerabilities that attackers would find. It is important to remember that attackers use fuzzing tools as well, and it is a tell-tale sign of a weak software security development program if fuzzing tools by discoverers or attackers find flaws in products you have already released to your customers. More sophisticated fuzzing techniques are used to improve and optimize coverage by using protocol specifications to target protocol areas most susceptible to vulnerabilities and to reduce the number of test cases needed without compromising test coverage. Static code analysis is used to ensure that secure coding policies are being followed, but protocol fuzzing tools are used to gain an attacker's perspective to the threat and risk.

Another advantage of fuzz testing is that it can be used with black-box, gray-box, or white-box testing and does not require source code access. Like the dynamic analysis tools discussed in this chapter, this feature makes it a great tool for testing third-party software or software that has been outsourced for development. One drawback of fuzz testing, however, is that it is intrusive and may well crash the system, which will likely require initial testing to occur in a separate environment such as a testing lab or virtualized environment.

There are two main types of fuzz testing: "smart" and "dumb."

- In "smart" (generational) fuzzing, the fuzzer pushes data to the program in a logical way, usually by waiting for responses and possibly altering the stack. This method requires in-depth knowledge of the target and specialized tools, but less crash analysis is required and also less duplication of findings than with dumb fuzzing.[25,26]
- In "dumb" (mutational) fuzzing, the fuzzer systematically pushes data to the program without waiting for proper responses. This method is closely tied to denial-of-service (DoS) attacks. This method requires no knowledge of the target and uses existing tools. However, more crash analysis is required, and there is more duplication of findings than with "smart" fuzzing.[27,28]

To carry out a fuzz test, the following steps are followed for each file or field that feeds into the application:

1. Enter random data or spaces to some part of the input file.
2. Execute the application with that input file.
3. Evaluate results. What broke? What ran as normal? What was expected to happen?
4. Number each test case and report findings to project management.[29]

6.4.4 Manual Code Review

Manual security code reviews are typically done as a line-by-line inspection of the software to determine any security vulnerabilities in the software product. This will include a thorough review of programming source code of multitier and multicomponent enterprise software products. After the use of multiple automated tools, which help quickly analyze flaws and vulnerabilities, the code is reviewed manually. Every issue discovered is validated, and the code is inspected to overcome the limitations of the automated tools and techniques. Coding errors can be found using different approaches, but even when compared to sophisticated tools, manual code reviews have clearly proven their value in terms of precision and quality. Unfortunately, manual code reviews are also the most expensive to execute.

Manual code reviews by definition are human-driven, and although the highest value-add for their use is for architectural design reviews, these software security reviews are done with a holistic approach that includes people, policies, and processes. Assuming limited resources, manual code review is best performed on only the most critical components of an application. These reviews will also include manually reviewing the documentation, secure coding policies, security requirements, and architectural designs. There is also a mentoring aspect of manual reviews, in that the software security architects will be able to teach others on the development team about the art of testing, how to understand the security process, policy awareness, and the appropriate skills for designing or implementing a secure application. Even with seasoned and security-savvy development teams, software security architects should adopt a trust-but-verify model. This process is enhanced by the fact that the architects usually analyze documentation together with the stakeholders and appropriate development team members and also interview the designers or system owners for their input.

It should be noted that if good software engineering processes are adhered to, they can alleviate many of the concerns that are being assessed by the code review team. In most cases, static and dynamic analysis or fuzz testing is more efficient at catching implementation bugs than code review, but if some of the security vulnerabilities that manual code review finds are rare, it is the only way they will be found. Once a type of security vulnerability has been found through manual code review, it should be incorporated into automatic code review tools. As mentioned previously, efficient and effective software security requires a holistic approach and includes not just manual software reviews but also mandatory software security training, security design reviews, threat modeling, fuzz testing, static and dynamic analysis, the identification of high-risk practices, and measurable criteria and requirements for each of the various phases in the software life cycle, including servicing and support.

The following steps are typically used for manual software security reviews:

- The threat model that was used to identify the risk and tell the development team which code to look at first and with the most scrutiny will also help the team to understand existing security threats in relation to the software's functionality.
- The various automated tools described above are used to assess the code for semantic and language security vulnerabilities and to optimize the search for the highest risk and the greatest effort to fix or mitigate.
- A line-by-line inspection of the software code is done manually to find logical errors, insecure use of cryptography, insecure system configurations, and other known issues specific to the platform.

Using a question-driven approach can help with the review activity. A list of standard questions can help you focus on common security vulnerabilities that are not unique to your software's architecture. This approach can be used in conjunction with techniques such as control flow and data flow analysis to optimize the ability to trace those paths through the code that are most likely to reveal security issues. Questions should address at least the most common coding vulnerabilities. Ask these questions while you are using control flow and dataflow analysis. Keep in mind that finding some vulnerabilities may require contextual knowledge of control and data flow, whereas others will be context-free and can be found using simple pattern matching. Some of the following techniques may be combined when doing a manual security review of the code:

- **Control flow analysis.** Control flow analysis is the mechanism used to step through logical conditions in the code. The process is as follows:
  1. Examine a function and determine each branch condition. These may include loops, switch statements, "if" statements, and "try/catch" blocks.
  2. Understand the conditions under which each block will execute.
  3. Move to the next function and repeat.

- **Data flow analysis.** Data flow analysis is the mechanism used to trace data from the points of input to the points of output. Because there can be many data flows in an application, use your code review objectives and the flagged areas from Step 2 to focus your work. The process is as follows:
  1. For each input location, determine how much you trust the source of input. When in doubt, you should give it no trust.
  2. Trace the flow of data to each possible output. Note any attempts at data validation.
  3. Move to the next input and continue.[30]

While performing data flow analysis, review the list of inputs and outputs, and then match this to the code that you need to review. You must pay particular attention to prioritizing any areas where the code crosses trust boundaries and where the code changes trust levels, just as you did during the threat modeling process. A set of common validation routines that your software can call as soon as it receives any untrusted data should be available which will give your software product a central validation area that can be updated as new information is discovered. As the data flow analysis is performed, give special attention to areas where the data is parsed and may go to multiple output locations, to ensure that the data is traced back to its source and trust is assigned based on the weakest link.

There are other lists of questions that should be considered. Some of these are organized into sets of key areas based on the implementation mistakes that result in the most common software vulnerabilities relevant to the software product or solution being developed, also called hotspots. These questions are typically developed by the software security architect and revolve around the last top 10 to 20 CVE or OWASP "Top 10" lists described earlier in the book.

A review for security issues unique to the architecture should also be conducted as part of the manual security review process. This step is particularly important if the software product uses a custom security mechanism or has features to mitigate known security threats. During this step, the list of code review objectives is also examined for anything that has not yet been reviewed. Here, too, a question-driven approach such as the following list will be useful, as the final code review step to verify that the security features and requirements that are unique to your software architecture have been met.

- *Does your architecture include a custom security implementation?* A custom security implementation is a great place to look for security issues for these reasons:
  - o It has already been recognized that a security problem exists, which is why the custom security code was written in the first place.
  - o Unlike other areas of the product, a functional issue is very likely to result in security vulnerability.
- *Are there known threats that have been specifically mitigated?* Code that mitigates known threats needs to be carefully reviewed for problems that could be used to circumvent the mitigation.

- *Are there unique roles in the application?* The use of roles assumes that there are some users with lower privileges than others. Make sure that there are no problems in the code that could allow one role to assume the privileges of another.[31]

We would like to reiterate that it is not an either/or proposition between different types of security testing. For a product to be secure, it should go through all types of security testing—static analysis, dynamic analysis, manual code review, penetration testing, and fuzzing. Often, trade-offs are made during the development cycle due to time constraints or deadlines, and testing is skipped as a product is rushed to market. This might save some time and a product may be released a few weeks/months sooner. However, this is an expensive proposition from a return on investment (ROI) point of view. Further, security problems found after a product is released can cause a lot of damage to customers and the brand name of the company.

6.5 Key Success Factors

The success of this fourth phase of the SDL depends on a review of policy compliance, security test case execution, completion of different types of security testing, and validation of privacy requirements. Table 6.1 lists key success factors for this phase.

Table 6.1 Key Success Factors

Key Success Factor	Description
1. Security test case execution	Coverage of all relevant test cases
2. Security testing	Completion of all types of security testing and remediation of problems found
3. Privacy validation and remediation	Effectiveness of privacy-related controls and remediation of any issues found
4. Policy compliance review	Updates for policy compliance as related to Phase 4

Success Factor 1: Security Test Case Execution

Refer to Section 6.2 for details on the success criteria for the security test execution plan.

Success Factor 2: Security Testing

It is critical to complete all types of security testing—manual code review, static analysis, dynamic analysis, penetration testing, and fuzzing. Issues found during each type of testing should be evaluated for risk and prioritized. Any security defect with medium or higher severity should be remediated before releasing or deploying a product. Defects with low severity should not be ignored but should be put on a roadmap for remediation as soon as possible.

Success Factor 3: Privacy Validation and Remediation

Validation of privacy issues should be part of security test plans and security testing. However, it is good to have a separate workstream to assess the effectiveness of controls in the product as related to privacy. Any issues identified should be prioritized and remediated before the product is released or deployed.

Success Factor 4: Policy Compliance Review (Updates)

If any additional policies are identified, or previously identified policies have been updated since the analysis was performed in Phase 3, updates should be reviewed, and changes to the product should be planned accordingly.

6.6 Deliverables

Table 6.2 lists deliverables for this phase of the SDL.

Table 6.2 Deliverables for Phase A4

Deliverable	Goal
Security test execution report	Review progress against identified security test cases
Updated policy compliance analysis	Analysis of adherence to company policies
Privacy compliance report	Validation that recommendations from privacy assessment have been implemented
Security testing reports	Findings from different types of security testing
Remediation report	Provide status on the security posture of product

Security Test Execution Report

The execution report should provide the status of the executed security tests and the frequency of tests. The report should also provide information on the number of retests performed to validate the remediation of issues.

Updated Policy Compliance Analysis

Policy compliance analysis artifacts (see Chapters 4 and 5) should be updated based on any new requirements or policies that might have come up during this phase of the SDL.

Privacy Compliance Report

The privacy compliance report should provide progress against privacy requirements provided in earlier phases. Any outstanding requirement should be implemented as soon as possible. It is also prudent to assess any changes in laws/regulations to identify (and put on a roadmap) any new requirements.

Security Testing Reports

A findings summary should be prepared for each type of security testing: manual code review, static analysis, dynamic analysis, penetration testing, and fuzzing. The reports should provide the type and number of issues identified and any consistent theme that can be derived from the findings. For example, suppose there are far fewer XSS issues in one component of the application compared to another. It could be because developers in the former were better trained or implemented the framework more effectively. Such feedback should be looped back into earlier stages of the SDL during the next release cycle.

Remediation Report

A remediation report/dashboard should be prepared and updated regularly from this stage. The purpose of this report is to showcase the security posture and risk of the product at a technical level.

6.7 Metrics

The following metrics should be collected during this phase of the SDL (some of which may overlap metrics we discussed earlier).

- Percent compliance with company policies (updated)
  - Percent of compliance in Phase 3 versus Phase 4
- Number of lines of code tested effectively with static analysis tools
- Number of security defects found through static analysis tools
- Number of high-risk defects found through static analysis tools
- Defect density (security issues per 1000 lines of code)
- Number and types of security issues found through static analysis, dynamic analysis, manual code review, penetration testing, and fuzzing
  - Overlap of security issues found through different types of testing
  - Comparison of severity of findings from different types of testing
  - Mapping of findings to threats/risks identified earlier
- Number of security findings remediated
  - Severity of findings
  - Time spent (approximate) in hours to remediate findings
- Number, types, and severity of findings outstanding
- Percentage compliance with the security test plan
- Number of security test cases executed
  - Number of findings from security test case execution
  - Number of retests executed

6.8 Summary

During our discussion of the design and development (A4) phase, we described the process for successful test case execution, the process of proper code review through the use of both automated tools and manual review, and the process for privacy validation and remediation to be conducted during this phase of the SDL. The most critical processes and procedures described in this chapter are those that provide the ability to effectively and efficiently test, tune, and remediate known vulnerabilities and to ensure that secure coding policies have been followed, which provide the necessary security and privacy vulnerability protections before moving on to the product ship (A5) phase of the SDL.

Chapter Quick-Check

1. The following are primary mitigation methods except:

   a. Locking down the environment
   b. Input validation
   c. Use of deprecated libraries for legacy code
   d. Output validation

2. Elements of defensive coding include all the following except:

   a. Custom cryptographic functions to avoid algorithm disclosure
   b. Exception handling to avoid program termination
   c. Interface coding efforts to avoid API-facing attacks
   d. Cryptographic agility to make cryptographic functions stronger

3. Static analysis can be used to check for:

   a. Approved function/library calls, examining rules and semantics associated with logic, and thread performance management
   b. Syntax, approved function/library calls, and race conditions
   c. Syntax, approved function/library calls, and memory management
   d. Syntax, approved function/library calls, and examining rules and semantics associated with logic and calls

4. Automated testing has the following advantages over manual code review except:

   a. Detection of unsafe or deprecated function calls
   b. Identification of obfuscated routines
   c. Speed of analysis
   d. Integration into the IDE

Exercises

The following exercises are based on the case study discussed in Appendix A. These exercises are intended to give you some practice in applying the steps and producing deliverables for Phase A4 of the SDL.

At this point, you've created a management plan and a roadmap to implement an SDL at Revvin' Engines. With a solid system and process that yields secure architecture and design for an API-based system of microservices that reflect the business requirements and the security and nonfunctional requirements for an application, you can gain assurance that the applications and infrastructure can stand up to the hostile public Internet.

As you move into the development activities, you'll need a plan and roadmap for security at development time, unit testing time, integration testing time, and pre-release testing for assurance that the applications are secure enough for release to production.

1. Revisit the initial testing plan and include all activities you deem are needed for the application(s) testing—both manual and tool-based.
2. Design processes to integrate testing activities in development pipelines for automation

of testing tasks that can be automated. Make certain that all testing results are reported to a gatekeeper function that will fail the build if the scan policies are unmet.

3. Establish the scanner policies needed for each scanning tool or process to determine pass/failure limits that trigger appropriate security events.

4. Determine the metrics needed across all mandated testing processes and determine the most appropriate reporting methods and mechanisms.

References

1. Kaner, C. (2008, April). "A Tutorial in Exploratory Testing," p. 36. Retrieved from http://www.kaner.com/pdfs/QAIExploring.pdf

2. Chmielewski, M., Clift, N., Fonrobert, S., and Ostwald, T. (2007, November). "*MSDN Magazine*: Find and Fix Vulnerabilities Before Your Application Ships." Retrieved from http://msdn.microsoft.com/en-us/magazine/cc163312.aspx

3. Microsoft Corporation. (2012). "How To: Perform a Security Code Review for Managed Code (.NET Framework 2.0)." Retrieved from http://msdn.microsoft.com/en-us/library/ff649315.aspx

4. Ibid.

5. Jackson, W. (2009, February). GCN—Technology, Tools and Tactics for Public Sector IT: "Static vs. Dynamic Code Analysis: Advantages and Disadvantages." Retrieved from http://gcn.com/Articles/2009/02/09/Static-vs-dynamic-code-analysis.aspx?p=1

6. Cornell, D. (2008, January). OWASP San Antonio Presentation: "Static Analysis Techniques for Testing Application Security." Retrieved from https://1library.net/document/y94orglq-static-analysis-techniques-testing-application-security-antonio-january.html

7. Jackson, W. (2009, February). GCN—Technology, Tools and Tactics for Public Sector IT: "Static vs. Dynamic Code Analysis: Advantages and Disadvantages." Retrieved from http://gcn.com/Articles/2009/02/09/Static-vs-dynamic-code-analysis.aspx?p=1

8. Cornell, D. (2008, January). OWASP San Antonio Presentation: "Static Analysis Techniques for Testing Application Security." Retrieved from https://1library.net/document/y94orglq-static-analysis-techniques-testing-application-security-antonio-january.html

9. Jackson, W. (2009, February). GCN—Technology, Tools and Tactics for Public Sector IT: "Static vs. Dynamic Code Analysis: Advantages and Disadvantages." Retrieved from http://gcn.com/Articles/2009/02/09/Static-vs-dynamic-code-analysis.aspx?p=1

10. Cornell, D. (2008, January). OWASP San Antonio Presentation: "Static Analysis Techniques for Testing Application Security." Retrieved from https://1library.net/document/y94orglq-static-analysis-techniques-testing-application-security-antonio-january.html

11. Jackson, W. (2009, February). GCN—Technology, Tools and Tactics for Public Sector IT: "Static vs. Dynamic Code Analysis: Advantages and Disadvantages." Retrieved from http://gcn.com/Articles/2009/02/09/Static-vs-dynamic-code-analysis.aspx?p=1

12. Cornell, D. (2008, January). OWASP San Antonio Presentation: "Static Analysis Techniques for Testing Application Security." Retrieved from https://1library.net/document/y94orglq-static-analysis-techniques-testing-application-security-antonio-january.html

13. The Open Web Application Security Project (OWASP). (2012). "Fuzzing." Retrieved from https://www.owasp.org/index.php/Fuzzing

14. R2Launch. (2012). "Fuzz." Retrieved from http://www.r2launch.nl/index.php/software-testing/fuzz

15. The Open Web Application Security Project (OWASP). (2012). "Testing Guide Introduction." Retrieved from https://www.owasp.org/index.php/Testing_Guide_Introduction#Manual_Inspections_.26_Reviews

16. The Open Web Application Security Project (OWASP). (2012). "Static Code Analysis." Retrieved from https://www.owasp.org/index.php/Static_Code_Analysis
17. Howard, M. (2006, July–August). "A Process for Performing Security Code Reviews." *IEEE Security & Privacy,* pp. 74–79.
18. Howard, M. (2004, November). "Mitigate Security Risks by Minimizing the Code You Expose to Untrusted Users." Retrieved from https://docs.microsoft.com/en-us/archive/msdn-magazine/2004/november/security-tips-minimizing-the-code-you-expose-to-untrusted-users
19. OWASP. (2013). "OWASP Top Ten." Retrieved from https://owasp.org/www-project-top-ten/
20. Peng, W., and Wallace, D. (1993, March). NIST Special Publication 500-209, "Software Error Analysis." Retrieved from https://nvlpubs.nist.gov/nistpubs/Legacy/SP/nistspecialpublication500-209.pdf
21. Ibid.
22. Ibid.
23. Ibid.
24. Ibid.
25. Royal, M., and Pokorny, P. (2012, April). Cameron University IT 4444—Capstone: "Dumb Fuzzing in Practice." Retrieved from https://www.pdffiller.com/12963674-5pdf-Dumb-Fuzzing-in-Practice-1-
26. Manion, A., and Orlando, M. (2011, May). ICSJWG Presentation: "Fuzz Testing for Dummies." Retrieved from https://fuzzinginfo.files.wordpress.com/2012/05/ag_16b_icsjwg_spring_2011_conf_manion_orlando.pdf
27. Royal, M., and Pokorny, P. (2012, April). Cameron University IT 4444—Capstone: "Dumb Fuzzing in Practice." Retrieved from https://www.pdffiller.com/12963674-5pdf-Dumb-Fuzzing-in-Practice-1-
28. Ibid.
29. Grembi, J. (2008). *Secure Software Development: A Security Programmer's Guide.* Boston, MA: Course Technology.
30. Meier, J., et al. (2005, October). Microsoft Corporation—MSDN Library: "How To: Perform a Security Code Review for Managed Code (.NET Framework 2.0)." Retrieved from http://msdn.microsoft.com/en-us/library/ff649315.aspx
31. Ibid.

Chapter 7

Ship (A5): SDL Activities and Best Practices

CHAPTER OVERVIEW

Now that you have reached the last phase of the software development life cycle (SDLC), you need to ensure that the software is secure and that privacy issues have been addressed to a level at which the software is acceptable for release and ready to ship. Software security and privacy requirements should have come from initial phases and been refined throughout the cycle. In this chapter, we will take you through the last stage of policy compliance review, followed by the final vulnerability scan, pre-release penetration testing, open-source licensing review, and the final security and privacy reviews.

CHAPTER TAKE-AWAYS

- Explore the practices that compose the Ship (Phase A5) of the security development life-cycle (SDL).
- Document the key success factors for completion of Phase A5.
- Create final deliverables for Phase A5 for the case study in Appendix A.
- Consolidate security testing reports for the case study in Appendix A.

Figure 7.1 illustrates the steps and activities found in Phase A5 of the SDL. As discussed in SDL Phases (A1)–(A4), SDL policy compliance covers all projects that have meaningful security and privacy risks and is analyzed in each phase and updated to cover new threats and practices. In the final policy compliance review, the SDL policy will be reviewed to ensure that the policy provides specific requirements based on different development criteria, such as product type, code type, and platform.

A vulnerability scan will look for any remaining vulnerabilities in your software and associated systems and report potential exposures. This process is usually automated, and it will

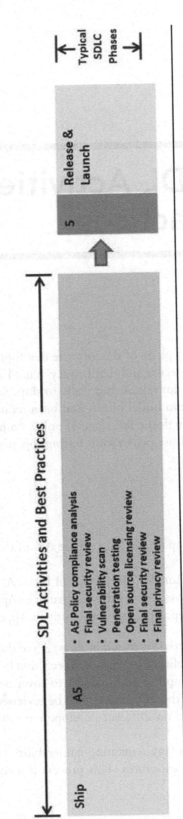

Figure 7.1 Ship (A5): SDL activities and best practices.

typically be run by somebody in your own organization. In contrast, a penetration test actually exploits weaknesses in the architecture of your systems and requires various levels of expertise within your scope of the software and associated systems you are testing. A seasoned security individual or team that is part of a third party to provide an independent point of view, high-level or specialized external expertise, and "another set of eyes" typically conducts the testing.

During the final phase of the SDL security review of the software being assessed, all of the security activities performed during the process, including threat models, tools outputs, and performance against requirements defined early in the process will be assessed to determine whether the software product is ready for release and shipping. We will discuss the three options that can occur as part of this process.

It is essential to be in compliance with applicable open-source requirements to avoid costly and time-consuming litigation. The two primary areas that need to be of concern for those managing the SDL where open-source software is used as part of the product or solution are license compliance and security.

The privacy requirements must be satisfied before the software can be released. Privacy requirement verification is typically verified concurrently with the final security review and, in many cases, is now considered part of the same process.

7.1 A5 Policy Compliance Analysis

As discussed for SDL Phases (A1)–(A4), SDL policy compliance covers all projects that have meaningful security and privacy risks and is analyzed in each phase and updated to cover new threats and practices. Specifically, activities and standards in the policy have been refreshed in each SDL phase, and they have incorporated lessons learned from root-cause analysis of security incidents, adapted to the changing threat environment, and will have resulted in tools and technique improvements. During the subsequent phases, SDL policy compliance has been tracked and, if needed, exceptions have been issued for high-risk projects. From the beginning of the SDL process, the SDL policy has formally defined which projects qualify for SDL mandates and what the requirements are for compliance. This policy has become a significant part in the governance of the SDL process in that it:

- Standardizes the types of projects that fall under the SDL mandate and activities.
- Defines the policy and processes that must happen at each phase of the SDL/SDLC for project compliance.
- Sets the requirements for the quality gates that must be met before release.

In the final policy compliance analysis, the policy will be reviewed to ensure that it provides specific requirements based on different development criteria, such as product type, code type, and platform.

7.2 Vulnerability Scan

Although there is no substitute for actual source-code review by a human, automated tools do have their advantages and can be used to save time and resources. They are particularly useful to conduct regression testing at this stage of the process, as a double check that any possible vulnerabilities have not inadvertently been re-introduced into the code and that all previously identified vulnerabilities have been mitigated throughout the process. It is also possible that other products with similar functionality have had publicly disclosed vulnerabilities since the beginning of the SDL for a particular software product, and these can be checked during the final security review as well. Given that software products commonly include 500,000 lines or more of code, vulnerability scanners can be very useful as a cost-effective and time-limited final check of the SDL. These scanners can carry out complex and comprehensive data flow analysis to identify vulnerability points that might be missed in the course of manual human review. These products are a much quicker and more efficient way to analyze every possible path through a compiled code base to find the root-cause-level vulnerabilities than using the human approach. They are also good tools to "check the checker," that is, the software security architect who has conducted manual reviews throughout the process.

Vulnerability scanning tools explore applications and use databases of signatures to attempt to identify weaknesses. Vulnerability scans are not the same as penetration tests and should not be categorized as such; however, some of the same tools may be used in both processes. A vulnerability scan is actually an assessment and, as such, will look for known vulnerabilities in the software and associated systems. It is automated, it can typically be run by a technician, and it will report potential exposures. Having your own development staff conduct the vulnerability scans will help them not only build up a baseline of what is normal for software security but also to understand it. In contrast, a penetration test actually exploits weaknesses in the architecture of your systems and requires various levels of expertise within your scope of the software and associated systems you are testing. Such testing is typically conducted by a seasoned software security professional such as a software security architect or seasoned software security engineer.

Vulnerability scanning is a necessary part of software security and the SDL. Given its automated nature and ease of performance, it should be run at various times through the SDL as a cost-effective, efficient, and minimally intrusive way to continually check your work. The results should be continually baselined to identify code or architectural changes that may have introduced new vulnerabilities during the process.

Although every effort must be taken to remediate all discovered vulnerabilities, there are some cases in which the scanner may falsely identify a vulnerability or exceptions are made. False positives are vulnerabilities where the scanner has identified the software as being vulnerable when, in fact, it is not. Of course, once this is proven, the false positive can be discounted. Exceptions are made because the remediation will prevent optimal software performance, restrict a critical function in the product, or even require a complete architecture redesign. The risk is deemed acceptable because compensating controls are in place or can be put in place with minimal effort to mitigate the risk. Exceptions may be permanent or they may have an expiration date attached. The typical vulnerability scan process is diagrammed in Figure 7.2.

Static or dynamic source-code vulnerability scanner tools, as discussed earlier in this book, can be used during this phase as appropriate. If the software is a web application, you must use tools designed specifically for web application vulnerability analysis. One mistake that should be avoided if you are using a web application vulnerability scanner is not to scan for just the OWASP "Top 10" vulnerabilities, but rather scan for all software application vulnerabilities. As with static or other dynamic vulnerability scanners, if critical, high, or severe application vulnerabilities are identified by scanning, those vulnerabilities must be fixed before the application is released to the production environment or shipped.

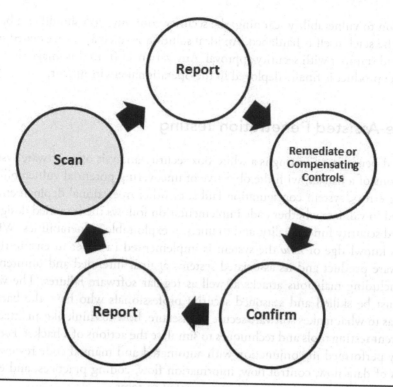

Figure 7.2   Typical vulnerability scan process.

You should use as many vulnerability scanners as possible across the stack. Web application scanning alone will not be sufficient, as the software stack (operating system, web servers, application servers, database servers) can also have vulnerabilities that need to be remediated. Vulnerability scanning should include external scans, internal scans and authenticated scans of the entire stack (especially in a cloud environment). External scans are primarily targeted at exploring security issues that can be found outside the firewall. Since a firewall often restricts ports, these scans may be of only limited utility at times; however, they can still be very valuable because findings from external scans are often also quite accessible to attackers. Internal scans are executed from inside firewalls, and, thus, findings are not restricted to ports everyone can see from outside firewalls. Internal scans allow us to identify security issues that an attacker or malicious insider can exploit if he or she gets inside the network (and is not outside restricted by firewalls). Authenticated scans are most comprehensive in that they not only identify issues covered by external and internal scans but also identify missing patches and reduce false positives. Authenticated scans require software to log on to a system to scan it, however, and thus are most intrusive.

Earlier in the process, security architecture should have laid out configuration requirements for the software stack to harden the stack and remove attack surfaces. Configuration guidelines exist in various forms, including hardening standards for operating systems and other software on which the product will be deployed. For example, off-the-shelf operating systems will have many unnecessary services and configurations that increase the attack surface on the stack. Hardening guidelines can be instrumental in reducing risk from the default configuration.

In addition to vulnerability scanning, the security configuration should also be validated to ensure that the stack itself is hardened. An ideal solution is to create a "hardened image" of the stack itself and stamp it with security approval. Any variances from this image should raise a red flag when the product is finally deployed in the operational environment.

7.3 Code-Assisted Penetration Testing

Code-assisted penetration testing is a white-box security analysis of a software system to simulate the actions of a hacker, with the objective of uncovering potential vulnerabilities resulting from coding errors, system configuration faults, or other operational deployment weaknesses. It is also used to validate whether code implementation follows the intended design, to validate implemented security functionality, and to uncover exploitable vulnerabilities. White-box testing requires knowledge of *how* the system is implemented in order to ensure the robustness of the software product and its associated systems against intended and unintended software behavior, including malicious attacks as well as regular software failures. The white-box test assessors must be skilled and seasoned security professionals who have the background and knowledge as to what makes software secure or insecure, how to think like an attacker, and how to use different testing tools and techniques to simulate the actions of a hacker. Penetration tests are typically performed in conjunction with automated and manual code reviews and require the analysis of data flow, control flow, information flow, coding practices, and exception and error handling within the software and its associated systems.

To successfully conduct a white-box security test of the code being developed and the systems with which it will be interacting, three basic requirements must be satisfied holistically, not independent of each other. The assessor(s)/tester(s) must:

1. Have access to and be able to comprehend and analyze available design documentation, source code, and other relevant development artifacts, and have the background and knowledge of what makes software secure
2. Be able to think like an attacker and have the ability to create tests that exploit software
3. Have knowledge and experience with the different tools and techniques available for white-box testing and the ability to think "outside the box" or unconventionally, as an adversary would use the same tools and techniques.

Independence is a key element and requirement for penetration testing, which is why engaging a third-party external security firm to conduct a security review and/or penetration testing should always be considered. This provides the benefit of both an "outside set of eyes" and independence and should be mandatory for all projects that are considered to be a high business risk. An outside view and perspective will help identify the types of vulnerabilities that other processes are not preventing and make the current state of security maturity clear to all. The third party should be afforded access to the threat models and architectural diagrams created during the SDL to determine priorities, test, and attack the software as a hacker might. The level of scrutiny will always be predicated on the available budget, since these types of firms typically charge a premium for their services. Any security issues or vulnerabilities identified during penetration testing must be addressed and resolved before the project is approved for release and shipping.

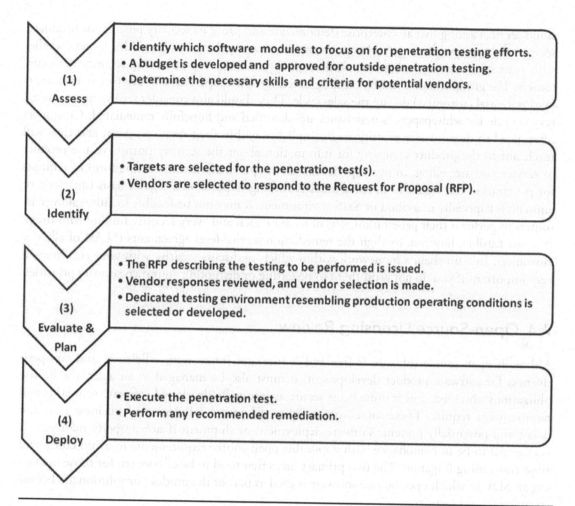

Figure 7.3   The four-phase process of penetration testing.

To achieve the minimum requirements for penetration testing, the four-phase process shown in Figure 7.3 should be followed.

The penetration test report is the final deliverable of the penetration test. The main body of the report should focus on what data was compromised and how, and provide the customer with the actual method of attack and exploit, along with the value of the data exploited. If needed or desired by the SDL and development teams, possible solutions can be included in the report as well. The detailed listing of the vulnerabilities that had attempted exploits and the false positives or vulnerabilities that were exploited but resulted in no data loss should be included in an appendix rather than the main body of the report in order to keep the primary part of this report succinct and to the point.

The long list of possible exposures typically generated from a vulnerability scan should be in the vulnerability scan report or readout and not part of the final penetration report. As mentioned in the previous section, the purpose of each activity and its results are different.

Security has been in the limelight for all the wrong reasons of late, given that some very well-known companies have been attacked, and some popular products have been in the news for having security holes. This has resulted in customers (whether for traditional software or SaaS/

cloud service) asking that an enterprise demonstrate and prove its security posture for products/ services they are purchasing. At this point in the release cycle, it is a good idea to get together with your sales and marketing team and create a framework for discussing security with customers. The group should consider creating a security whitepaper that can be given to customers (and potential customers) during the sales cycle. They should also consider setting up an annual review cycle for whitepapers as new issues are identified and hopefully remediated. Customers often need to demonstrate security and compliance within their own company, and thus will reach out to the product company for information about the security posture of the product or service you are selling. In our experience, such requests often come in the form of requests for penetration test results or detailed security findings reports on a regular basis (quarterly or annually). Especially in a cloud or SaaS environment, it may not be feasible to either allow customers to perform their penetration tests or to share each and every security finding with them. It is not feasible, however, to align the remediation service-level agreements (SLAs) of all your customers. In a nutshell, a framework within which to discuss security with your customers is very important if you do not want them to be setting or disrupting your own security priorities.

7.4 Open-Source Licensing Review

Although open-source software is free and it increases innovation, efficiency, and competitiveness for software product development, it must also be managed as an asset, the license obligations observed, and it must be as secure as internally developed software standards and requirements require. These sometimes unique and complex license and business risks can delay, and potentially prevent, software deployment or shipment if not properly managed. It is essential to be in compliance with applicable open-source requirements to avoid costly and time-consuming litigation. The two primary areas that need to be of concern for those managing an SDL in which open-source software is used as part of the product or solution are license compliance and security.

1. **Open-source software license compliance.** Noncompliance with open-source software licensing requirements can result in costly and time-consuming litigation, court time, copyright infringement, public press exposure, bad publicity, and negative risk to the noncompliant organization's reputation and business relationships. Mismanagement and noncompliance with open-source licenses may also result in the difficulty or inability to provide software product support, the delay of current release and ship dates, or the stoppage of orders currently scheduled to ship.
2. **Open-source software security.** SDL and development teams, as well as their executive sponsors, need to be aware of and understand vulnerabilities associated with open-source software code to be used in their own software product. As with the software being developed in-house, all vulnerabilities known to the open-source and software security community must be identified, assessed, and mitigated throughout the SDL process and include the same threat modeling, architectural security and privacy review, and risk assessment rigor and as the code being developed in-house.

To put this into perspective, a few examples of the consequences of not properly managing open-source software license or security are given below.

- **Diebold® and PES.** Artifex® Software, the company behind the open-source Ghostscript® PDF processing software, filed a lawsuit against voting machine vendor Diebold and its subsidiary Premier Election Solutions. Artifex said that Diebold violated the General Public License (GPL) by incorporating Ghostscript into commercial electronic voting machine systems. Ghostscript, which was originally developed in the late 1980s, is distributed free under the GNU® GPL. This license permits developers to study, modify, use, and redistribute the software but requires that derivatives be made available under the same terms. Companies that want to use Ghostscript in closed-source proprietary software projects can avoid the copyright requirement by purchasing a commercial license from Artifex. Among commercial Ghostscript users who have purchased licenses from Artifex are some of the biggest names in the printing and technology industries, including HP®, IBM®, Kodak®, Siemens®, SGI®, and Xerox®.[1]
- **Skype®.** Skype was found guilty of violating the GNU GPL by a Munich, Germany, regional court. This decision has influenced the way companies have approached GPL compliance since then.[2]
- **Verizon®.** Two software developers reached a settlement in a lawsuit against Verizon Communications in which they claimed the telecom giant's broadband service violated the terms of the widely used open-source agreement under which their product was licensed. The issue centered on claims that a subcontractor used an open-source program called BusyBox in Verizon's wireless routers. As part of the settlement, Verizon subcontractor Actiontec Electronics must pay an undisclosed sum to developers Erick Andersen and Rob Landley. It must also appoint an internal officer to ensure that it is in compliance with licenses governing the open-source software it uses.[3]
- **Google®.** Google and other companies continue to receive bad publicity because they use the Android™ mobile platform, which was launched with known security vulnerabilities and continues to be a major target for hackers. Mobile malware tracked by McAfee® exploded in 2012, growing almost 700 percent over the 2011 numbers. Close to 85 percent of this malware targets smart phones running Android. The big surprise in the huge increase is not that Android is being attacked: Google's smartphone platform has been a key focus for the bad guys for some time. The big surprise is that Google has not managed to stem the tide in any significant way. Security concerns about Android should not be news to Google, and Google should be putting security at the top of its list of priorities.[4]
- **Oracle®.** Security experts accused Oracle of not paying attention to its flagship database software and underreporting the severity of a "fundamental" flaw. Even as Oracle fixed numerous flaws across multiple products in their January 2013 Critical Patch Update, security experts criticized the company for the low number of database fixes and claimed that the company is downplaying the severity of a flaw in its flagship relational database. As Oracle expands its product portfolio and increases the total number of products patched through the quarterly CPU, there appears to be a "bottleneck" in Oracle's patching process. This CPU was the first time Oracle included the open-source MySQL database, which it acquired in 2010 as part of the Sun Microsystems® acquisition.[5]
- **CNET Download.com.** CNET Download.com was caught adding spyware, adware, and other malware to thousands of software packages that it distributes, including their Nmap Security Scanner. They did this even though it clearly violated their own anti-adware policy. (They did remove the anti-adware/spyware promise from the page.) After widespread criticism of the practice, Download.com removed its rogue installer from Nmap®

and some other software, but the company still uses it widely and has announced plans to expand it. For these reasons, we suggest avoiding CNET Download.com entirely. It is safer to download apps from official sites or more ethical aggregators such as FileHippo®, NiNite, or Softpedia®.[6]

Using manual methods to find, select, monitor, and validate open-source code is time-consuming, inefficient, and an unnecessary drain on scarce development team resources. Automation through tools such as Black Duck Software® (www.blackducksoftware.com) or Revenera™ (http://www.revenera.com) is essential to effectively and efficiently incorporate open-source software into SDLC development efforts to drive down development costs and manage the software and its security throughout the SDL. Black Duck Software's products and services allow organizations to analyze the composition of software source code and binary files, search for reusable code, manage open-source and third-party code approval, honor the legal obligations associated with mixed-origin code, and monitor related security vulnerabilities.[7–9] Revenera enables organizations to manage the growing complexity of multisource development environments by answering the question, "What's in your code?" Through detailed analysis of the code base, customers gain insight into their code inventory—a critical component of quality control, risk mitigation, and vulnerability assessment, with the goal of eliminating legal and vulnerability concerns associated with its use.[10]

7.5 Final Security Review

During the final security review of software being developed, all of the security activities performed, including threat modeling, tools output, and performance against requirements defined early in the process, are assessed again to determine whether the software product is ready for release and shipping. This process will result in one of three outcomes:

1. **The final security review is passed.** In this case, all final security review issues that have been identified have been corrected, the software is certified to have met all SDL requirements, and it is ready for release from a security perspective.

2. **The final security review is passed with exceptions.** In this case, not all issues that have been identified have been corrected, but an acceptable compromise has been made for one or more exceptions that the SDL and development team were not able to resolve. As exceptions, the unresolved issues will not be resolved in the current release and will be addressed and corrected in the next patch or release.

3. **The final security review is not passed and requires an escalation.** In this case, the SDL and development team cannot reach a compromise on a specific security vulnerability and its remediation, and so the software cannot be approved for release and shipment. There is typically a business justification identified earlier in the SDL process that prevents the identified issue from being compliant with an SDL security requirement. The SDL requirements that are blocking the release cannot be resolved by the two teams and must be escalated to higher management for a decision, which of course will take into account the risk and consequences identified if the software is released without meeting the requirement. The escalation to management should be a consolidated report composed by both the SDL and development teams that includes a description and rationale of the security risk.

The final security review must be scheduled carefully in order to maximize the time needed to fully analyze and remediate both known and any security issues that may be discovered during the final review, in ample time to account for the software product release and ship dates.

The final security review process should include the following:

- **Scheduling.** The product security review must be scheduled so that all required information from the SDL to complete this step has been acquired and is available, and enough time has been allowed to minimize any delay in the release date. The start date cannot be set until all security review activities defined and agreed to at the beginning of the SDL process have been completed, including in-depth security vulnerability reviews, threat modeling, and appropriate and relevant static, dynamic, and fuzz testing tool analysis.
- **Specific final security review tasks.**
  - The SDL and development team will meet to review and ensure that satisfactory responses have been made for all questions that have arisen and documented during the SDL process.
  - Threat models developed earlier in the process have been reviewed and updated as of the start date of the final security review to ensure that all known and suspected threats identified through the process have been mitigated.
  - All security vulnerabilities have been reviewed against the criteria established for release early in the process, and at least the minimum security standard has been enforced throughout the SDL. Any security vulnerabilities that were rejected or deferred for the current release of the software product must be reviewed as well. It is important to note that if the SDL and development team is not constantly evaluating the severity of security vulnerabilities against the standard that is used during the SDL process, then a large number of security vulnerabilities may re-appear or be discovered during the final security review and result in unnecessary and possibly significant use of resources and time, thus delaying the release of the product.
  - The static, dynamic, and fuzz testing tools should be run before final security review so that results can be fully evaluated before a decision is made for final release. In some cases, the tools may provide inaccurate or unacceptable results, in which case you may need to re-run the tools or find more acceptable alternatives to the ones used during the process.
  - You must review and ensure that all of the relevant internal security policies and external regulatory requirements have been followed and that software being reviewed is in compliance with the requirements for each.
  - If a specific SDL security requirement cannot be met and the overall security risk is tolerable, an exception must be requested, preferably well in advance of the final security review and as early as possible in the process.

The final product security review can be described as a four-step process as outlined below and represented graphically in Figure 7.4.

1. **Assess resource availability.** In this step, the resources that will be required and available in order to conduct the final security review are identified. The ability to enforce the quality gates required before the software can be released is also assessed. Minimum acceptable levels of security as it relates to quality are established through quality gates.

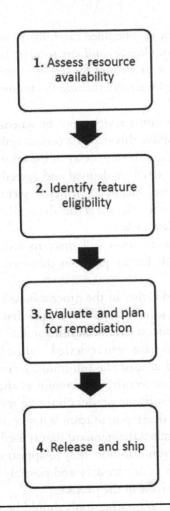

Figure 7.4 Four-step final security review process.

Having the quality gates early in the SDLC process so that security risks are understood early in the SDL process helps ensure that vulnerabilities are identified and fixed early, which will avoid unnecessary work and delays later in the process. The SDL and development team must show compliance with the quality gates as part of the final security review. If security has truly been built into the SDLC process as a result of the SDL, the time required to complete the final security review will be minimal; if not, more time and resources will be required, which might delay the ability to release and ship on time.

2. **Identify feature eligibility.** During this step, security tasks that are eligible for work in the final security review are identified. Feature eligibility should have been done earlier in the SDL process to avoid unfinished security work in the final security review. Scrutiny should have also been given to areas or sub-teams where vulnerabilities have not been reported yet during the SDL process but that have a history of vulnerabilities with high scores that could bring a surprise task to the teams during the final security review.

3. **Evaluate and plan for remediation.** During this step, the stakeholders responsible for the tasks identified in the previous step are notified, and scheduling for the final security review is set.

4. **Release and ship.** The product security review is completed after all SDL requirements, such as fuzzing, vulnerability scans, secure coding policies review, and other current security practices, as well as any exceptions to quality gates or vulnerabilities, have been formally reviewed and approved. Functional regression will have typically taken place during the final security review as well. Regression testing is used to discover new software vulnerabilities or regressions from what was already discovered, hence the term regression. These regressions can be a result of changes in the existing functional and nonfunctional areas of the software or the system after changes have been made. In short, regression testing assesses whether a change in one part of the software has resulted in a change in other parts of the software or system it interacts with.

7.6 Final Privacy Review

Typically, privacy requirements must be satisfied before the software can be released. Although the final security review must be completed before release, security exceptions as discussed previously highlight that not all security issues have to be satisfied before release. Privacy requirement verification is typically verified concurrently with the final security review and, in many cases, is now considered part of the same process. This requires that significant changes that occurred after the completion of the general privacy questionnaire, such as collecting different data types, substantively changing the language of a notice or the style of consent, or identification of new software behavior that negatively affects the protection of privacy, are addressed. This entails reviewing the software for any relevant changes or open issues that were identified during previous privacy reviews or as part of the final security review. Specific privacy requirements for the final review should include the following:

- If the project has been determined to be a P1 project, then the SDL team and privacy lead must review the Microsoft® SDL Privacy Questionnaire (Appendix C)[11] mentioned in the previous chapter or its equivalent to determine whether a privacy disclosure is required. If the privacy lead determines that a privacy disclosure is waived or covered, then there is no need to meet this requirement. The privacy lead will give final approval for release of the privacy disclosure statement.
- If the project has been determined to be a P2 project, then the privacy lead will determine if a privacy design review is being requested, provide a confirmation that the software architectural design is compliant with privacy standards applicable to this software product, or determine if an exception request is needed. The privacy lead typically works with the SDL and developer lead and legal advisor, as appropriate, to complete the privacy disclosure before public release of the product and ensure that the privacy disclosure is posted appropriately for web-centric products.
- If the project is a P3 project, then no changes affecting privacy requirements compliance have been identified, no additional reviews or approvals are needed, and the final privacy review is complete. If not, then the SDL team and privacy lead will provide a list of required changes.

In addition to the responsibilities, process, and procedures required for a response to software product security vulnerabilities discovered after release and shipment, a similar function to the product security incident response team (PSIRT) is created for response to privacy issues discovered after release and shipment. This element will be discussed in the next chapter in relation to the post-release support activities.

7.7 Key Success Factors

The success of this fifth phase of the SDL depends on the final review of policy compliance, comprehensive vulnerability scanning and penetration testing, and final security and privacy reviews. Table 7.1 lists key success factors for this phase, as discussed below.

Table 7.1 Key Success Factors

Key Success Factor	Description
1. Policy compliance analysis	Final review of security and compliance requirements during the development process
2. Vulnerability scanning	Scanning of the software stack for identifying security issues
3. Penetration testing	Exploiting any/all security issues on the software stack
4. Open-source licensing review	Final review of open-source software used in the stack
5. Final security review	Final review of compliance against all security requirements identified during the SDL cycle
6. Final privacy review	Final review of compliance against all privacy requirements identified during the SDL cycle
7. Customer engagement framework	The framework that defines the process for sharing security-related information with customers

Success Factor 1: Policy Compliance Analysis

If any new security requirements have been identified (based on threats or updates to policies), they need to be vetted for the feasibility of implementation so late in the development process. Some requirements may not make it into the product, whereas others might be important enough to delay the release date.

Success Factor 2: Vulnerability Scanning

Vulnerability scanning and security configuration validation provide one final opportunity to identify and remediate security issues across the software stack. Vulnerability scanning and security configuration validation should include assessments from different vantage points (external, internal, and authenticated). It should also cover all layers in the stack, from the operating system to applications.

Success Factor 3: Penetration Testing

Ensuring that there is no confusion between penetration testing and vulnerability scanning is essential. Vulnerability scanning provides a list of validated security findings. Penetration testing goes one step further and is more of an attack simulation on your target environment.

The outcome often depends on the penetration testers' skills, imagination, and experience. Vulnerability scanning feeds into penetration testing.

Success Factor 4: Open-Source Licensing Review

Final review of open-source software that ensures all licensing requirements have been met is essential to mitigate legal liability. It also enables the identification of technologies that need to feed into a different type of security testing (vulnerability scanning and penetration testing).

Success Factor 5: Final Security Review

It is critical that a final security review be performed before this phase of the SDL ends. If all requirements are met, then security can say "Go" without any exceptions. If there are exceptions to security requirements, they must be well documented and time-bound. An example is a "conditional go," under which unmet requirements do not stop release but will be remediated by an agreed-upon date.

Success Factor 6: Final Privacy Review

Similar to Factor 5, this step allows final review of the product against privacy requirements laid out at the start of the cycle and that have been updated or refined since then. If any requirements are unmet, they should be documented as time-bound exceptions and require remediation by a definite date.

Success Factor 7: Customer Engagement Framework

As discussed earlier in the chapter, it is important that a framework be defined to engage customers in security-related discussions both during and after the sale process. This can limit ad hoc requests and escalations from customers and give them confidence that your company has a handle on security.

7.8 Deliverables

Table 7.2 lists deliverables for this phase of the SDL.

Table 7.2 Deliverables for Phase A5

Deliverable	Goal
Updated policy compliance analysis	Analysis of adherence to company policies
Security testing reports	Findings from different types of security testing in this phase of the SDL
Remediation report	Provide status on the security posture of product
Open-source licensing review report	Review of compliance with licensing requirements if open-source software is used
Final security and privacy review reports	Review of compliance with security and privacy requirements
Customer engagement framework	Detailed framework to engage customers during different stages of the product life cycle

Updated Policy Compliance Analysis

Policy compliance analysis artifacts (see Chapters 4, 5, and 6) should be updated based on any new requirements or policies that may have come up during this phase of the SDL.

Security Testing Reports

The findings summary (discussed in Chapter 6) should be updated to include vulnerability scans (external, internal, and authenticated) and penetration testing findings during this phase. A customer-facing report should also be prepared to share with enterprise customers.

Remediation Report

In addition to updating security testing reports (or findings), the remediation report should also be updated to give a better idea of the product's security posture going into the release. Any findings that have not been remediated by now (and are not to be remediated before the release date), should be discussed and put on a roadmap.

Open-Source Licensing Review Report

A formal review report of open-source software used in the software stack should be prepared that outlines different licensing requirements (The MIT® License, GNU® General Public License, GNU® Lesser General Public License, BSD® License) and how they are being met. The security and privacy officers should review the report and sign off on it.

Final Security and Privacy Review Reports

After a final review of compliance against security and privacy requirements, a formal sign-off by security and privacy officers should be required.

Customer Engagement Framework

A formally documented process to share security information with customers should be delivered as part of this phase. The process should include types of information (and frequency) shared with customers, notification in case of security incidents, security findings, and remediation SLAs.

7.9 Metrics

The following metrics should be collected during this phase of the SDL:

- Percent compliance with company policies (updated)
  - Percent of compliance in Phase 5 versus Phase 4
- Number, type, and severity of security issues found through vulnerability scanning and penetration testing
  - Overlap of security issues found through different types of testing

- ○ Comparison of severity of findings from different types of testing
- ○ Mapping of findings to threats/risks identified earlier
- Number of security findings remediated (updated)
  - ○ Severity of findings
  - ○ Time spent (approximate) in hours to remediate findings
- Number, types, and severity of findings outstanding (updated)
- Percentage compliance with security and privacy requirements

7.10 Summary

In this chapter, we have described the requirements for successful release and ship of the software product after it has finished the SDLC and associated SDL activities and best practices (see Figure 7.5). Now that we have made it through SDL Phase A5 and the product has been released, the next chapter will describe SDL Phase A6, which will outline the SDL post-release support activity (PRSA) phase of our SDL. After a software product is released and shipped, the software security, development, and privacy teams, with support from the corporate public relations, legal, and other groups, must be available to respond to any possible security vulnerabilities or privacy issues that warrant a response. In addition, a response plan detailing appropriate processes and procedures must be developed that includes preparations for potential post-release issues. In addition to external vulnerability disclosure responses, this phase should include internal review for new product combinations or cloud deployment, post-release certifications, security architectural reviews, and tool-based assessments of current, legacy, and M&A products and solutions, as well as third-party reviews of released software products that may be required by customers, regulatory requirements, or industry standards.

Chapter Quick-Check

1. The post-release plan should have a policy to allow:
   a. Rules
   b. Deviations
   c. Procedures
   d. Practices

2. Management reviews recommend:
   a. Best practices
   b. Roles
   c. Accountability
   d. Corrective or remedial action

3. The aim of black-box testing is to confirm that a given input:
   a. Is correct
   b. Can be processed accurately
   c. Produces a predictable output
   d. Will not cause a defect

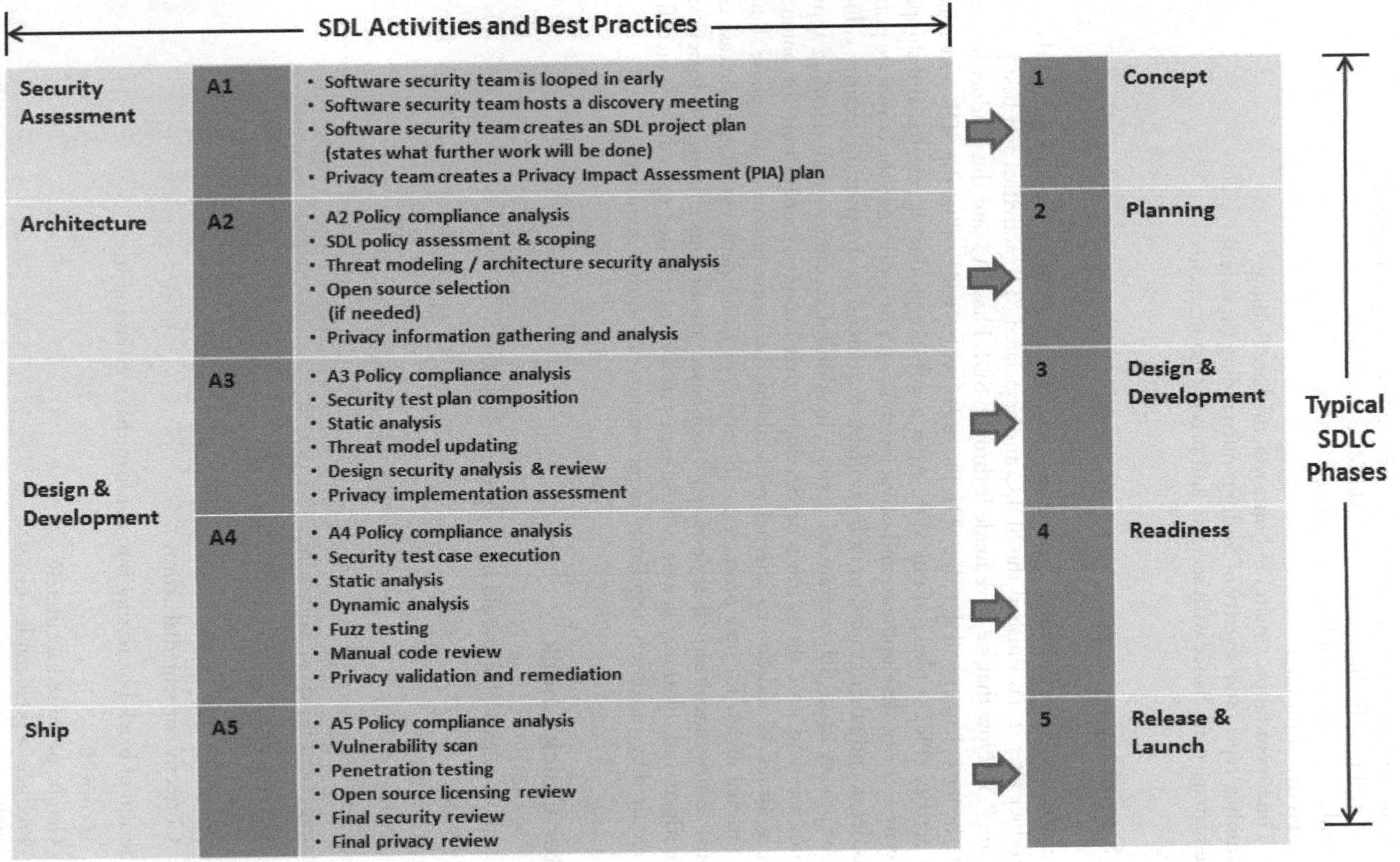

SDL Activities and Best Practices

			Typical SDLC Phases	
Security Assessment	A1	• Software security team is looped in early • Software security team hosts a discovery meeting • Software security team creates an SDL project plan (states what further work will be done) • Privacy team creates a Privacy Impact Assessment (PIA) plan	1	Concept
Architecture	A2	• A2 Policy compliance analysis • SDL policy assessment & scoping • Threat modeling / architecture security analysis • Open source selection (if needed) • Privacy information gathering and analysis	2	Planning
Design & Development	A3	• A3 Policy compliance analysis • Security test plan composition • Static analysis • Threat model updating • Design security analysis & review • Privacy implementation assessment	3	Design & Development
	A4	• A4 Policy compliance analysis • Security test case execution • Static analysis • Dynamic analysis • Fuzz testing • Manual code review • Privacy validation and remediation	4	Readiness
Ship	A5	• A5 Policy compliance analysis • Vulnerability scan • Penetration testing • Open source licensing review • Final security review • Final privacy review	5	Release & Launch

Figure 7.5 A1 to A5 SDL activities and best practices.

4. Configuration management exercises:
   a. Rational control over the code
   b. Rational control over the design
   c. Rational control over the change process
   d. Enforcement of the change process

5. The management level authorized to approve changes must be:
   a. As high as possible
   b. As simple as possible
   c. Clearly defined
   d. Approved

Exercises

The following exercises are based on the case study discussed in Appendix A. These exercises are intended to give you some practice in applying the steps and producing deliverables for Phase A5 of the SDL.

Within the last phase of the software development life cycle (SDLC), you need to ensure that the software from the Revvin' Engines team is sufficiently secure, that regulations and industry requirements are met, and that privacy issues have been addressed to a level at which the software is acceptable for release and ready to ship.

1. Conduct a final policy compliance analysis that answers the question of whether all internal application security requirements and all industry requirements are met or not.
2. Create the plans for final security testing to include:
   a. Static code testing for any residual vulnerabilities not addressed in earlier phases.
   b. A penetration test from a qualified penetration tester or firm.
   c. A final open-source and third-party library composition review to assure that only the latest versions of libraries used within the application are present.
3. Conduct a final security review with the compliance reviews and testing results to establish the parameters for release of the system.
4. Conduct a final privacy review to assure compliance with all privacy requirements in addition to all security requirements.
5. Develop a plan for communication of security-related information that customer service and the application support team will need to operate the system once customers begin using it.

References

1. Paul, R. (2008, November 4). "Diebold Faces GPL Infringement Lawsuit over Voting Machines: Artifex Software, the Company Behind Ghostscript, Has Filed a Lawsuit Against. . . ." *Arstechnica: Technology Lab/Information Technology*. Retrieved from http://arstechnica.com /information-technology/2008/11/diebold-faces-gpl-infringement-lawsuit-over-voting-machines

2. Broersma, M. (2007, July 26). "Skype Found Guilty of GPL Violations." IDG News Service. Retrieved from https://www.itworldcanada.com/article/skype-found-guilty-of-gpl-violations/9161

3. McDougall, P. (2008, March 17). "Verizon Settles Open Source Software Lawsuit: The Issue Centered on Claims That a Subcontractor Used an Open Source Program Called BusyBox in Verizon's Wireless Routers." *Information Week*. Retrieved from https://www.informationweek.com/software/verizon-settles-open-source-software-lawsuit

4. Koetsier, J. (2012, September 4). "Sorry, Google Fanboys: Android Security Suffers as Malware Explodes by 700%." *VentureBeat*. Retrieved from http://venturebeat.com/2012/09/04/sorry-google-fanboys-android-security-sucks-hard-as-malware-explodes-by-700/#FKvUAhZrG8g5jywy.99

5. Rashid, F. (2012, January 1). "Oracle Accused of Downplaying Database Flaws, Severity." *eWeek*. Retrieved from https://www.eweek.com/security/oracle-accused-of-downplaying-database-flaws-severity/

6. Insecure.org. (2013). "Download.com Caught Adding Malware to Nmap & Other Software." Retrieved from http://insecure.org/news/download-com-fiasco.html

7. Schwartz, E. (2007, August 6). "Open Source Lands in the Enterprise with Both Feet: Major Business Applications on Linux Turns OS into a Commodity." *Infoworld*. Retrieved from http://www.infoworld.com/t/applications/open-source-lands-in-enterprise-both-feet-576

8. Worthington, D. (2007, August 6). "Quacking Through Licensing Complexity: Black Duck's Open Source Licensing Solution Tackles GPLv3." *SDTimes*. Retrieved from http://www.sdtimes.com/link/31007

9. Boston Business Journal Staff. (2007, December 17). "Battles over Open Source Carve Niche for Startup." *Boston Business Journal*. Retrieved from http://www.bizjournals.com/boston/stories/2007/12/17/story13.html?page=all

10. Revenera. (2021). Revenera home page. Retrieved from https://www.revenera.com

11. Microsoft Corporation. (2012). "Appendix C: SDL Privacy Questionnaire." Retrieved from http://msdn.microsoft.com/en-us/library/windows/desktop/cc307393.aspx

Chapter 8

Post-Release Support (PRSA1–5)

CHAPTER OVERVIEW

Many of the functions and their associated activities and best practices described in this chapter are handled by groups other than the software security group that would have the principal oversight over SDL activities and best practices (A1–A5) described in the previous chapters. Here we'll describe them as activities that are the responsibility of the centralized software security group in an organization.

CHAPTER TAKE-AWAYS

- Explore the practices that compose the post-release support activities (PRSA) of the security development lifecycle (SDL).
- Document the key success factors for implementing the PRSA deliverables.
- Prepare plans and deliverables for the PRSA using the case study in Appendix A.

Figure 8.1 illustrates the post-release support activities (PRSA) and best practices.

Organizing the software security group with matrixed relationships enables the complete implementation and operation of the SDL. The authors have found that this is a much more cost-effective and efficient way to manage these activities with existing resources. This is precisely the reason we highly recommend that the core software security group be composed of senior software security architects who have hard "dotted-line" relationships with the software security champions, who in turn have the same relationships with the software security evangelists. There should also be a strong relationship between the software security architects in the centralized software security group and the product managers of each Tier 1 software product, just as there is for the software security champions. It is also important that the software security group and function be in the right organization so they can be most successful.

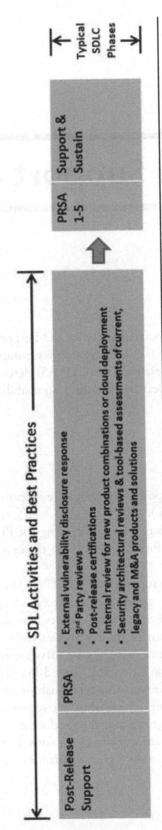

Figure 8.1 Post-release support (PRSA1–5): SDL activities and best practices.

8.1 Right-Sizing Your Software Security Group

First, we will walk through each of the software security group relationships and the importance of putting everything into perspective in order to "right-size" the building of a successful software security program. Doing this means having

- The right organizational location
- The right people
- The right process

8.1.1 The Right Organizational Location

Although there have been great advances in software security technology over the last few years, we believe that people are still the most important element of a successful software security program that includes the implementation and management of the activities and best practices. To facilitate the best use of the people responsible for software security, they must be part of the right organization (see Figure 8.2). Having been in seven Chief Security Officer (CSO)

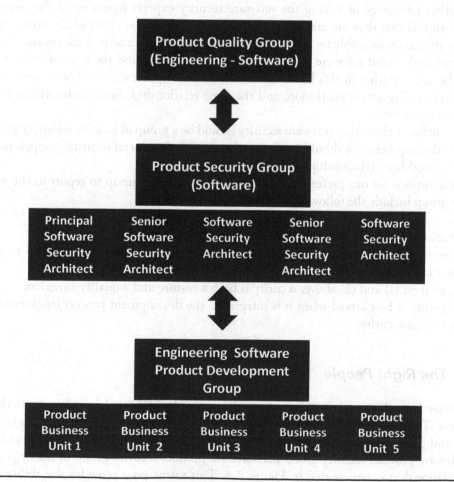

Figure 8.2   The right organizational location.

and Chief Information Security Officer (CISO) roles, James Ransome, one of the co-authors of this book, has had software security reporting to him in several of his roles. Based on both his experience and communication with his peers in the industry, it is clear that the software security function ideally should fall within the engineering (software development) function and, in particular, within the quality function. The general consensus is that the application security role typically reports to the centralized information security role CSO/CISO position and should not be confused with the software security function. Typically, those who are in an application security role within an IT security organization are great at running tools but do not have the software development background necessary to fully interpret the results. To make this point clear, it is important to differentiate between software and application security. Perhaps the best way to clarify this distinction is with a quote from Gary McGraw:

> Software security is about building secure software: designing software to be secure; making sure making sure that software is secure; and educating software developers, architects, and users about how to build security in. On the other hand, application security is about protecting software and the systems that software runs in a post facto way, only after development is complete.[1]

Another advantage of having the software security experts reporting to the engineering organization is that they are empowered by the fact that they are part of the same organization; are directly responsible for implementing the SDL policies and procedures and associated tools; and understand software development, its architecture, and the level of effort required to fix the same. Earlier in this book, we described the importance of software security as an element of quality and organization, and the same relationship should exist within the engineering organization.

The authors believe that software security should be a group of its own within engineering/software development and should work very closely with the central security group; it may even have a "dotted-line" relationship to the CSO/CISO.

A few reasons for our preference for the software security group to report to the software quality group include the following:

1. Security vulnerabilities are, by definition, quality issues.
2. Security features are architectural functions with a very close relationship to product management.
3. Based on (1) and (2) above, security is both a feature and a quality function.
4. Quality is best served when it is integral to the development process (engineering) and includes security.

8.1.2 The Right People

In Chapter 2, we discussed the talent required to make the SDL model we describe in this book a success. This will include a minimum of one principal software security architect, a mix of senior and general software security architects, and, ideally, one software security architect in the software product security group per software product security group in the organization. This relationship is represented in Figure 8.3. This talent pool provides the ability to scale

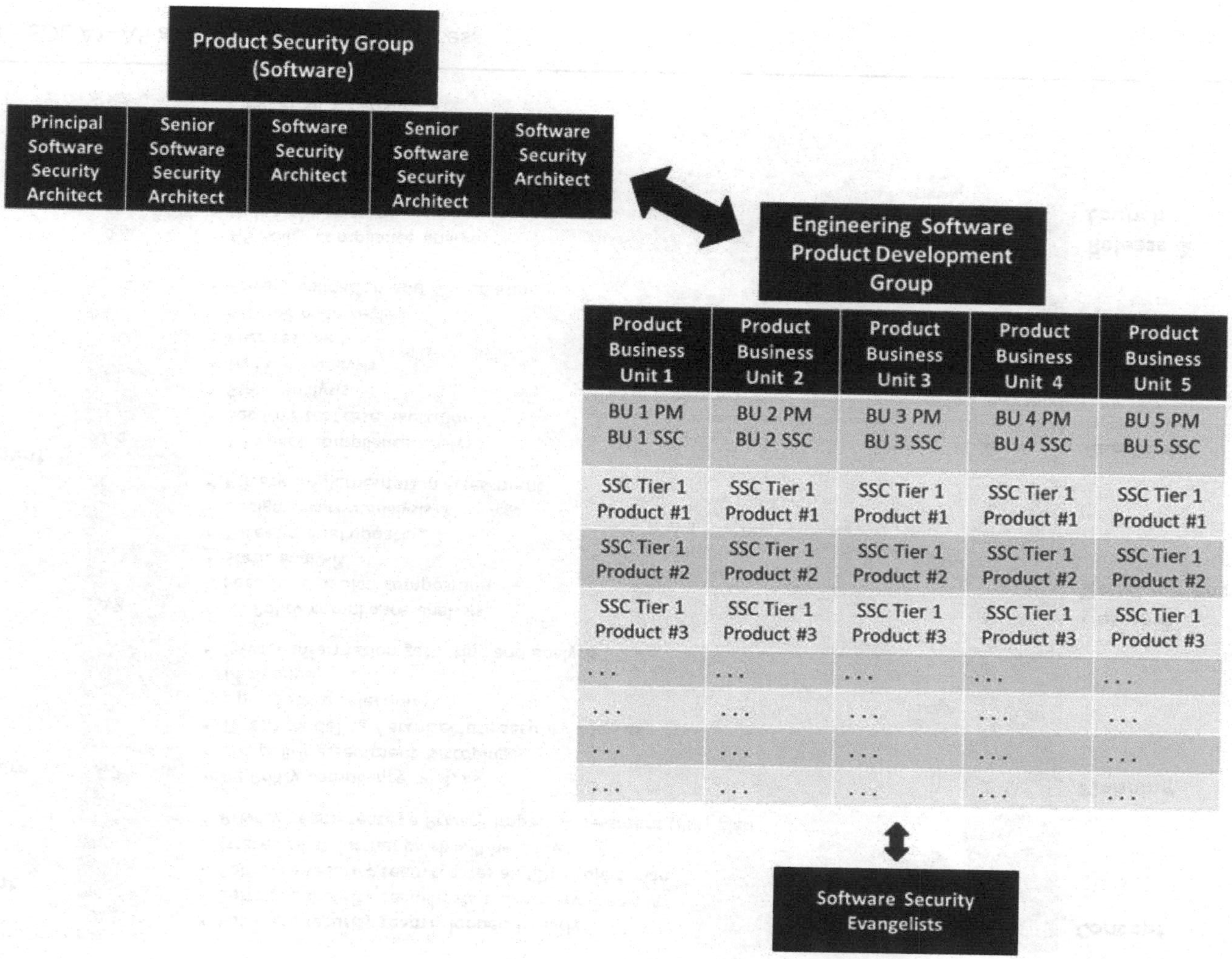

Product Security Group (Software)

Principal Software Security Architect	Senior Software Security Architect	Software Security Architect

Engineering Software Product Development Group

Product Business Unit 1	Product Business Unit 2	Product Business Unit 3	Product Business Unit 4	Product Business Unit 5
BU 1 PM / BU 1 SSC	BU 2 PM / BU 2 SSC	BU 3 PM / BU 3 SSC	BU 4 PM / BU 4 SSC	BU 5 PM / BU 5 SSC
SSC Tier 1 Product #1	SSC Tier 1 Product #1	SSC Tier 1 Product #1	SSC Tier 1 Product #1	SSC Tier 1 Product #1
SSC Tier 1 Product #2	SSC Tier 1 Product #2	SSC Tier 1 Product #2	SSC Tier 1 Product #2	SSC Tier 1 Product #2
SSC Tier 1 Product #3	SSC Tier 1 Product #3	SSC Tier 1 Product #3	SSC Tier 1 Product #3	SSC Tier 1 Product #3
...	...	...	...	...
...	...	...	...	...
...	...	...	...	...

Software Security Evangelists

Figure 8.3 The right people.

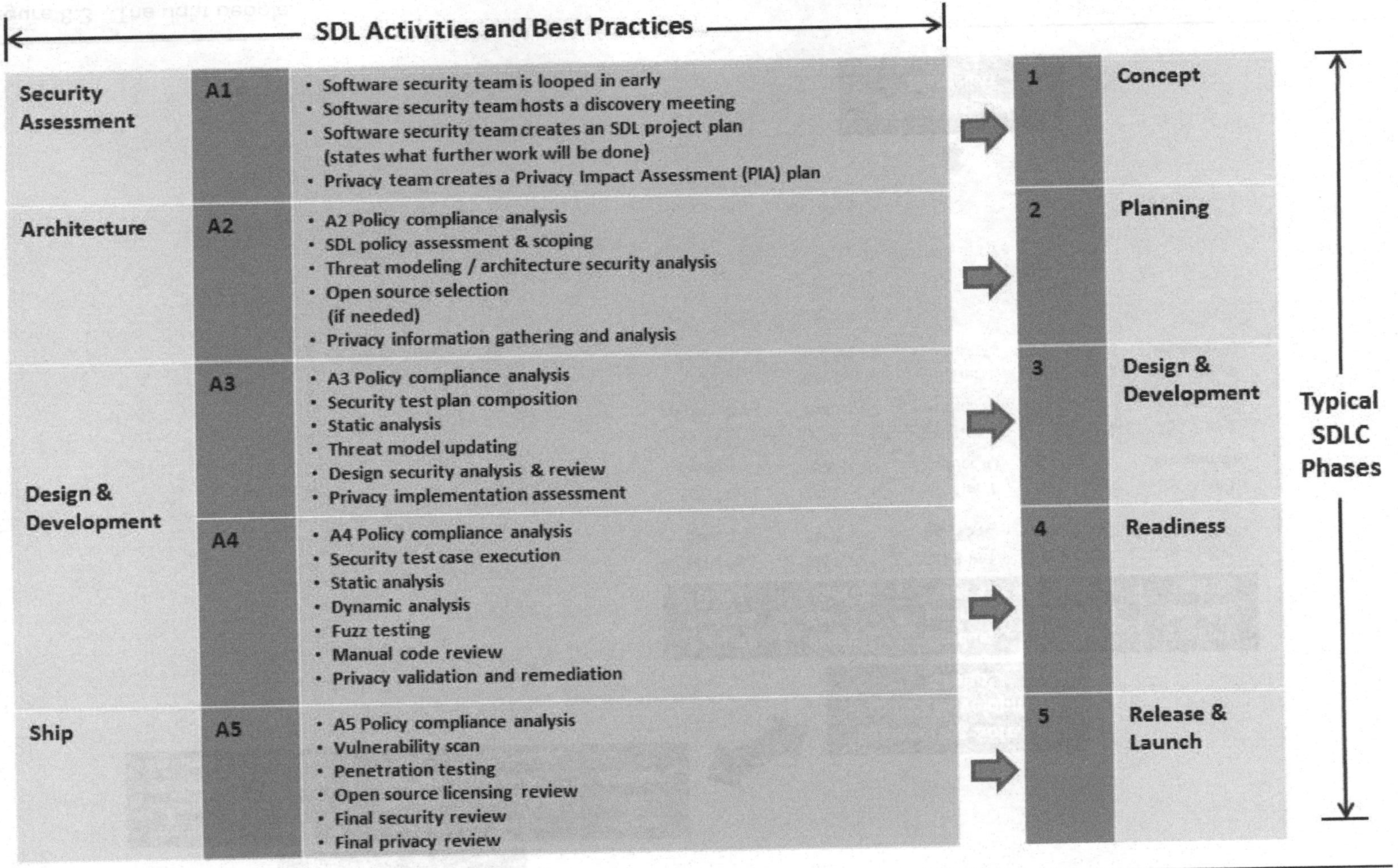

SDL Activities and Best Practices

Security Assessment	A1	• Software security team is looped in early • Software security team hosts a discovery meeting • Software security team creates an SDL project plan (states what further work will be done) • Privacy team creates a Privacy Impact Assessment (PIA) plan
Architecture	A2	• A2 Policy compliance analysis • SDL policy assessment & scoping • Threat modeling / architecture security analysis • Open source selection (if needed) • Privacy information gathering and analysis
	A3	• A3 Policy compliance analysis • Security test plan composition • Static analysis • Threat model updating • Design security analysis & review • Privacy implementation assessment
Design & Development	A4	• A4 Policy compliance analysis • Security test case execution • Static analysis • Dynamic analysis • Fuzz testing • Manual code review • Privacy validation and remediation
Ship	A5	• A5 Policy compliance analysis • Vulnerability scan • Penetration testing • Open source licensing review • Final security review • Final privacy review

Typical SDLC Phases

1	Concept
2	Planning
3	Design & Development
4	Readiness
5	Release & Launch

Figure 8.4 SDL A1–A5 activities and best practices.

in that there will also ideally be one software security champion (SSC) per Tier 1 software product within each engineering software product development group. Another element of the talent is the software security evangelists (SSEs) for organizations that are large enough to have extra candidates for the software security champions' (SSCs) role, who can be candidates for SSEs until there is a slot for them as SSCs. An SSE has two roles—as an SSC in training and as an evangelist for the overall software product security program promulgating policy, enforcing policy, and evangelizing the overall SDL process.

8.1.3 The Right Process

The right process comprises the core SDL activities and best practices described in this book so far and summarized in Figure 8.4. In addition to the core activities and best practices, we have added the activities and best practices highlighted in Figure 8.1. Given the continued pressure to do more with less, we don't believe most organizations will have the luxury of having most of the elements of PRSAs 1–5 as separate organizations but will need to provide for innovative ways to include them in their overall software security program to optimize the leverage of use of available resources. Sections 8.2–8.6 of this chapter will provide our approach to the activities and best practices required to make this a success in every organization in which it is appropriate.

8.2 PRSA1: External Vulnerability Disclosure Response

One of the key elements of our post-release methodology is that the typical Product Security Incident Response Team (PSIRT) function can be a shared responsibility within our proposed leveraged organizational structure for software security and privacy that covers responses to both post-release security vulnerability and privacy issue discoveries. No matter how good your software security program and associated SDL is, the fact is that something will be missed at some point, and you need a plan to respond to this. Most important, if discovery of software security vulnerabilities and privacy issues in post-release software products is a common occurrence, that is a clear sign that building security into the organization's software development life cycle (SDLC) through an SDL-like process is weak or nonexistent. Such weakness can result in negative visibility due to publicly disclosed exploitation of vulnerabilities or security flaws inherent to the post-release software, subsequent loss of market share due to brand defamation, lawsuits or breach of contracts, and a resultant major target for further exploitation by adversarial opportunists.

Based on our experiences, we cannot emphasize enough how important it is to have a single group that acts as a focal point for all communications with customers about security vulnerabilities. Often, we have seen at least three different groups communicating with customers: customer support, sales, and an information security group. PSIRT may or may not be part of the information security organization in a particular company, though this is certainly desirable. To summarize, a clearly defined chain of communications with customers is of critical importance to prevent disclosure of unintended information and to avoid panic and putting entire accounts at stake.

8.2.1 Post-Release PSIRT Response

In relation to software security, a PSIRT is responsible for responding to software product security incidents involving external discoveries of post-release software product security vulnerabilities. As part of this role, the team manages the investigation of publicly discovered security vulnerabilities of their company's software products and the systems they interact with. The external discoverers might be independent security researchers, consultants, industry organizations, other vendors, or benevolent or possibly even nefarious hackers who identify possible security issues with software products for which the PSIRT is responsible. Issues identified are prioritized based on the potential severity of the vulnerability, typically using the CVSS scoring system described earlier in the book as well as other environmental factors. The resolution of a reported incident may require upgrades to products that are under active support from the PSIRT's parent company.

Shortly after its identification and during the investigation of a claim of vulnerability, the PSIRT should work collaboratively with the discoverer to confirm the nature of the vulnerability, gather required technical information, and ascertain appropriate remedial action.

When the initial investigation is complete, the results are delivered to the discoverer along with a plan for resolution and public disclosure. If the incident reporter disagrees with the conclusion, the PSIRT should attempt to address those concerns.

The discoverer(s) will be asked to maintain strict confidentiality until complete resolutions are available for customers and have been published by the PSIRT on the company's website through the appropriate coordinated public disclosure typically called a security bulletin (SB). During the investigation and pre-reporting process, the PSIRT coordinates communications with the discoverer, including status and documentation updates on the investigation of the incident. Further information may also be required from the discoverer to validate the claim and the methods used to exploit the vulnerability. Discoverers will also be notified that if they disclose the vulnerability before publication by the PSIRT, then the discoverers will not be given credit in the public disclosure by the company and the case will be treated as a "zero day," no-notice discovery that has been reported publicly by an external source. In the case of a zero-day discovery, the PSIRT and development teams work together to remediate the vulnerability as soon as possible, according to the severity of the Common Vulnerability Scoring System (CVSS) (https://www.first.org/cvss/v3.1/specification-document) scoring for the particular vulnerability. In the case of a zero-day, highly scored vulnerability, the company's PR team will work closely with the PSIRT to manage potential negative press and customer reaction.

During the investigation of a reported vulnerability, the PSIRT coordinates and manages all sensitive information on a highly confidential basis. Internal distribution is limited to those individuals who have a legitimate need to know and can actively assist in the resolution of the vulnerability.

The PSIRT will also work with third-party coordination centers, such as the CERT® Coordination Center (CERT/CC) (https://www.kb.cert.org/vuls/), and others to manage a coordinated industry disclosure for reported vulnerabilities affecting the software products they are responsible for. In some cases, multiple vendors will be affected and will be involved in the coordinated response with centers such as CERT. If a coordination center is involved, then, depending on the circumstances, the PSIRT may contact the center on the behalf of the discoverers, or assist them in doing it themselves.

If a third-party component of the product is affected, this will complicate the remediation process because the PSIRT will be dependent on a third party for remediation. A further complication is that the PSIRT will have to coordinate and, in many cases, notify the vendor directly to ensure coordination with the third-party coordination center and, likely, direct involvement with the discoverer. Even though a third-party component has been used, the assumption is that the owner of the primary software product is ultimately responsible for all components of the software, whether they own them or not.

As mentioned above, PSIRTs generally use the CVSS to assess the severity of a vulnerability as part of their standard process for evaluating reported potential vulnerabilities in their products and determining which vulnerabilities warrant external and internal reporting.

The CVSS model uses three distinct measurements or scores that include base, temporal, and environmental calculations, and the sum of all three scores should be considered the final CVSS score. This score represents a single moment in time; it is tailored to a specific environment and is used to prioritize responses to a particular externally discovered vulnerability. In addition, most PSIRTs will consider modifying the final score to account for factors that are not properly captured in the CVSS score. PSIRTs typically use the following CVSS guidelines when determining the severity of a particular vulnerability and the need to report it:

- Critical (C)— CVSS base score of 9.0–10.0
- High (H)— CVSS base score of 7.0–8.9
- Medium (M)—CVSS base score of 4.0–6.9
- Low (L)—CVSS base score of 0.1–3.9[2]

If there is a security issue involving a third-party software component in the product the PSIRT is responsible for, then, depending on the situation and whether the third party has a CVSS score, the PSIRT may use the CVSS score provided by the component creator and/or may adjust the score to reflect the impact on the overall software product.

Public disclosure, including the relevant base and temporal CVSS scores and a CVE® ID[3] report, is typically made for an external post-release discovery event when one or more of the following have occurred:

- The incident response process has been completed and has determined that enough software patches or other remediations exist to address the vulnerability. Public disclosure of code fixes can be issued to address high-severity vulnerabilities.
- Active exploitation of a vulnerability that could lead to increased risk for the PSIRT company's customers has been observed that requires a published security vulnerability announcement. The announcement may or may not include a complete set of patches or other remediation steps. When possible, compensating controls are included in the public announcement to provide interim protection that will limit exposure until the permanent fix is announced.
- A zero-day announcement or other potential for increased public awareness of a vulnerability affecting the PSIRT company's product is probable, which could lead to increased risk for customers. In these cases, the PSIRT has worked closely with the company's PR team to help assess public indicators and warnings, such as Twitter feeds and blogs, that this exposure is imminent, and it will have prepared a statement ahead of time. Again,

this accelerated public vulnerability announcement will not include a complete set of patches or other remediation steps, but, ideally, interim compensating controls to limit exposure can be identified.

A typical step-by-step PSIRT case-handling process will include the following steps:

1. Notification of vulnerability as assessed by an individual discoverer or organization is received.
2. The responsible software product development group is identified, together with resources required for assessment of the discoverers' vulnerability claim.
3. If the claim is credible, an impact assessment is made and a timeline for a fix is determined. The level of effort needed and priority to develop a fix is balanced against the likelihood of public disclosure of the severity and risk of the vulnerability. In some cases, external resources may be required due to other critical tasks the development team is carrying out. If the claim is not credible, additional information is requested from the discoverer to ensure that the threat was properly recreated in the testing environment. If it is not credible after the testing environment has been confirmed, then the discoverer is notified of the company's findings. If the discoverer goes public claiming the vulnerability is credible even though the company has determined it is not, then the PSIRT typically works with the company's PR team to publish the results of the company's finding as a counter to the discoverer.
4. The time frame for remediation, the resources needed to fix a confirmed vulnerability, and the reporting format (e.g., security bulletin, knowledge base article, or other form of public notification) are committed to.
5. After patch or other remediation methods have been identified, all customers are notified simultaneously on the date of the availability of the fix through the reporting format determined in Step 4.

8.2.1.1 ISO 29147 and ISO 30111

Two International Organization for Standardization (ISO®) standards relate to the proper functioning of a vendor PSIRT:

1. ISO/IEC 29147:2018 [ISO/IEC 29147:2018]—Information technology—Security techniques—Vulnerability disclosure

This standard provides requirements and recommendations to vendors on the disclosure of vulnerabilities in products and services and is applicable to vendors who choose to practice vulnerability disclosure to reduce risk to users of vendors' products and services.

Vulnerability disclosure enables users to perform technical vulnerability management as specified in ISO/IEC 27002:2013, 12.6.1. Vulnerability disclosure helps users protect their systems and data, prioritize defensive investments, and better assess risk. The goal of vulnerability disclosure is to reduce the risk associated with exploiting vulnerabilities. Coordinated vulnerability disclosure is especially important when multiple vendors are affected. This standard provides:

- Guidelines on receiving reports about potential vulnerabilities
- Guidelines on disclosing vulnerability remediation information
- Terms and definitions that are specific to vulnerability disclosure
- An overview of vulnerability disclosure concepts
- Techniques and policy considerations for vulnerability disclosure
- Examples of techniques, policies (Annex A), and communications (Annex B)[4]

2. ISO/IEC 30111:2019 [ISO/IEC 30111:2019]—Information technology—Security techniques—Vulnerability handling processes

This standard provides requirements and recommendations for how to process and remediate reported potential vulnerabilities in a product or service and is applicable to vendors involved in handling vulnerabilities. Other related activities that take place between receiving and disclosing vulnerability reports are described in ISO/IEC 30111.[5]

8.2.2 Post-Release Privacy Response

In addition to post-release security issues that may be discovered and disclosed, potential privacy issues may also be discovered. In our experience, privacy-related issues do not get as much attention as security vulnerabilities, nor is a group charted specifically to deal with such issues. A software development company may have a chief privacy officer (CPO) or equivalent, such as a specialized counsel on retainer, but most do not have a staff and are likely limited to one privacy support expert, at best. This necessitates a close alignment and working relationship between the PSIRT function and the centralized software security group and the privacy function of the company, whether the latter is in-sourced or out-sourced. A post-release privacy response should be built into the PSIRT process just as security should be built into the SDLC. Given the potential legal nature of privacy issues or privacy control vulnerability exploitations, the privacy advisor should script basic talking points, response procedures, and legal escalation requirements for the response team to use to respond to any potential privacy issues discovered post-release. Some basic guidelines follow:

- Privacy experts should be directly involved in all incidents that fall into the P1 and P2 categories described earlier in this book.
- Additional development, quality assurance, and security resources appropriate for potential post-release privacy discovery issues should be identified during the SDL process so that can participate in post-release privacy incident responses.
- Software development organizations should develop their own privacy response plans or modify the Microsoft® SDL Privacy Escalation Response Framework (Appendix K)[6] for their own use. This should include risk assessment, detailed diagnosis, short-term and long-term action planning, and implementation of action plans. As with the PSIRT responses outlined above, the response might include creating a patch or other risk-remediation procedures, replying to media inquiries, and reaching out to the external discoverer.

8.2.3 Optimizing Post-Release Third-Party Response

Collaboration between different teams and stakeholders provides the best possible chance of success of post-release response. The collective of software security champions, software security evangelists, and an ongoing formal software security programmatic relationship with the software development product managers and quality team to support and collaborate with the centralized software security team as proposed in this book provides several distinct advantages over teams solely dedicated to handle post-release PSIRT and privacy support:

- Direct PSIRT and privacy response ownership is achieved by embedding these functions into the engineering and development groups directly responsible for fixing the product directly affected by the discovered vulnerability or privacy issue.
- Direct knowledge of the code, architecture, and overall software product design and functionality with a direct influence on the remediation process will result in increased efficiency, control, and response over an external organizational entity without direct knowledge of the product. Essentially, this removes the middleman and streamlines the process.
- This process provides for better return on investment (ROI) for both the PSIRT and the privacy response function through the leverage of resources and direct knowledge of the software product at the source through the direct involvement and ownership by the development teams.
- Direct empowerment of the development teams and project managers, their more direct ownership of the remediation process, and a centralized software security group embedded in the engineering/software development group provide single-organizational responsibility for the response.
- Software security champions and software security evangelists operate locally with the software product manager and appropriate product development resources to directly drive the assessment and remediation (if needed) of the claimed vulnerability by an external discoverer.
- All the above result in faster time to execution and response and, most important, help speed up the mitigation of negative press exposure and customer risk. We believe there is an advantage to our proposed organizational infrastructure in providing a cost-effective, minimal resource, and efficient way to respond to this type of incident while reducing the burden on resources dedicated to the development of the software itself.

8.3 PRSA2: Third-Party Reviews

Over the last few years, customers of software vendors have increasingly requested independent audits to verify the security and quality of software applications that they have either purchased or are evaluating for purchase. Software vulnerabilities have increasingly been tied to high-profile data breaches over the last few years and have resulted in more customers requiring independent and visible proof that the software they purchase is secure. This, of course, has helped put pressure on companies that develop software to ensure that the secure software development processes are built into the SDLC to avoid the very costly discovery of vulnerabilities that are caught post-release—often a sign of an immature, ineffective, or non-existent software security program. Because of the preponderance of post-release code having security vulnerabilities and privacy issues that should have been caught during development, third-party assessment of post-release or near-release code has become the norm in the industry, whether the company producing the software has a reputation for producing secure code or not. In some cases, it is demanded by the prospective or current customer, and in other cases, it is conducted proactively by the company producing the code.

Even for companies that have outstanding software security programs, software applications can alternate in and out of compliance with policies or regulatory requirements over long periods of time for a variety of reasons. For example, a new functionality or use case in a new version of the application may introduce new vulnerabilities or planes of attack, causing the application to drop out of compliance. Additionally, these requirements may change over time. Many companies use third-party code reviews to help identify these situations rather than spend the limited resources of their internal teams.

Third-party testing should include testing the entire stack, not just your product. That means performing testing as outlined in earlier chapters as well as continuous post-release testing. At a minimum, post-release testing should include annual penetration testing (application and software stack). Any new code released after initial release should follow the SDL requirements outlined in previous chapters.

The biggest challenge is to do this in a timely and cost-effective manner while also protecting the source code and other intellectual property during the process. Some of the choices for third-party testing include the following.

1. *Hand over source code to a third party for inspection.* This is not a real option for those who want to protect the most precious intellectual property that a software development organization possesses—their source code.
2. *Contract manual penetration testing services that can also do deep-dive code and software architectural design reviews for each new release.* To avoid the risk of source code leaving the control of the company that is developing it, contractors must be required to work on-site in a controlled environment, under special nondisclosure agreements and under specific guidelines. These typically include a source-code protection policy and IP protection guidelines. An alternative to this approach is to employ a company that uses tools that require the exposure of binary code only. In this case, the contractor inspects the application at the same level as it is attacked—the binaries—and can ensure that all threats are detected. This type of testing can be done on-site or remotely as a service.
3. *Purchase, install, and train development teams to use on-premise tools and function as lower-level software security architects as an extension of the software security group to conduct the "people side" of the software security architectural review.* Then invite auditors into your organization to document your processes. Many mature software security organizations have done this. A mature software security program such as that described in this book will help scale and reduce the need for additional headcount to do this work. Building this into your SDL/SDLC process is a cost-effective, efficient, and manageable way to do this.
4. *Require third-party suppliers of code in your application to do the same.* In today's software development environments, a majority of software development organizations make use

of code developed elsewhere, either commercial off-the-shelf (COTS) or open-source software. Just as with internally developed software, a third party should prepare an attestation report per the software application owner's requirements, which may include an attack surface review, review of cryptography, architecture risk analysis, technology-specific security testing, binary analysis if source code is unavailable, source code analysis if it is, and fuzz testing in addition to a general penetration testing routine.

8.4 PRSA3: Post-Release Certifications

There are numerous security-focused certifications that a software development team may face after the release of the product that are added on as a requirement rather than during the development process, for a variety of reasons. These reasons may include use of the software in industry or government sectors that were not planned for during design and development, new uses for the software, and new government, country, regional, business or industry sector, or regulatory requirements that did not exist prior to the release of the product. Post-release certification requirements that did not exist prior to the release of the product are a forgivable offense, but missing any that are currently required and were missed early in the SDL is not. Avoiding noncompliance to certifications required for the use of the software that is being developed requires either an internal resource in the company dedicated to following software-use certifications and other requirements, including privacy requirements, or an individual or organization that specializes in this area of experience. This becomes particularly challenging as the number of these types of certifications and requirements increases rapidly around the globe. Following is a short list of examples of security or privacy certifications or standards that could become necessary for a software product to comply with post-release requirements due to market or use-case changes:

- The Federal Information Security Management Act (FISMA)[7]
- Federal Information Standard 140-2 (FIPS 140-2)—Security Requirements for Cryptographic Modules[8]
- The U.S. Department of Defense Information Assurance Certification and Accreditation Process (DIACAP)[9,10]
- The Health Insurance Portability and Accountability Act of 1996 (HIPAA) (privacy and security rules)[11]
- Safe Harbor (privacy)[12]

8.5 PRSA4: Internal Review for New Product Combinations or Cloud Deployments

In our profession, we continue to encounter the misconception that once software has been through an SDL, you can reuse the software code any way you want. This presumption is false because any architectural changes that have occurred after release of a software product will likely introduce new attack vectors in the previously secure code. For this reason, software code must be put through the SDL process again when there is a new use of the software or an architectural change to the code post-release. Any new code must also be vetted through the various types of security testing outlined in earlier chapters.

8.6 PRSA5: Security Architectural Reviews and Tool-Based Assessments of Current, Legacy, and M&A Products and Solutions

8.6.1 Legacy Code

Although they may have once been viewed as an unnecessary cost burden, the best activities and best practices we have outlined in our SDL are a consequence of the discovery that security was not always a key element of the software development process and sometimes led to security vulnerabilities and risk mitigation costs that rivaled the initial cost of the software to be developed. The acceptance of legacy code is based on an assumption of what is expected to happen, in that the software must be proven to be functionally correct and operationally viable. However, when it comes to software security, the unexpected is what typically causes the vulnerabilities. Not only are these security vulnerabilities financially unacceptable, they are also unacceptable from an operational, functional, and overall risk perspective. This is particularly true when the software supports embedded critical systems and applications such as those found in national and regional infrastructures, transportation, defense, medicine, and finance. In these applications, the liabilities, costs, mission, and business impacts associated with unexpected security software and system vulnerabilities are considered unacceptable. Unless the architecture of legacy software is correctly assessed and analyzed from a security perspective, the impact of changes cannot be predicted, nor can changes be applied effectively. This is why the same testing and review rigor that is followed during the SDL must be followed during legacy code reviews: as a means of mitigating the unexpected. If done with the proper process and rigor, this will go far in ensuring secure code implementation that is consistent between legacy and new code.

A legacy software application is one that continues to be used because of the cost of replacing or redesigning it and often despite its poor competitiveness and compatibility with newer equivalents. The most significant issue in this regard is that the organization has likely been depending on this legacy software application for some time, and it predates software development security activities such as those described in our SDL and the mandates that currently drive these practices. Further, a considerable amount of money and resources may be required to eliminate this security "technical debt." Technical debt is the difference between what was delivered and what should have been delivered. The importance of working with legacy code and technical debt is critical for most companies that develop software.[13]

Legacy code with technical debt can also exist because even though the product should have been put in "end-of-life" status, one or more customers do not or cannot upgrade to a newer version of the software, and that customer happens to be a critical customer who considers this product essential to its business. This "critical customer" status often leads to legacy code and products staying in service so that the relationship with the customer(s) still using the product is not jeopardized.

It is not always necessary to pay your technical debt, as it is your financial debt. There may be parts of the code that should be fixed, but the software product still works as advertised; optimizing the code and removing known technical debt may not yield a worthwhile ROI. You may also decide to just take the code out of the program because it no longer serves a purpose. In cases like these, you may never need to pay off that technical debt.

Most important to this discussion is that the technical debt in legacy software may contain security vulnerabilities. Over the course of a project, it is tempting for an organization to become lax regarding software quality and security. Most commonly, this results when teams are expected to complete too much functionality in a given time frame, or quality and security are simply not considered high-priority characteristics for the software.[14] In these situations, there may be security vulnerabilities in the legacy code that exist as a result of the technical debt. From a software product security perspective, the key task when looking at legacy code is to balance the ROI of addressing the security technical debt against the risk of leaving it in. Two primary decisions must be considered:

1. How much new code presumably scrubbed by the SDL are you writing to replace the existing old code? At what rate will the volume of old code be replaced, and what security risk is there for whatever remains?
2. Reviewing old code is a slow and tedious process. Serious ROI decisions must be made. You must reserve resources for this work to reduce the technical security debt for current resources. The level of effort for this work will depend on whether the SDL existed at the time the code was developed. If there was no SDL at the time the legacy code was being developed, the level of effort will be high.

This is the basic process for assessing the security of legacy software applications:

- Assess the business criticality of the application. The software application has likely been successfully relied on for years, and this may be the first time it has been looked at from a security perspective. In fact, it is highly probable that this is the first time it has been examined with this level of scrutiny. If any security vulnerabilities or flaws are discovered, even though there may be only one or two, they will likely require a large-scale effort and significant resources to mitigate. It is important to identify business criticality in order to balance the business risk versus the security risk and ROI in these cases.
- Identify someone who is very familiar with the code. Since the legacy code is "old" code, it most likely has not been updated recently, and there may be few if any people in the organization who understand the software anymore. Further, it may have been developed on top of an old language base and/or poorly documented or commented. If this is the case, then the next step will be to conduct a software security assessment very similar to what is done during the SDL process. If the original developers, documentation, and history exist for the legacy software, and some security was built into the software, then the security assessment process can be shortened to focus just on assessing the gaps in current knowledge.
- Other basic questions should also be asked, such as:
  - Has this application previously been exploited because of a known security vulnerability or flaw?

- ○ Has it been fixed? If not, what can be done about it now?
- ○ Have there been any changes in the software architecture, function, or use that may have added new security vulnerabilities or new planes of attack?
- Assess the security of the software using the key software security assessment techniques of the SDL.
- Create a proposal that will tell the business how to remediate the security vulnerabilities or flaws in the software (cost + time) or how quickly they should think about replacing it (cost). If it is determined that the software is to be replaced, there will be risks in the interim, so you need to make sure you know where the security vulnerabilities and flaws are and develop a plan to mitigate and limit any damage that may result from an adversarial attack or exploitation of the software until the legacy code is replaced.
- If the cost of remediation is considered unacceptable by the business and there are no customer, industry, or regulatory requirements that require that security vulnerability or flaws be fixed, then the senior management for the business unit developing the software and possibly the head of the software engineering development organization and legal counsel will be required to sign off on accepting the risk for continued use of the legacy software.

8.6.2 Mergers and Acquisitions (M&As)

To be competitive, most companies want to develop new products and access new markets and will seek alternatives, such as a merger and acquisition (M&A), when they cannot do this with their current resources. M&As occur for many reasons but are typically driven by the desire to improve competitiveness, profitability, or other value to the company and its products. In the software world, this is typically a function that you need in your solution set or in the product itself. The talent that may come with acquisition will be a bonus if the primary focus of the M&A is the software of the target company. The activities of an M&A start when the initial discussions for the M&A begin and continue through the due diligence phase and on to the integration of the target company and/or the acquired technology into the parent company. The level of effort and scope of work in the process will depend on the size and complexity of the effort. It should be noted that M&As do not always include all of the resources of the target company. They may include the code for one software product, or multiple technologies or products that are attractive and of value to the acquiring company.

The due-diligence phase of an M&A is critical, and security plays a vital role in helping make it successful. If software is included as part of the M&A, a security architectural review and use of automated tools will be required. This may be done either through the use of the potential acquirer's software security staff or through a third party, depending on the restrictions that are imposed as part of the assessment and whether source code can be reviewed. Due to the proprietary nature of source code, most target companies with not allow a review of their source code during the M&A assessment process. Thus, an automated tool will be needed that can conduct comprehensive code review via static binary analysis. This is done by scanning compiled or "byte" code at the binary level rather than reviewing source code and typically includes static, dynamic, and manual techniques.

Perhaps the best checklist for conducting a M&A software security assessment can be found in Table 1, "Software Assurance (SwA) Concern Categories," and Table 2, "Questions for GOTS

(Proprietary & Open Source) and Custom Software," in the Carnegie Mellon "US CERT Software Supply Chain Risk Management & Due-Diligence, Software Assurance Pocket Guide Series: Acquisition & Outsourcing, Volume II, Version 1.2,[15]" which can be accessed at http://osgug.ucaiug.org/utilisec/Shared%20Documents/Security%20Procurement%20Guidelines%20and%20Language/DHS%20-%20Building%20Security%20In%20-%20Software%20Supply%20Chain%20Risk%20Management%20and%20Due-Diligence.pdf. Another similar and useful resource is the Carnegie Mellon Software Engineering Institute Working Paper, "Adapting the SQUARE Method for Security Requirements Engineering to Acquisition,"[16] which can be accessed at www.cert.org/.../SQUARE_for_Acquisition_Working_Paper_v2.pdf. SQuaRE stands for Systems Quality Requirements Engineering and defined in ISO/IEC 25010:2011 (https://www.iso.org/standard/35733.html). This particular paper describes the SQuaRE for acquisition (A-SQuaRE) process for security requirements engineering and is adapted for different acquisition situations.

Some key items that a software security assessor should keep in mind during an M&A software security review include the following:

1. The intent of the M&A software security review is not to focus on getting rid of elements of the target software but rather to assess any business risk that could result from any security risks identified.
2. Highlight anything that may shift the nature of the deal or negatively affect the integration.
3. Look for anything that may be a possible deal breaker.

8.7 Key Success Factors

External Vulnerability Disclosure Response Process

In this post-release phase of the SDL cycle, it is critical to have a well-defined and documented external vulnerability disclosure response process. Stakeholders should be clearly identified, and a responsibility assignment or responsibility assignment matrix (Responsible, Accountable, Consulted, and Informed [RACI] matrix) should be created. Most important, only one team should be responsible for interfacing with customers to discuss vulnerabilities and remediation. All other teams and stakeholders should work with that team and assure that there are no other channels of communication or any information leaked selectively to customers. It is often the case that large accounts or enterprise customers are given preferential treatment and are privy to information that small- and medium-sized businesses are not. This is not a good security practice. Vulnerability information should be disclosed to everyone or no one. Selective disclosure is not a good idea, plays favorites with customers, and, in some cases, may be illegal and counter what constitutes fair and equitable treatment of all customers.

It is also important to define and formalize the internal vulnerability-handling process as part of overall vulnerability management and remediation programs. In addition to security teams and external researches, employees or internal customers of the products/services will often identify security problems and communicate them to the product or operations team. There needs to be a well-defined process to make sure all relevant security vulnerabilities are captured and put through the remediation queue.

Post-Release Certifications

Relevant certifications needed after the product is released (or deployed in the cloud) should have been identified in one of the earlier phases of the SDL cycle. Requirements for certifications should have been included in security and privacy requirements. This will prevent any retrofitting or findings during compliance audits for certifications. Certifications often do require annual audits or surveillance audits. The security team should work with the security compliance team to ensure that all relevant controls requirements are met.

Third-Party Security Reviews

As we have discussed, third-party reviews are often critical to demonstrate "security" to end users and customers. A preferred list of vendors should be created by the software team, and these vendors should be vetted for their skills as well as ability to handle sensitive information. Since these vendors will be handling sensitive security information, it is important to note if they use full disk encryption, communicate securely, dispose of any customer data as soon as testing ends, and so on. Any time there is a need for security testing, one of these vendors should be selected for the testing. Security testing of the entire software stack and product portfolio should be performed at least annually.

SDL Cycle for Any Architectural Changes or Code Reuses

Any architectural or code changes or code/component reuses should trigger SDL activities (though not all may be needed, depending on the significance of the changes).

Security Strategy and Process for Legacy Code, M&A, and EOL Products

Legacy code most likely will never be updated or modified. In addition, a legacy software stack will also never be patched or upgraded. Software running on old Apache web server will have severe dependencies on it as well as the operating system and thus will not be upgraded without the application itself being changed. Any security issues identified in legacy code will take a long time to remediate (if at all). The best way to deal with legacy code is to move away from it as soon as you can. Alternatives include defining a security process for managing security vulnerabilities in legacy code, monitoring legacy code closely (at least annually), and quarantining products running legacy code so that they pose minimal risk to the environment.

M&A security assessment strategy is one of the key success factors in the post-release phase. As mentioned earlier, you may not have access to source code, so assessment strategies need to take this into account—that is, you may need to use binaries rather than source code. In the end, M&A security assessment should provide input into the overall quality of the software being acquired. If this assessment is not thought through carefully or done correctly, the software security group or the information security group may end up dealing with repercussions for a long time to come. A weakness in acquired software may weaken the software posture of other products deployed in the environment.

In addition to a strategy for treating legacy code and products and M&A, it is important to define end-of-line plans for the current version of the product/release. An end-of-line roadmap can guide security strategy from this point on.

8.8 Deliverables

Key deliverables for this phase are listed in Table 8.1.

Table 8.1 Key Deliverables

Deliverable	Description
External vulnerability disclosure response process	The process to define evaluation and communication of security vulnerabilities
Post-release certifications	Certifications from external parties to demonstrate the security posture of products/services
Third-party security reviews	Security assessments performed by groups other than internal testing teams
Security strategy and process for legacy code, M&A, and EOL plans	Strategy to mitigate security risk from legacy code and M&As

External Vulnerability Disclosure Response Process

This deliverable should clearly identify stakeholders in the process and create a RACI for their role in it. In addition, communication cadence with customers should be formalized and published so that everyone in the company is aware of it and can invoke it if needed. Most important, the process should be followed every time a security vulnerability comes from external channels or needs to be disclosed to customers.

Post-Release Certifications

Post-release certifications may include multiple deliverables or certifications based on target markets, regulatory needs, and customer requests. Any one of these factors may drive a certification strategy. Certification should be renewed if drivers for these certifications are still present.

Third-Party Security Reviews

This deliverable consists of multiple security assessments from independent third parties. At least two reports based on assessments should be created: one for internal consumption and one for external use. External reports should not list details of security vulnerabilities or expose critical information. Reports for internal consumption should be as detailed as possible and provide short- as well as long-term remediation recommendations.

Security Strategy for Legacy Code, M&A, and EOL Plans

There are three different deliverables under this umbrella: security strategy for legacy code and products, security strategy for M&As, and end-of-life plans. Each of these should be vetted with relevant stakeholders and implemented in practice only once they have been signed off by everyone.

8.9 Metrics

The following metrics should be captured as part of this phase of the SDL:

- Time in hours to respond to externally disclosed security vulnerabilities
- Monthly FTE (full-time employee) hours required for the external disclosure process
- Number of security findings (ranked by severity) after the product has been released
- Number of customer-reported security issues per month
- Number of customer-reported security issues not identified during any SDL activities

8.10 Summary

This chapter concludes the step-by-step overview of our SDL and covers what we believe to be a unique, practical, timely, and operationally relevant approach to post-release security and privacy support. This approach not only brings the tasks and organizational responsibilities back into the SDL but also keeps the centralized software security group and engineering software development teams empowered to own their own security process for products they are directly responsible for. Most important, we covered the organizational structure, people, and process required to do this both effectively and efficiently while maximizing the ROI for security and privacy support in the post-release environment. In the next chapter, we will take everything we have discussed so far and make it relevant to the various software development methodologies, whether Waterfall, Agile, a blend, or something in between. We have included deliverables and metrics (Chapters 3 through 8), which can be used by organizations to manage, optimize, and measure the effectiveness of their software security programs. In Chapter 9, we bring it all together to apply elements of the SDL framework as solutions to real-world problems.

Chapter Quick-Check

1. Product deployment and post-release assurance requires:
   a. Secure coding
   b. Object-oriented management
   c. Problem resolution
   d. Configuration management

2. Incident response processes should be:
   a. Routinely executed and tested.
   b. Operationally complex
   c. Strategically planned
   d. Totally constrained

3. The incident management team is:
   a. A strictly technical operation
   b. Composed of the best programmers

c. Strictly composed of managers
d. Often a diverse bunch of people representing all relevant disciplines

4. The operations and management processes are lumped together into sustainment because:
   a. They are at the end of the life cycle.
   b. They are the major activities during the software use life cycle period.
   c. They are neither development nor acquisition.
   d. They are strictly control processes for sustaining assurance.

Exercises

The following exercises are based on the case study discussed in Appendix A. These exercises are intended to give you some practice in applying the steps and producing deliverables for the PRSA Phase of the SDL.

With the completion of the development under your new SDL, it's time to revisit some of the choices you've made along the way and take a critical view of your new system and processes. Is it right-sized in the right-way? Do supporting processes operate as intended and desired? Are all supporting processes—inside and outside of IT—in place and operating as expected?

In the PRSA Phase, you're given the opportunity to adjust your team, your expectations, and your results, while fortifying these processes with policy changes, operational support, and engagement with outside parties for testing, certification, and accreditation of your application and your program.

1. Prepare a draft statement for an External Vulnerability Disclosure Response Process (e.g., a bug bounty program) following the guidance in Chapter 8.
2. Consider the needs for post-release assessments and certifications from regulatory bodies, such as the Payment Card Industry Data Security Standard (PCI-DSS).
3. Develop a plan for contracting and acquiring the services from a professional penetration testing firm to gain an attacker's view of your system.
4. Develop a draft strategy for addressing security risk from associated legacy systems, M&As, and software end-of-life planning.
5. Document the key performance and key risk indicators as metrics for the ongoing operation of the system and sustainment of the overall SDL.

References

1. McGraw, G. (2006). *Software Security: Building Security In*. Addison Wesley/Pearson Education, Boston, p. 20.
2. first.org. (2021). "Common Vulnerability Scoring System v3.1: Specification Document." Retrieved from https://www.first.org/cvss/v3.1/specification-document
3. cve.org. (2021). "Overview—About the CVE Program." Retrieved from https://www.cve.org /About/Overview

4. ISO®. (2018). "ISO/IEC 29147:2018 [ISO/IEC 29147:2018]—Information technology—Security techniques—Vulnerability disclosure." Retrieved fromhttps://www.iso.org/standard/72311.html

5. ISO®. (2019). "ISO/IEC 30111:2019 [ISO/IEC 30111:2019]—Information technology—Security techniques—Vulnerability handling processes." Retrieved from https://www.iso.org/standard/53231.html

6. Microsoft Corporation. (2013). "Appendix K: SDL Privacy Escalation Response Framework (Sample)." Retrieved from http://msdn.microsoft.com/en-us/library/windows/desktop/cc307401.aspx

7. U.S. Cybersecurity & Infrastructure Security Agency. (2021). "Federal Information Security Management Act (FISMA)." Retrieved from https://www.cisa.gov/federal-information-security-modernization-act

8. National Institute of Standards and Technology. (2001). "Federal Information Standard 140-2 (FIPS 14-2)—Security Requirements for Cryptographic Modules." Retrieved from http://csrc.nist.gov/publications/fips/fips140-2/fips1402.pdf

9. U.S. Department of Defense. (2013). "Department of Defense Information Assurance Certification and Accreditation Process (DIACAP)." Retrieved from https://www.acqnotes.com/Attachments/DoD%20Information%20Assurance%20Certification%20and%20Accreditation%20Process%20(DIACAP)%20-BRIEF.pdf

10. U.S. Department of Defense. (2003). "Department of Defense Instruction Number 8500.2, February 6, 2003—Information Assurance (IA) Implementation." Retrieved from https://irp.fas.org/doddir/dod/d8500_2.pdf

11. U.S. Government Printing Office. (1996). "Health Insurance Portability and Accountability Act of 1996 (HIPAA)," Public Law 104-191, 104th Congress. Retrieved from http://www.gpo.gov/fdsys/pkg/PLAW-104publ191/html/PLAW-104publ191.htm

12. ftc.gov. (2015). "U.S.-EU & U.S.- Safe Harbor Framework." Retrieved from http://export.gov/safeharbor

13. Mar, K., and James, M. (2010). "CollabNet Whitepaper: Technical Debt and Design Death." Retrieved from https://www.scribd.com/document/2680060/Technical-Debt

14. Ibid.

15. United States Government—US CERT. (2009). "Software Supply Chain Risk Management & Due-Diligence, Software Assurance Pocket Guide Series: Acquisition & Outsourcing, Volume II Version 1.2," June 16, 2009. Retrieved from http://osgug.ucaiug.org/utilisec/Shared%20Documents/Security%20Procurement%20Guidelines%20and%20Language/DHS%20-%20Building%20Security%20In%20-%20Software%20Supply%20Chain%20Risk%20Management%20and%20Due-Diligence.pdf

16. Mead, N. (2010). "Carnegie Mellon Software Engineering Institute Working Paper: Adapting the SQUARE Method for Security Requirements Engineering to Acquisition." Retrieved from https://resources.sei.cmu.edu/asset_files/WhitePaper/2010_019_001_51613.pdf

Chapter 9

Adapting Our Reference Framework to Your Environment

CHAPTER OVERVIEW

Software is determined to be secure as a result of an analysis of how the program is to be used, under what conditions, and the security requirements it must meet in the environment in which it is to be deployed. The security development lifecycle (SDL) must also extend beyond the release of the product. Therefore, if the assumptions underlying the software and their previously implied requirements do not hold in an unplanned operational environment, the software may no longer be secure, and the SDL process may need to start over, in part or as a whole, if a complete product redesign is required. In this sense, we have established the need for accurate and meaningful security requirements and the metrics to govern them, as well as examples of how to develop them. It is also assumed that the security requirements are not all known prior to the development process, and we have described the process by which they are derived, analyzed, and validated.

CHAPTER TAKE-AWAYS

- Adapt your SDL to include key deliverables, metrics, and measurement tools for sustaining growth and operation.
- Examine the two leading SDL maturity models—OWASP®'s Security Assurance Maturity Model (SAMM)™ and Synopsys®'s Building Security In Maturity Model (BSIMM).
- Apply a seven-step recipe for detailed threat modeling and design vulnerability remediation techniques.
- Learn how to apply the MITRE ATT&CK® and D3FEND® knowledge bases to your threat management practices.
- Detemine how to adapt your SDL to future growth, expansion, and roadmaps for establishing maturity levels over time.

Software executives, leaders, and managers must support the robust coding practices and necessary security enhancements as required by a business-relevant SDL as well as supporting the staffing requirements, scheduling, budgeting, and resource allocations required for this type of work. We have described the process, requirements, and management of metrics for people in these roles so that they can accurately assess the impact and resources required for an SDL that is relevant to and will work best in their organization and environment. Our approach has been designed from real-life, on-the-ground challenges and experiences, and we have described how to think about issues in order to develop effective approaches and manage them as a business process.

One style of SDL isn't relevant to all environments. What we have done in this book is provide you with a detailed framework in a Waterfall-type format that provides lists from which you can pick and choose to meet the needs of your environment or for full or partial (upgrade) software development needs. We will start this chapter with an overview of the top four environments you are likely to deploy your SDL in; then, we will summarize the key elements of our SDL reference framework as well as the top maturity models you are likely to build your SDL around, some final thoughts on enhancing your threat modeling practice as part of the SDL, and, finally, guidance on pulling it all together.

9.1 Overview of the Top Four Environments in Which You Are Likely to Deploy Your SDL

You can "build your own" SDL to build security into a process that is appropriate for your specific needs and environment, whether it be Agile, DevOps, Cloud, Digital Enterprise, or a combination of two or more of these. Each environment is described below.

9.1.1 Agile

Agile software development refers to software development life cycle (SDLC) methodologies based on the idea of iterative development, in which requirements and solutions evolve through collaboration between self-organizing, cross-functional teams. Agile development is designed to enable teams to deliver value faster, with greater quality and predictability and greater abilities to respond to change.[1]

Scrum and Kanban are the dominant implementations of Agile, and Scrum is the one most often found in software development organizations. There's Agile/Scrum as a formal, strict, tightly controlled process, and then there's Agile/Scrum as it's implemented in the real world. Implementation of Agile will vary from the fundamentalist and purist views to various elements that appear as Agile-like processes, and everything in between. It's less important HOW it's implemented in your environment than it is to understand WHAT your specific implementation means to your SDL.

9.1.2 DevOps

With the successful rise and proof of the viability of Scrum to speed up software development, further changes made to speed up HOW software is deployed came on the scene with the marriage of development and operations.

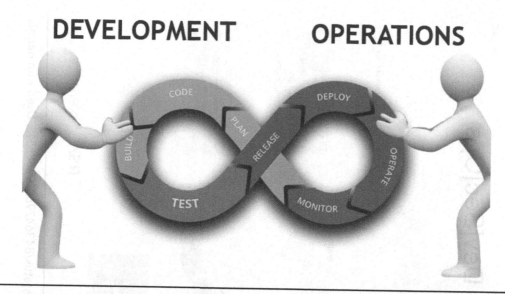

DEVELOPMENT   **OPERATIONS**

Figure 9.1   Agile/Scrum framework (*Source*: Neon Rain Interactive, licensed under CC BY-ND 3.0 NZ).

Now, development teams and operations teams work together as partners for ongoing operations, enhancements, defect removal, and optimization of resources as they learn how their product operates in the real world.

As AppSec professionals engage in the planning for continuous integration/continuous deployment (CI/CD), DevOps, and new models for data center operations, DevOps began to transform into what we'll call DevSecOps.

Figure 9.1 is a simple depiction of how Agile and DevOps work in unison.[2]

Figure 9.2 shows what the marriage of Dev and Ops teams looks like when comprehensive security controls transform DevOps into DevSecOps.[3]

9.1.3 Cloud

As organizations migrated to new uses of cloud technology, such as Platform as a Service (PaaS), Infrastructure as a Service (IaaS), and containerization, it became obvious that a lift and shift strategy was not going to fly. Rather, these new ways of operating data centers required rethinking how applications are built, deployed, and used. Large, monolithic applications started undergoing a refactoring process to break up the applications. This activity involves isolating functions (services) around a central concept or entity—for example, one microservice might deal with all the functions needed to create a client entity, another microservice might represent the sales entity, yet another might represent order processing, and so on. These microservices are activated using an application programming interface (API) that describes what functions are available to access and what attributes are involved. These APIs are most often developed using the representational state transfer,[4] or REST, architectural style.

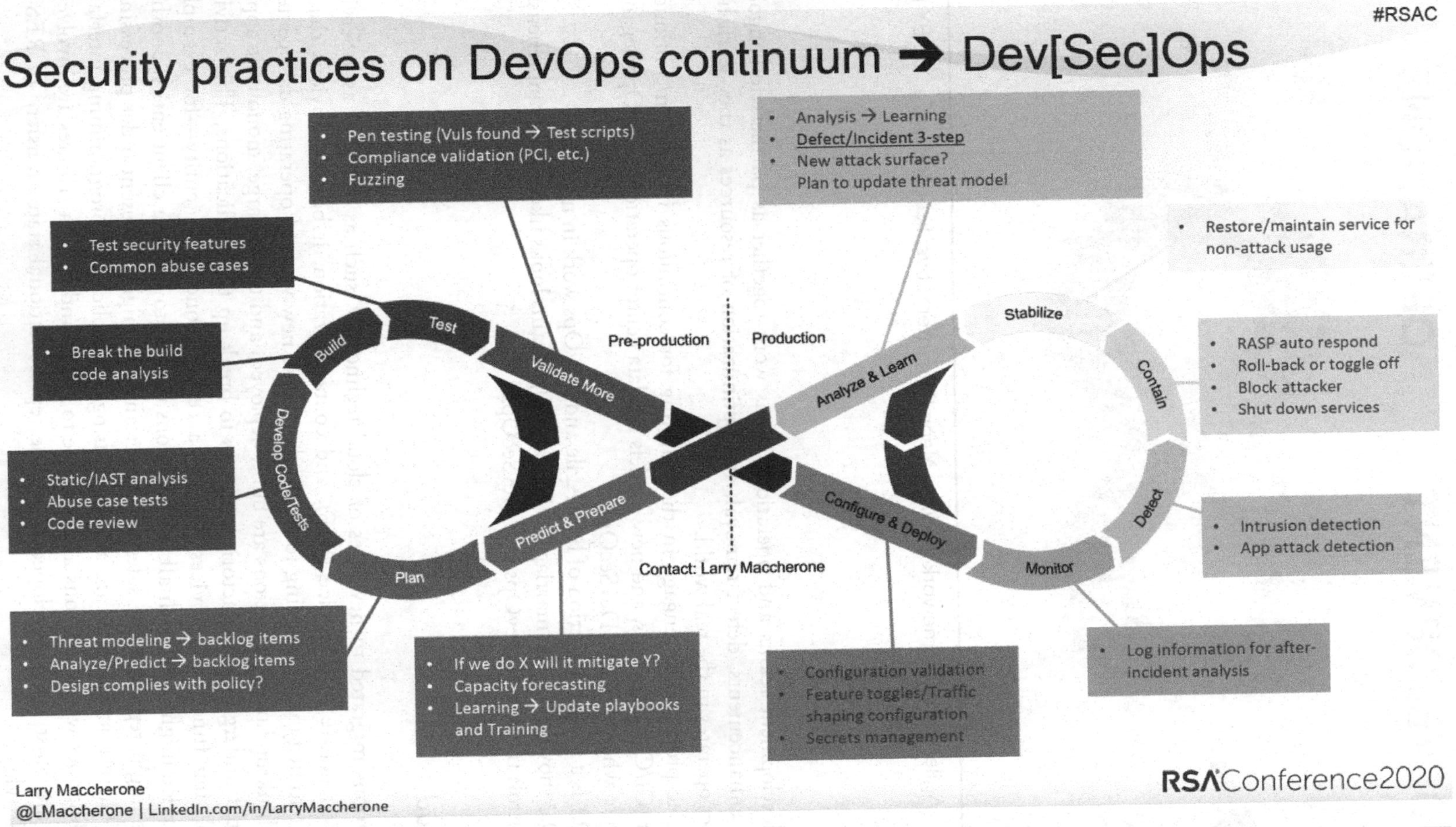

Security practices on DevOps continuum → Dev[Sec]Ops

- Restore/maintain service for non-attack usage

- RASP auto respond
- Roll-back or toggle off
- Block attacker
- Shut down services

- Intrusion detection
- App attack detection

- Log information for after-incident analysis

- Analysis → Learning
- Defect/Incident 3-step
- New attack surface?
- Plan to update threat model

Contain

Defend

Stabilize

Monitor

Analyze & Learn

Configure & Deploy

Production

- Configuration validation
- Feature toggles/Traffic shaping configuration
- Secrets management

Pre-production

Validate More

Predict & Prepare

Contact: Larry Maccherone

- If we do X will it mitigate Y?
- Capacity forecasting
- Learning → Update playbooks and Training

- Pen testing (Vuls found → Test scripts)
- Compliance validation (PCI, etc.)
- Fuzzing

Test

Plan

Build

Develop Code/Tests

- Test security features
- Common abuse cases

- Break the build
- code analysis

- Static/IAST analysis
- Abuse case tests
- Code review

- Threat modeling → backlog items
- Analyze/Predict → backlog items
- Design complies with policy?

Larry Maccherone
@LMaccherone | LinkedIn.com/in/LarryMaccherone

Figure 9.2 DevSecOps cycle (Source: Retrieved from https://twitter.com/lmaccherone/status/8436479607978851 2. Used with permission of L. Maccherone, Jr.).

Application development using these microservices entails developing a series of API invocation processes that perform useful work without concern for how these services are implemented, while permitting enhancement and changes to occur without interface changes to isolate the need for rebuilding every application that needs those services.

Traditional SDL mapping needs to be adapted to make it feasible to build and deploy code where the velocity of deployments can be 100s or 1000s of changes a day. It increases the need to make accurate threat models with a granular understanding of trust boundaries (e.g., between microservices).

One should ask if every API update needs all SDL activities. For feasible SDL activities, triggers should be defined to kick off high-impact ones (e.g., dynamic security testing).

9.1.4 Digital Enterprise

A digital enterprise uses technology to enable and improve business activities to achieve a competitive advantage. This is why many start-ups have an advantage over established competitors. They are able to start out small with agile business practices that are fast, agile, innovative, and disruptive. Larger institutionalized companies must now move quickly to digitize all of their operations to compete. This typically involves rapid and dramatic change. The ability to respond to a changing marketplace is critical for their success. The principles used for Agile, DevOps, and the cloud described in Sections 9.1.1 to 9.1.3 are used to build and enhance the successful operations for a digital enterprise.

The traditional Waterfall method for software development is not feasible or practical for the iterative product release cycle required for the digital enterprise. The elements of the Agile development process and CI/CD should use early user testing, customer analytics, and prioritization based on user feedback, thus providing a smoother path toward enhancing the business value chain. Agility is achieved by eliminating wasted effort, thereby speeding up the product release lifecycle. Automation, orchestration technology, and APIs are used to reduce or eliminate manual security processes and interactions to shorten development times and deliver new features, fixes, and updates aligned with the business. This will reduce the release times, raise quality levels, and increase the productivity of the team members, as well as facilitate security operating at speeds required in a cloud environment. Enterprise environments typically include employee productivity tools (Slack®, Office 365®, messaging, emails) and business systems such as CRM and HR (e.g., Workday®). Similar to the cloud, enterprise development needs can be quite different from traditional products. The technology stack is likely to be Microsoft®-based. Increasingly, on-prem business applications are being replaced by Software-as-a-Service (SaaS) applications.

As more companies have moved to public cloud services due to the end-to-end digital transformation, from the customer interface through the back-office processes, security challenges have significantly increased with the ever-changing and increasing footprint and attack surfaces. Building security into the software development process as described in this book has never been more important, and it is core to the successful operation of a digital enterprise. Integrating third-party SaaS applications through APIs increases the attack surface and changes trust boundaries in many cases. This supply-chain integration risk is enhanced today; in all likelihood, the application stack is changing every day. SDL managers should pay special attention to location-specific regulatory and privacy requirements.

Table 9.1 Key Success Factors for Each Phase of the Security Development Lifecycle (SDL)

Phase	Key Success Factor	Description
Security Assessment (A1): SDL Activities and Best Practices	1. Accuracy of planned SDL activities	All SDL activities are accurately identified.
	2. Product risk profile	Management understands the true cost of developing the product.
	3. Accuracy of threat profile	Mitigating steps and countermeasures are in place for the product to be successful in its environment.
	4. Coverage of relevant regulations, certifications, and compliance frameworks	All applicable legal and compliance aspects are covered.
	5. Coverage of security objectives needed for software	"Must have" security objectives are met.
Architecture (A2): SDL Activities and Best Practices	1. Identification of business requirements and risks	Mapping of business requirements and risks defined in terms of CIA.
	2. Effective threat modeling	Identifying threats for the software.
	3. Effective architectural threat analysis	Analysis of threats to the software and probability of threat materializing.
	4. Effective risk mitigation strategy	Risk acceptance, tolerance, and mitigation plan per business requirements.
	5. Accuracy of DFDs	Data flow diagrams (DFDs) used during threat modeling.
Design and Development (A3): SDL Activities and Best Practices	1. Comprehensive security test plan	Mapping types of security testing required at different stages of the software development life cycle (SDLC).
	2. Effective threat modeling	Identifying threats to the software.
	3. Design security analysis	Analysis of threats to various software components.
	4. Privacy implementation assessment	Efforts required for the implementation of privacy-related controls based on assessment.
	5. Policy compliance review (updates)	Updates for policy compliance as related to Phase 3.

Design and Development (A4): SDL Activities and Best Practices		
1. Security test case execution		Coverage of all relevant test cases.
2. Security testing		Completion of all types of security testing and remediation of problems found.
3. Privacy validation and remediation		Effectiveness of privacy-related controls and remediation of any issues found.
4. Policy compliance review		Updates for policy compliance as related to Phase 4.
Ship (A5): SDL Activities and Best Practices		
1. Policy compliance analysis		Final review of security and compliance requirements during the development process.
2. Vulnerability scanning		Scanning of the software stack for identifying security issues, including open-source and third-party libraries.
3. Penetration testing		Exploiting any/all security issues on the software stack.
4. Open-source licensing review		Final review of open-source software used in the stack.
5. Final security review		Final review of compliance against all security requirements identified during the SDL cycle.
6. Final privacy review		Final review of compliance against all privacy requirements identified during the SDL cycle.
7. Customer engagement framework		The framework that defines the process for sharing security-related information with customers.

(A description of Table 9.1 can be found on the following page.)

9.2 Key Success Factors, Deliverables, and Metrics for Each Phase of Our SDL Reference Framework

In Chapters 3 through 7, we have outlined key success factors, deliverables, and metrics that should be captured as part of our SDL model. In Chapter 8, the SDL post-release phase, we outline the key deliverables and metrics. The key success factors, deliverables, and metrics are not set in stone and may need to be tweaked as you map the SDL to your own SDLC. In Table 9.1, we have summarized the key success factors that are described in Chapters 3 through 8. The Deliverables and Metrics are found at the end of this chapter to help you adapt to your own SDL.

9.3 Software Security Maturity Models and the SDL

In this section, you will find a detailed examination of two measurement and metrics models intended to help you determine the baseline maturity of the secure development integration into your SDLC and the pathways to further improve the maturity of your program.

We'll take a look at the two leading software security maturity approaches:

- OWASP's Open Software Assurance Maturity Model (OpenSAMM)
- Building Security In Maturity Model (BSIMM v11)

9.3.1 Maturity Models for Security and Resilience

Jeremy Epstein, a senior computer scientist at SRI International, wrote about the value of a software security maturity model[5]:

> So how do security maturity models like OpenSAMM and BSIMM fit into this picture? Both have done a great job cataloging, updating, and organizing many of the "rules of thumb" that have been used over the past few decades for investing in software assurance. By defining a common language to describe the techniques we use, these models will enable us to compare one organization to another and will help organizations understand areas where they may be more or less advanced than their peers. . . . Since these are process standards, not technical standards, moving in the direction of either BSIMM or OpenSAMM will help an organization advance—and waiting for the dust to settle just means it will take longer to catch up with other organizations. . . . [I]n short: do not let the perfect be the enemy of the good. For software assurance, it's time to get moving now.

9.3.2 Software Assurance Maturity Model—OpenSAMM

OpenSAMM is an open framework developed by the Open Web Application Security Project (OWASP) to help organizations formulate and implement a strategy for software security that is tailored to the specific risks facing the organization. OpenSAMM offers a roadmap and a well-defined maturity model for secure software development and deployment, along with useful tools for self-assessment and planning. OpenSAMM comes as a 96-page PDF file with detailed descriptions of each core activity and corresponding security processes.[6]

The resources provided by OpenSAMM aid in:

- Evaluating an organization's existing software security practices.
- Building a balanced software security program in well-defined iterations.
- Demonstrating concrete improvements to a security assurance program.
- Defining and measuring security-related activities within an organization.

SAMM was defined with flexibility in mind so that it can be utilized by small, medium, and large organizations using any style of SDLC. The model can be applied organization-wide for a single line of business, or even on an individual project.

OpenSAMM was beta released under a Creative Commons Attribution Share-Alike license. The original work was donated to OWASP and is currently being run as an OWASP project.

OpenSAMM starts with the core activities that should be present in any organization that develops software:

- Governance
- Construction
- Verification
- Deployment

In each of these core activities, three *security practices* are defined for 12 practices that are used to determine the overall maturity of your program. The security practices cover all areas relevant to software security assurance, and each provides a "silo" for improvement. These three security practices for each level of core activities are shown in Figure 9.3.

9.3.2.1 OpenSAMM Business Functions

Each of these business functions is described below:

- **Governance** is centered on the processes and activities related to how an organization manages overall software development activities. More specifically, this includes concerns confronting cross-cut groups involved in development as well as business processes that are established at the organization level.
- **Construction** concerns the processes and activities related to how an organization defines goals and creates software within development projects. In general, this includes product management, requirements gathering, high-level architecture specifications, detailed design, and implementation.
- **Verification** is focused on the processes and activities related to how an organization checks and tests artifacts produced throughout software development. This typically includes quality assurance (QA) work such as testing, but it can also include other review and evaluation activities.

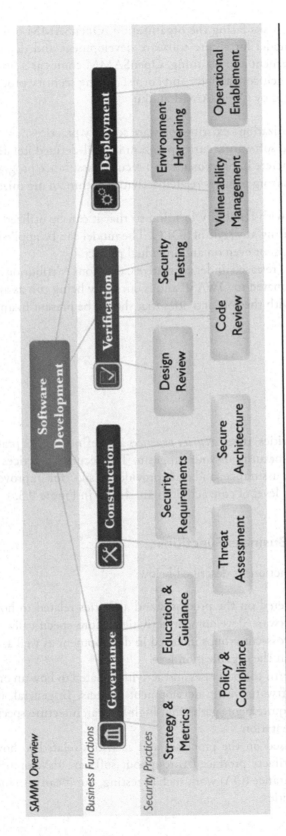

Figure 9.3 OpenSAMM model (*Source:* OpenSAMM by OWASP is licensed under CC-BY-SA).

- **Deployment** entails the processes and activities related to how an organization manages the release of software that has been created. This can involve shipping products to end users, deploying products to internal or external hosts, and normal operations of software in the runtime environment.

Objectives under each of the 12 practice areas define how each practice can be improved over time and establish a maturity level for any given area. The four *maturity levels* for a practice correspond to:

0: Implicit starting point with the practice unfulfilled
1: Initial understanding and ad hoc provision of the practice
2: Increase efficiency and/or effectiveness of the practice
3: Comprehensive mastery of the practice at scale

9.3.2.2 Core Practice Areas

In this section, we'll break down each of the practice areas into specific practices within it.

Governance Core Practice Areas

- **Strategy and Metrics (SM)** involves the overall strategic direction of the software assurance program and the instrumentation of processes and activities to collect metrics about an organization's security posture.
- **Policy and Compliance (PC)** involves setting up a security and compliance control and audit framework throughout an organization to achieve increased assurance in software under construction and in operation.
- **Education and Guidance (EG)** involves increasing security knowledge among personnel in software development through training and guidance on security topics relevant to individual job functions.

Construction Core Practice Areas

- **Threat Assessment (TA)** involves accurately identifying and characterizing potential attacks on an organization's software in order to better understand the risks and facilitate risk management.
- **Security Requirements (SR)** involve promoting the inclusion of security-related requirements during the software development process in order to specify correct functionality from inception.
- **Secure Architecture (SA)** involves bolstering the design process with activities to promote secure-by-default designs and control over technologies and frameworks on which software is built.

Verification Core Practice Areas

- **Design Review (DR)** involves inspection of the artifacts created from the design process to ensure the provision of adequate security mechanisms and adherence to an organization's expectations for security.

- **Code Review (CR)** involves the assessment of an organization's source code to aid vulnerability discovery and related mitigation activities as well as establish a baseline for secure coding expectations.
- **Security Testing (ST)** involves testing the organization's software in its runtime environment in order to both discover vulnerabilities and establish a minimum standard for software releases.

Deployment Core Practice Areas

- **Vulnerability Management (VM)** involves establishing consistent processes for managing internal and external vulnerability reports to limit exposure and gather data to enhance the security assurance program.
- **Environment Hardening (EH)** involves implementing controls for the operating environment surrounding an organization's software to bolster the security posture of applications that have been deployed.
- **Operational Enablement (OE)** involves identifying and capturing security-relevant information needed by an operator to properly configure, deploy, and run an organization's software.

9.3.2.3 Levels of Maturity

Each core practice area is further detailed with a defined level of maturity using the following structure:

- Objective
- Activities
- Results
- Success Metrics
- Costs
- Personnel
- Related Levels

9.3.2.3.1 Objective

The *objective* is a general statement that captures the assurance goal of attaining the associated level. As the levels increase for a given practice, the objectives characterize more sophisticated goals in terms of building assurance for software development and deployment.

9.3.2.3.2 Activities

The *activities* are core requisites for attaining the level. Some are meant to be performed organization-wide, and some correspond to actions for individual project teams. In either case, the activities capture the core security function, and organizations are free to determine how they fulfill the activities.

9.3.2.3.3 Results

The *results* characterize capabilities and deliverables obtained by achieving the given level. In some cases, these are specified concretely; in others, a more qualitative statement is made about increased capability.

9.3.2.3.4 Success Metrics

The *success metrics* specify example measurements that can be used to check whether an organization is performing at the given level. Data collection and management are left to the choice of each organization, but recommended data sources and thresholds are provided.

9.3.2.3.5 Costs

The *costs* are qualitative statements about the expenses incurred by an organization attaining the given level. Although specific values will vary for each organization, these are meant to provide an idea of the one-time and ongoing costs associated with operating at a particular level.

9.3.2.3.6 Personnel

These properties of a level indicate the estimated ongoing overhead in terms of human resources for operating at the given level:

- Developers—individuals performing detailed design and implementation of the software
- Architects—individuals performing high-level design work and large-scale system engineering
- Managers—individuals performing day-to-day management of development staff
- QA testers—individuals performing quality assurance testing and prerelease verification of software
- Security auditors—individuals with technical security knowledge related to software being produced
- Business owners—individuals performing key decision making on software and its business requirements
- Support operations—individuals performing customer support or direct technical operations support

9.3.2.3.7 Related Levels

The *related levels* are references to levels within other practices that have some potential overlaps, depending on the organization's structure and progress in building an assurance program. Functionally, these indicate synergies or optimizations in activity implementation if the related level is also a goal or already in place.

9.3.2.3.8 Assurance

Because the 12 practices are each a maturity area, the successive objectives represent the "building blocks" for any assurance program. OpenSAMM is designed for use in improving an assurance program in phases by:

- Selecting security practices to improve in the next phase of the assurance program.
- Achieving the next objective in each practice by performing the corresponding activities at the specified success metrics.

9.3.2.4 Using OpenSAMM to Assess Maturity Levels

Each security practice also includes an assessment worksheet, with the answers indicating the current level of maturity for that practice. A sample assessment worksheet extract for the education and guidance (EG) activities is shown in Figure 9.4.

Based on the scores assigned to each security practice, an organization can create a scorecard to capture those values. Functionally, a scorecard can be the simple set of 12 scores for a particular time. However, selecting a time interval over which to generate a scorecard facilitates the understanding of overall changes in the assurance program during the time frame.

Using interval scorecards is encouraged for several situations:

- Gap analysis
  - Capturing scores from detailed assessments versus expected performance levels.
- Demonstrating improvement
  - Capturing scores from before and after an iteration of assurance program build-out.
- Ongoing measurement.
  - Capturing scores over consistent time frames for an assurance program that is already in place.

One of the main uses of OpenSAMM is to help organizations build software security assurance programs. That process is straightforward and generally begins with an assessment to determine if the organization is already performing some security assurance activities.

Several roadmap templates for common types of organizations are provided. Thus, many organizations can choose an appropriate match and then tailor the roadmap template to their needs. For other types of organizations, it may be necessary to build a custom roadmap. Roadmap templates are provided for:

- Independent software vendors
- Online service providers
- Financial services organizations
- Government organizations

These organization types were chosen because:

- They represent common use cases.

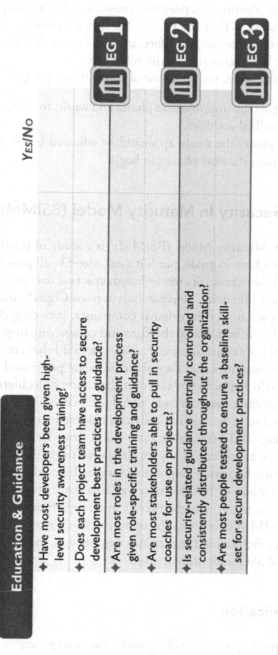

Education & Guidance

Yes/No

- ◆ Have most developers been given high-level security awareness training?
- ◆ Does each project team have access to secure development best practices and guidance?
- ◆ Are most roles in the development process given role-specific training and guidance?
- ◆ Are most stakeholders able to pull in security coaches for use on projects?
- ◆ Is security-related guidance centrally controlled and consistently distributed throughout the organization?
- ◆ Are most people tested to ensure a baseline skill-set for secure development practices?

EG 1
EG 2
EG 3

Figure 9.4 Sample OpenSAMM assessment worksheet extract (*Source:* OpenSAMM by OWASP is licensed under CC-BY-SA).

- Each organization has variations in typical software-induced risk.
- Optimal creation of an assurance program is different for each.

Roadmaps consist of phases in which several practices are each improved by one level. Building a roadmap entails selecting practices to improve in each planned phase. Organizations are free to plan into the future as far as they want, but they are encouraged to iterate based on business drivers and organization-specific information to ensure that the assurance goals are commensurate with their business goals and risk tolerance.

Once a roadmap is established, the build-out of an assurance program is simplified.

- An organization begins the improvement phases and works to achieve the stated levels by performing the prescribed activities.
- At the end of each phase, the roadmap should be adjusted based on what was actually accomplished, and then the next phase can begin.

9.4 The Building Security In Maturity Model (BSIMM)

The Building Security In Maturity Model (BSIMM)[7] is a study of existing software security initiatives. BSIMM is not a how-to guide, nor is it a one-size-fits-all prescription. The project's primary objective was to build a maturity model based on actual data gathered from nine large-scale software development initiatives. Representatives from Cigital® and Fortify® conducted interviews and collected data from nine original companies, including Adobe®, Dell® EMC®, Google®, Microsoft, and five others. Using this data and conducting in-person executive interviews, the team developed a Software Security Framework (SSF) that creates buckets and three maturity levels for the 116 activities that they observed being performed in software development organizations. BSIMM has been updated over the course of its lifetime. Now, in its 11th edition, it includes new activities that have been added to clearly show that AppSec in the cloud is becoming mainstream and indicates that activities observed among independent software vendors, Internet of Things (IoT) companies, and cloud firms have begun to converge, suggesting that common cloud architectures require similar software security approaches.

BSIMM is meant for use by anyone responsible for creating and executing a software security initiative (SSI). The authors of BSIMM observed that successful SSIs are typically run by a senior executive who reports to the highest levels in an organization. These executives lead an internal group that BSIMM refers to as the *software security group* (SSG), which is charged with directly executing or facilitating the activities described in the BSIMM. The BSIMM is written with the SSG and SSG leadership in mind.

9.4.1 BSIMM Organization

This model is divided into 12 practices, falling under four categories:

- Governance
- Intelligence
- Software security development lifecycle (SSDL) touchpoints
- Deployment

BSIMM indicates that SSGs should emphasize security education and mentoring rather than policing for security errors. BSIMM is not explicitly intended for software developers. Instead, it's intended for people who are trying to teach software developers how to do proper software security.

Properly used, BSIMM can help you determine where your organization stands with respect to real-world software security initiatives, what peers in your industry are doing, and what steps you can take to make your approach more effective.

A maturity model is appropriate because improving software security *almost always* means changing the way an organization works—something that never happens overnight. BSIMM provides a way to assess the state of an organization, prioritize changes, and demonstrate progress. Not all organizations need to reach the same security goals, but by applying BSIMM, all organizations can be *measured with the same yardstick.*

9.4.2 BSIMM Software Security Framework

The BSIMM Software Security Framework (SSF) is shown in Figure 9.5.

9.4.2.1 Governance

Governance includes those practices that help organize, manage, and measure a software security initiative. Staff development is also a central governance practice. In the governance domain, the strategy and metrics practice encompasses planning, assigning roles and responsibilities, identifying software security goals, determining budgets, and identifying metrics and gates. The compliance and policy practices focus on:

- Identifying controls for compliance requirements such as PCI-DSS and HIPAA.
- Developing contractual controls such as service-level agreements (SLAs) to help control commercial off-the-shelf (COTS) software risk.
- Setting organizational software security policy and auditing against that policy.
- Training, because it fills a critical role in software security—software developers and architects often start out with very little security knowledge.

9.4.2.2 Intelligence

Intelligence includes those practices that result in collections of corporate knowledge used in carrying out software security activities throughout the organization. Collections include both proactive security guidance and organizational threat modeling.

The intelligence domain is meant to create organization-wide resources. Those resources are divided into three practices:

- Attack models capture information used to think like an attacker: threat modeling, abuse-case development and refinement, data classification, and technology-specific attack patterns.

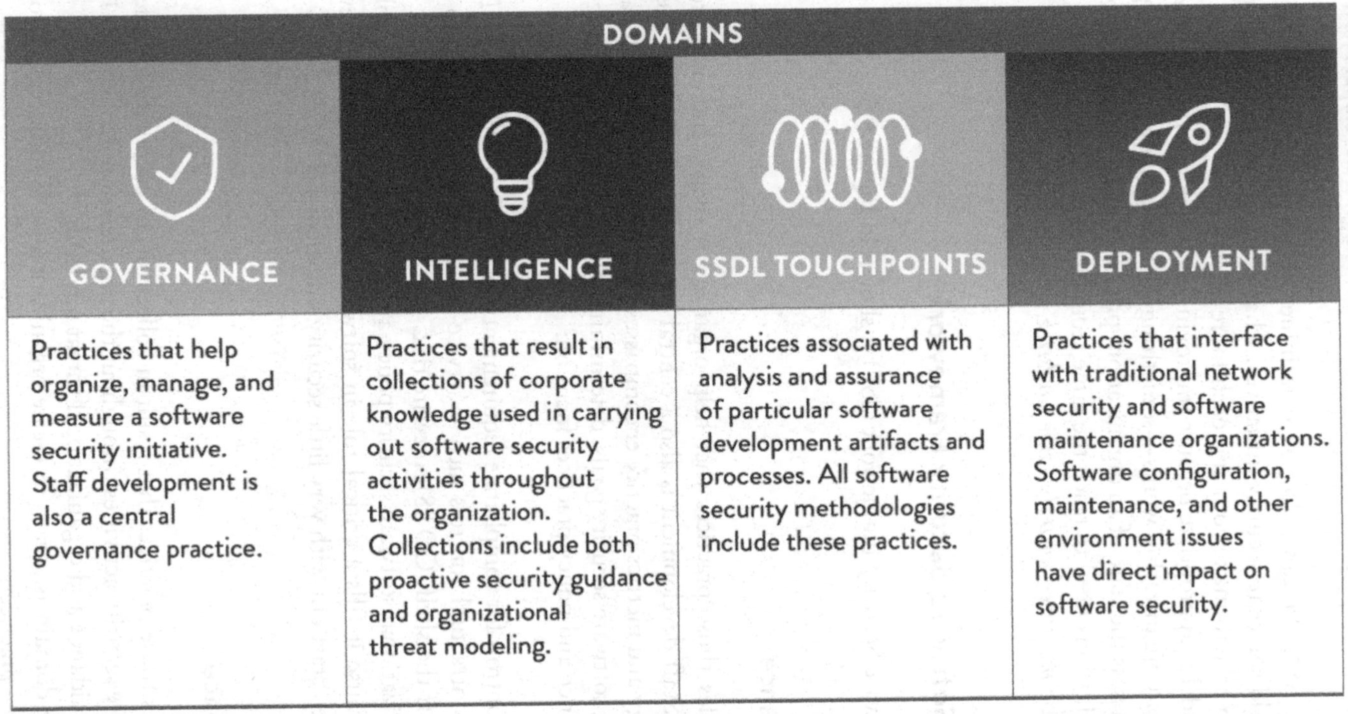

DOMAINS

GOVERNANCE	INTELLIGENCE	SSDL TOUCHPOINTS	DEPLOYMENT
Practices that help organize, manage, and measure a software security initiative. Staff development is also a central governance practice.	Practices that result in collections of corporate knowledge used in carrying out software security activities throughout the organization. Collections include both proactive security guidance and organizational threat modeling.	Practices associated with analysis and assurance of particular software development artifacts and processes. All software security methodologies include these practices.	Practices that interface with traditional network security and software maintenance organizations. Software configuration, maintenance, and other environment issues have direct impact on software security.

Figure 9.5 The BSIMM software security framework.

- The security features and design practice are charged with creating usable security patterns for major security controls (meeting the standards defined in the next practice), building middleware frameworks for those controls, and creating and publishing other proactive security guidance.
- The standards and requirements practice involves eliciting explicit security requirements (nonfunctional requirements [NFRs] as acceptance criteria) from the organization, determining which COTS software to recommend, building standards for major security controls (such as authentication, input validation, etc.), creating security standards for technologies in use, and creating a standards review board.

9.4.2.3 SDL Touchpoints

SDL touchpoints include those practices associated with the analysis and assurance of particular software development artifacts and processes. All software security methodologies include these practices.

The SDL touchpoints domain is probably the most familiar of the four domains. This domain includes essential software security best practices that are integrated into the SDLC. The two most important software security practices are *architecture analysis* and *code review.*

Architecture analysis encompasses capturing software architecture in concise diagrams, applying lists of risks and threats, adopting a process for review (such as STRIDE or architectural risk analysis), and building an assessment and remediation plan for the organization.

The code review practice includes the use of code review tools, development of customized rules, profiles for tool use by different roles (e.g., developers versus analysts), manual analysis, and tracking/measuring results. The security testing practice is concerned with prerelease testing, including integrating security into standard QA processes. This practice includes the use of black box security tools (including fuzz testing) as a smoke test in QA, risk-driven white box testing, application of the attack model, and code coverage analysis. Security testing focuses on vulnerabilities in construction.

9.4.3 Deployment

Deployment includes those practices that interface with traditional network security and software maintenance organizations. Software configuration, maintenance, and other environmental issues have direct impacts on software security.

By contrast, in the deployment domain, the penetration testing practice involves more standard outside-in testing of the sort carried out by security specialists. Penetration testing focuses on vulnerabilities in the final configuration and provides direct feeds to defect management and mitigation. The software environment practice concerns itself with operating system and platform patching, web application firewalls, installation and configuration documentation, application monitoring, change management, and, ultimately, code signing. Finally, the configuration management and vulnerability management practice is concerned with patching and updating applications, version control, defect tracking and remediation, and incident handling.

9.4.4 BSIMM's 12 Practice Areas

Under each BSIMM category, there are a number of objectives and associated activities that determine the current level of maturity for that category. As you work your way down the list, the evidence of additional activities moves the organization further along the maturity levels, so that those organizations that claim to conduct all the activities in a specific category wind up as the most mature, at Level 3. The 12 practices are shown in Figure 9.6.

9.4.5 Measuring Results with BSIMM

Figure 9.7 shows a spider graph of the average maturity levels from the 130 organizations that have completed a BSIMM assessment by Synopsys. The average maturity is used to compare a specific organization's maturity to help determine gaps and areas for improvement, or to compare among overall industries (i.e., healthcare, insurance, financial services, etc.), as shown in the example in Figure 9.8.

9.4.6 The BSIMM Community

The 130 firms participating in BSIMM form the community. A private online community platform with nearly 600 members provides software security personnel a forum to discuss solutions with others who face the same issues, refine strategy with someone who has already addressed an issue, seek out mentors from those further along a career path, and band together to solve hard problems. Community members also receive exclusive access to topical webinars and other curated content. The BSIMM community also hosts annual private conferences during which representatives from each firm gather in an off-the-record forum to discuss software security initiatives.

9.4.7 Conducting a BSIMM Assessment

The BSIMM document is published under the Creative Commons Attribution-Share Alike 3.0 License, and you can use the documentation to conduct your own assessment for internal purposes. If you want your firm's data and outcomes included in the BSIMM data pool that's used for updating BSIMM, you'll need a contract with Synopsys to conduct an official assessment and report.

In preparation for that formal assessment, you'll need to consider which application development teams to engage for the interviews. BSIMM assessments are conducted as a series of interviews with subject matter experts (SMEs) and knowledgeable people in your organization who are involved with your software security initiative. You can slice the potential assessment population into any cross sections that you'd like, but try to select those teams that represent actual outcomes from your efforts to roll out AppSec. In other words, you want teams who have engaged in AppSec practices you've helped to implement and are showing positive outcomes from those engagements. To gain a representative view of the SSI itself, you'll need a good cross section of those whose lives you've touched with your program and who have a good understrating of your mission and objectives for AppSec.

GOVERNANCE	INTELLIGENCE	SSDL TOUCHPOINTS	DEPLOYMENT
1. Strategy & Metrics (SM)	4. Attack Models (AM)	7. Architecture Analysis (AA)	10. Penetration Testing (PT)
2. Compliance & Policy (CP)	5. Security Features & Design (SFD)	8. Code Review (CR)	11. Software Environment (SE)
3. Training (T)	6. Standards & Requirements (SR)	9. Security Testing (ST)	12. Configuration Management & Vulnerability Management (CMVM)

Figure 9.6 BSIMM's 12 practices (*Source:* BSIMM 11 by Sammy Migues, John Steven, and Mike Ware is licensed under CC-BY-SA).

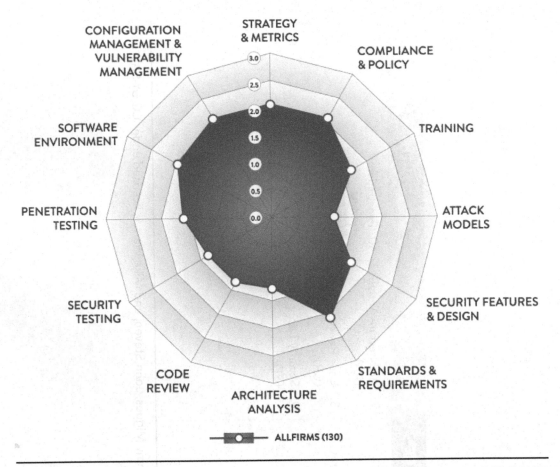

Figure 9.7 BSIMM average world maturity levels across the 130 participants in BSIMM V11 (*Source:* BSIMM 11 by Sammy Migues, John Steven, and Mike Ware is licensed under CC-BY-SA).

9.4.8 Section Summary

You saw two approaches to developing, collecting, and assessing metrics to help determine an overall maturity level of your secure development implementation efforts and programs. Although both models should lead you to improved and measurable processes, selecting the one to use must be determined by your own organization's structure, its internal development processes, and your own good judgment. Although we won't recommend one approach over the other, you should be able to see the overlaps between them and use the one that best fits your purposes. As we mentioned early in this chapter, don't let the perfect be the enemy of the good. For software assurance, the time to get moving is now!

9.5 Enhancing Your Threat Modeling Practice As Part of the SDL

Everyone recognizes that, in most software development projects, time and budget are fixed values, and the introduction of the "extra work" tied to security and resilience requirements

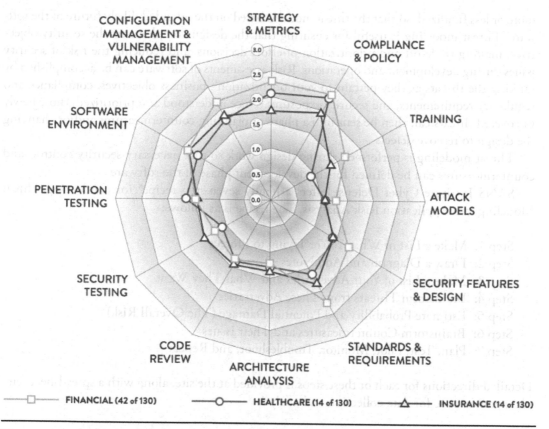

CONFIGURATION
MANAGEMENT &
VULNERABILITY
MANAGEMENT

STRATEGY
& METRICS

COMPLIANCE
& POLICY

SOFTWARE
ENVIRONMENT

TRAINING

PENETRATION
TESTING

ATTACK
MODELS

SECURITY
TESTING

SECURITY FEATURES
& DESIGN

CODE
REVIEW

STANDARDS &
REQUIREMENTS

ARCHITECTURE
ANALYSIS

FINANCIAL (42 of 130)   HEALTHCARE (14 of 130)   INSURANCE (14 of 130)

Figure 9.8 BSIMM average maturity levels across financial services, insurance, and health-care (*Source:* BSIMM 11 by Sammy Migues, John Steven, and Mike Ware is licensed under CC-BY-SA).

are generally not well received by software development teams. The best place to introduce the security design and architecture review is when the team is engaged in the functional design and architecture review of the software.

Learning to see your network through the eyes of your adversaries is an important part of the risk analysis and hardening process. Risk analysis involves identifying assets and the threats to these assets, and hardening is about how to protect your assets. A risk analysis and hardening process can range in character from overly rigorous to very casual and informal. Practical risk analysis and hardening lies somewhere in between these two extremes.

What follows is a recipe to perform a practical risk analysis and get a hardening plan started. It's not intended to be perfect or comprehensive—it's intended to be *practical*.

9.5.1 Practical Threat and Application Risk Modeling

Threat modeling includes determining the attack surface of the software by examining its functionality for trust boundaries, entry points, data flow, and exit points. Threat models are only useful once the design documentation that represents the entire application's architecture is more or less finalized, so that the threat model is based on the intended, likely future of the software. Threat modeling is useful for ensuring that the design complements the security objectives, making trade-off and prioritization-of-effort decisions, and reducing the risk of security issues during development and operations. Risk assessments of software can be accomplished by ranking the threats as they pertain to your organization's business objectives, compliance and regulatory requirements, and security exposures. Once understood and prioritized, those newly uncovered threats can then be sent into a phase of planning countermeasures and/or changing the design to remove defects.

Threat modeling is performed during design work so that necessary security controls and countermeasures can be defined for the development phase of the software.

SANS Institute Cyber Defense offers a handy seven-step recipe[8] for conducting Threat Modeling and Application Risk Analysis. The recipe is as follows:

Step 1: Make a List of What You're Trying to Protect
Step 2: Draw a Diagram and Add Notes
Step 3: Make a List of Your Adversaries and What They Want
Step 4: Brainstorm Threats from These Adversaries
Step 5: Estimate Probability and Potential Damage (The Overall Risk)
Step 6: Brainstorm Countermeasures and Their Issues
Step 7: Plan, Test, Pilot, Monitor, Troubleshoot, and Repeat

Detailed directions for each of these steps is provided at the site, along with a spreadsheet template you can use for data collection and analysis.

9.5.1.1 Brainstorming Threats

Step 4 of the recipe calls for brainstorming threats from your adversaries. One of the more popular brainstorming techniques was popularized by Microsoft and is called STRIDE. STRIDE is a mnemonic for:

- **Spoofing**
- **Tampering**
- **Repudiation**
- **Information disclosure**
- **Denial of service**
- **Elevation of privilege**

Section 4.3.3 covers the details for each category of STRIDE. The central idea behind STRIDE is that you can classify all your threats according to one of these six STRIDE categories. Since each category has a specific set of potential mitigations, once you have analyzed the threats, categorized them, and prioritized them, you will know how to mitigate or eliminate the defect that could lead to an exploit.

The STRIDE process is really a brainstorming activity conducted in person or via media-sharing channels (e.g., Zoom®, Microsoft Teams®, etc.). Participants use the documentation to identify assets in the architecture, their purpose, and their relative value. These become the targets for would-be attackers. Next, they identify possible attackers and what they would want from the system:

- Who are your actual or likely adversaries?
- What do they want to achieve?
- What are their skills and resources?
- How determined are they?
- What would they be willing to risk or give up to achieve their goals?
- What about insiders?

As you collect these across projects, you can also build a reusable catalog of attack profiles with enough details to make them suitable for anyone who wants to conduct threat modeling.

Next, imagine that you are one of those adversaries and try to see your network *through their eyes*. You know what you want; how would you try to get at it by misusing the application?

Just like the product backlog and user stories, a threat model is a living document—as you change the design, you need to go back and update your threat model to see if any new threats appear.

9.5.1.2 Risk Analysis and Assessment

For Step 5 of the recipe, we turn to another mnemonic from Microsoft, called DREAD, described in Section 4.3.3.4. It scores 5 categories,[9] which are added together and divided by 5, yielding a result from 0 to 10, where 0 indicates little or no impact and 10 is the house-on-fire situation.

Other risk analysis considerations include:

- Threats and vulnerabilities that exist in the project's environment or that result from interaction with other systems.
- Code that was created by external development groups in either source or object form. It's vitally important to carefully evaluate any code from sources external to your team, including purchased libraries and open-source components and libraries that may be present. Failing to do so might cause security vulnerabilities the team does not know about or learns about too late.
- Threat models should include all legacy code if the project is a new release of an existing program. Such code could have been written before much was known about software security and, therefore, likely contains vulnerabilities.
- A detailed privacy analysis to document your project's key privacy aspects. Important issues to consider include:
  - What personal data is collected?
  - What is the compelling customer value proposition and business justification?
  - What notice and consent experiences are provided?
  - What controls are provided to both internal and external users of the application?
  - How is unauthorized access to personal information prevented?

Once your threat identification and prioritization steps are completed, you should have the following sets of information available for the next steps, which comprise identifying different design choices, countermeasures that should be added, and improvements in the design based on the reviews. Completed threat-model documentation should include:

- A diagram and an enumeration and description of the elements in your diagram.
- A threat and risk analysis, since that is the core of the threat model.

In addition:

- For each mitigated threat that you identify in the threat analysis, you should include the bug or defect number associated with the mitigation plan to add to your backlog of required work.
- You should also have a one- or two-paragraph description of your software components and what they do. Maintaining a list of key contacts for questions is also useful.
- You should confirm that threat model data and associated documentation (functional/design specifications) is stored using the document control system used by the development team.
- You should consider reviews and approvals of threat models and referenced mitigations reviewed by at least one developer, one tester, and one program or project manager. Ask architects, developers, testers, program managers, and others who understand the software to contribute to the threat models and to review them. Solicit broad input and reviews to ensure that the threat models are as comprehensive as possible.

And remember that threat modeling is never complete as long as the application continues to gain features, is ported to other operating environments (e.g., cloud) or is rewritten as web services, APIs, and microservices to take advantage of modern computing practices.

9.5.2 MITRE ATT&CK[10] and MITRE D3FEND[11]

MITRE ATT&CK is a globally accessible knowledge base of adversary tactics and techniques that is based on real-world observations and is developed and published by the MITRE Corporation. The ATT&CK knowledge base can save you countless hours of research time and effort for conducting threat intelligence and threat management practices in your own SDL. A companion MITRE project, MITRE D3FEND, is useful for protecting even the most targeted IT infrastructures and applications.

The ATT&CK knowledge base is used as a foundation for the development of specific threat models and methodologies in the private sector, in government, and in the cybersecurity product and service community. ATT&CK is open and available to any person or organization for use at no charge. ATT&CK was created out of a need to systematically categorize adversary behavior as part of conducting structured adversary emulation exercises within MITRE's FMX research environment.

The first ATT&CK model was created in September 2013 and was primarily focused on the Windows enterprise environment. It was further refined through internal research and development and subsequently publicly released in May 2015 with 96 techniques under 9 tactics. Since then, ATT&CK has experienced tremendous growth based on contributions from the cybersecurity community. MITRE has created several additional ATT&CK-based models that were created based on the methodology used to create the first ATT&CK.

The knowledge base is a valuable resource for vulnerability managers with information and insights:

- **Detections and Analytics**
  ATT&CK can help cyber defenders develop analytics that detect the techniques used by an adversary.

- **Threat Intelligence**
  ATT&CK gives analysts a common language to structure, compare, and analyze threat intelligence.

- **Adversary Emulation and Red Teaming**
  ATT&CK provides a common language and framework that red teams can use to emulate specific threats and plan their operations.

- **Assessment and Engineering**
  ATT&CK can be used to assess your organization's capabilities and drive engineering decisions, such as what tools or logging you should implement.

The MITRE D3FEND knowledge base is a framework that provides defensive techniques that system administrators can apply to counter the practices detailed in the ATT&CK knowledge base.

9.6 Pulling It All Together

Cyber threats result from software flaws, which are weakness that can be exploited by a cyber attack or exploitation of a software application or system. In this book, we have covered strategies for implementing specific aspects of software security in the form of SDL best practices to assist software development organizations in avoiding and reducing software flaws as an essential element of effective core software security by providing security at the source.

Although achieving a vulnerability-free product is exceedingly difficult, maybe even impossible, it should always be your goal. By applying the best practices in this book, the software you develop will be as free from security vulnerabilities as possible. The fewer the number of vulnerabilities, the harder it will be for an attacker to exploit a given application.

By no means are we going to stop all threats through the use of software security best practices, but maximizing the reduction of the attack surface is our ultimate goal in that it makes our job as software security professionals easier and that of our adversaries more difficult. By implementing the practices outlined in this book, you will be able to mitigate threats coming from most threat actors.

This section describes how to apply everything you have learned in this book to the real world through the use of a flexible, agile, and business-relevant SDL.

9.7 Overcoming Organizational and Business Challenges with a Properly Designed, Managed, and Focused SDL

We have outlined an organizational structure with associated roles and responsibilities specific to the tasks that are identified in our SDL model and that have been field-tested and optimized by the authors of this book. This previously described structure will serve you well to effectively and efficiently create, deliver, and manage the best practices described in this book. It will also assist in the successful buy-in and management of the tasks through A1–A5 in our SDL model. As an added benefit, by using the organizational structure suggested, you will be able to deliver the tasks described in Chapter 8 for post-release support (PRSA1–5), which are typically conducted by other organizations than your own. By using the metrics described in each section of the SDL model, you will not only be able to effectively manage and track your software security programs and SDL success but also provide a dashboard to your corporate management and internal customers as to the current state of your program. This dashboard can also be used to identify gaps, which can be used to justify headcount, funding, and other resources, when needed. Most important, by building security in, you will maximize the ability to avoid post-release discoveries of security vulnerabilities in your software and increase your ability to successfully manage these discoveries on the occasions when they do occur.

9.8 Software Security Organizational Realities and Leverage

Although an incremental headcount hire plan based on a progressive increase in workload is typically the norm for most organizations, incremental growth isn't the right model for what has been proposed in this book and certainly isn't a reality for those going through austerity realities within their organizations. Doing more with less is a reality we all face, regardless of the risks we are facing. To help solve this conundrum, we have proposed a model for a software security group that doesn't depend on continual growth, linear or otherwise. The virtual team grows against linear growth, allowing a fully staffed, centralized software security group to remain relatively stable. We believe that a centralized group comprising one seasoned software security architect per main software product group and one for each software product within that group in your software engineering development organization will be sufficient to scale quite nicely as long as the software security champion program is adhered to, as proposed in this book. In addition, by sharing the responsibility for a typical product security incident response team (PSIRT) among the key software security champions for each software product in a development organization, a single PSIRT manager should suffice, given the shared responsibilities of the task throughout the organization. As described earlier in the book, excellence is not about increasing numbers; it is about the quality of the staff you hire. Each of these seasoned software security architects can coordinate and support the implementation of the SDL within each business unit and software product line and will:

- Provide the associated software security champion with the centralized software security group process and governance.
- Mentor the software security champions in security architecture and reviews.
- Support the associated business unit software security champion in the mentorship of each software product line software security champion.
- Coordinate with product management for early and timely security requirements.

- Help to calculate project security risk.
- Help to ensure that software security champions institute appropriate and full security testing.
- Ensure that appropriate security testing tools are available (static, dynamic, fuzzing) for use in the SDL, as appropriate.

Although these tasks benefit greatly from senior experience and discretion, there is a significant opportunity in having these senior technical leaders' mentor the software security champions and software security architects, as both a wonderful growth opportunity for the individuals involved and a cost savings to the company and the organization. Someone with the potential to grow into a leader through experience and mentorship is a perfect candidate for the software security champions in our model. We are the sum of everything we have ever done, which is constantly being revised and remembered. The same can be said of software security architects; it is a journey, not a point in time, and requires constant learning, mentoring, and collaboration with those who have been there before.

In our model, there are multiple paths to appropriate "coverage." Unlike a fully centralized function, a virtual team, handled with care, can be coalesced and led by a far smaller central team. The authors have made this model work, sometimes numerous times in a number of disparate organizations, and consider this a proven track record for a model that will constantly evolve with the ever-changing realities we are faced with in software security. Each member of the centralized software security group must be able to inspire, encourage, and lead a virtual team such that the virtual members contribute key subject matter expert (SME) tasks but at the same time do not become overloaded with additional or operational tasks. "Just enough," such that the PSIRT function can reap huge benefits through having true SMEs contribute and enable, while at the same time making sure that no one person bears the entire brunt of a set of operational activities that can't be dodged.

Since our model for a centralized software security group makes use of an extended virtual team, the need for a large central PSIRT staff, as may be found in other organizations, is not needed. Tasks that can be managed in a decentralized manner are performed, such as technical investigations, release planning, and fix development. However, there is a coordination role that must be sophisticated enough to technically comprehend the implications and risks involved in various responses. Peer review is a powerful tool for avoiding missteps. Further, the central role within the engineering software development group itself provides coordination across teams, something that is lacking in most organizations. We must not respond individually to a vulnerability that affects many software products in unique and idiosyncratic ways. Further, it is essential to provide an interface between PR (and sometimes marketing) support and the technical teams who are involved in responding. You want your response to vulnerability reporters to be consistent and to avoid putting your company and your brand at risk, externally.

9.9 Future Predictions for Software Security

We have divided this section into to two parts. First, the bad news, which is the things that we see that will likely continue on in industry but that should be changed; and second, the good things we see with regard to software security in the future—the light at the end of the tunnel, if you will.

9.9.1 The Bad News

We'll start with the bad news. For the most part, other than threat modeling and architectural security reviews, which are an art—not a science, software security isn't that difficult, but it is an area that industry has known about for many years and yet has chosen to do almost nothing about. This is evident in the top software vulnerabilities in the Common Vulnerabilities and Exposures (CVE®) and the OWASP® and CWE™/SANS Top 25 vulnerability lists, which have remained essentially the same over the last 10 years. Although industry has started to take leadership in this area over the last few years, we see software security as an ongoing problem for the foreseeable future, and it will take time to finally steer industry in the right direction. As discussed throughout the book, building security into the software development process is more about an attitude change, management acceptance, and business/operational process changes than blazing new trails in new scientific or technical disciplines.

The price of fixing vulnerabilities later in the cycle is very high. The effort required to tune and maintain current product security tools can be more expensive than buying new tools. Although much of the burden of making this change is on vendors, we have some thoughts that may help change this paradigm. We propose a paradigm shift away from vulnerabilities in software security. Not every vulnerability gets exploited, or is even exploitable. Often, mitigations that are not obvious to vanilla vulnerability scanners make even garden-variety vulnerabilities unattractive to attackers. We are not suggesting that we stop fixing bugs in code. Quite the opposite, as should be clear from the contents of this book. Still, delivering reports with thousands of vulnerabilities have not made software secure. However, as a collective whole, the security industry continues to focus on vulnerability: every new type of attack, every new variation, and every conceivable attack methodology. Instead, a focus on correct program behavior aligns well with how developers approach designing and creating code.

Correctness goes to the heart of the software process. In our experience, developers are rewarded for correctness. And it should be obvious that vulnerabilities are errors, plain and simple. Focusing on correctness would, unfortunately, be a sea change in software security. Tools today often don't report the one, single bug that will respond to multiple variations of a particular type of attack. Instead, too often, tools report each variation as a "vulnerability" that needs to be addressed by the developer. This is the way security people think about the situation. It's an attacker's view: Which attack methods will work on this particular system? That is the question that most vulnerability scanners address today (as of this writing).

However, people who write code simply want to know what the coding error is, where it is in the code, and what the correct behavior is that must be programmed. Often, if the tool contains any programming hints, these tend to be buried in the tool's user interface. Instead, we propose that a tool should be no more difficult to use than a compiler. The results could be a list of code errors, coupled to line numbers in the code, with a code snippet pointing out where the error lies. Of course, this is an oversimplification. Some kinds of security vulnerabilities lie across code snippets, or even across a whole system. Still, focus could be on what is the coding error and what is its solution. Logical errors could be described in terms of the design solution: things such as randomizing session IDs properly or including nonpredictable session identifiers with each web input (to prevent cross-site request forgery, for instance). In a world in which tens of millions of people are writing web code, and a great deal of that code contains exploitable vulnerabilities, we need an approach that simplifies the finding of the actual coding errors.

Massive counts of the millions of vulnerabilities have not reduced the attack surface. We like to suggest calling this new approach "developer-centric software security." "Developer centric" means that security people should understand developers' focus and developers' problems. The security industry must begin to address these in order to get security considered in its rightful place, right next to maintainability, correctness of algorithm, correctness of calculation, and all the other problems that a skilled programmer must face.

9.9.2 The Good News

As discussed throughout the book and in the previous section, industry knows what to do, that they should do it, and how to do it, but they don't do it. Knowing what to do is a significant portion of the battle that needs to be won. And we believe that pressure resulting from ISO standards (27034, 29147, and 30111) and the recent increase in business and government community awareness and oversight for software security that is built into the software development process will finally make software security a priority and business enabler. Other good news is that the tools and training for software security continue to improve. We also see more and more mentoring of the next generation of software security architects, which will serve our industry well over time. Most important, new organizational and management SDL models based on real-life experiences and successes, such as the one described in this book, are being developed.

9.10 Comprehensive SDL Review

Earlier in this chapter, we summarizied the Key Success Factors for each phase of the SDL (see Table 9.1). Here we include both the deliverables and metrics that should be included as regular artifacts of your specific SDL. Table 9.2 summarizes the deliverables from each phase, and Table 9.3 suggests some metrics that practitioners have found useful. With measurements of program maturity that you have seen in this chapter, you should be able to further customize the deliverables and metrics you need for operating the SDL and planning for its next evolution.

9.11 Conclusion

The criticality of software security as we move quickly toward this new age of tasks previously relegated to the human mind and now being replaced by software-driven machines cannot be underestimated. It is for this reason that we have written this book. In contrast and for the foreseeable future, humans will continue to write software programs. This also means that new software will keep building on legacy code or software that was written prior to security being taken seriously or before sophisticated attacks became prevalent. As long as humans write the programs, the key to successful software security is to make the software development program process more efficient and effective. Although the approach of this book includes people, process, and technology approaches to software security, the authors believe that the people element of software security is still the most important part to manage. This will remain true as long as software is developed, managed, and exploited by humans. This book has outlined

Table 9.2 Deliverables for Each Phase of the Security Development Lifecycle (SDL)

Phase	Deliverable	Goal
Security Assessment (A1): SDL Activities and Best Practices	Product risk profile	Estimate actual cost of the product.
	SDL project outline	Map SDL activities to the development schedule.
	Applicable laws and regulations	Obtain formal sign-off from stakeholders on applicable laws.
	Threat profile	Guide SDL activities to mitigate threats.
	Certification requirements	List requirements for product and operations certifications.
	List of third-party software	Identify dependence on third-party software.
	Metrics template	Establish cadence for regular reporting to executives.
	Business requirements	Software requirements, including CIA.
	Threat modeling artifacts	Data flow diagrams, elements, threat listing.
	Architecture threat analysis	Prioritization of threats and risks based on threat analysis.
	Risk mitigation plan	Plan to mitigate, accept, or tolerate risk.
	Policy compliance analysis	Analysis of adherence to company policies.
Design and Development (A3): SDL Activities and Best Practices	Updated threat modeling artifacts	Data flow diagrams, elements, threat listing.
	Design security review	Modifications to the design of software components based on security assessments.
	Security test plans	Plan to mitigate, accept, or tolerate risk.
	Updated policy compliance analysis	Analysis of adherence to company policies.
	Privacy implementation assessment results	Recommendations from privacy assessments.

Design and Development (A4): SDL Activities and Best Practices	Security test execution report	Review progress against identified security test cases.
	Updated policy compliance analysis	Analysis of adherence to company policies.
	Privacy compliance report	Validation that recommendations from privacy assessment have been implemented.
	Security testing reports	Findings from different types of security testing.
	Remediation report	Provide status on the security posture of the product.
Ship (A5): SDL Activities and Best Practices	Updated policy compliance analysis	Analysis of adherence to company policies.
	Security testing reports	Findings from different types of security testing in this phase of the SDL.
	Remediation report	Provide status on the security posture of the product.
	Open-source licensing review report	Review of compliance with licensing requirements if open-source software is used.
	Final security and privacy review reports	Review of compliance with security and privacy requirements.
	Customer engagement framework	Detailed framework to engage customers during different stages of the product life cycle.
Post-Release Support (PRSA1–5)	External vulnerability disclosure response process	The process to define evaluation and communication of security vulnerabilities.
	Post-release certifications	Certifications from external parties to demonstrate the security posture of products/services.
	Third-party security reviews	Security assessments performed by groups other than internal testing teams.
	Security strategy and process for legacy code, M&As, and EOL plans	Strategy to mitigate security risk from legacy code and mergers and acquisitions (M&As).

Table 9.3 Metrics for Each Phase of the Security Development Lifecycle (SDL)

Phase	Metric
Security Assessment (A1): SDL Activities and Best Practices	Time in weeks when software security team was looped in
	Percent of stakeholders participating in the SDL activities
	Percent of SDL activities mapped to development activities
	Percent of security objectives met
Architecture (A2): SDL Activities and Best Practices	List of business threats, technical threats (mapped to business threats), and threat actors
	Number of security objectives unmet after this phase
	Percent compliance with company policies (existing)
	Number of entry points for software (using data flow diagrams [DFDs])
	Percent of risk (and threats) accepted, mitigated, and tolerated
	Percent of initial software requirements redefined
	Number of planned software architectural changes (major and minor) in a product
	Number of software architectural changes needed based on security requirements
Design and Development (A3): SDL Activities and Best Practices	Threats, probability, and severity
	Percent compliance with company policies (updated)
	Percent of compliance in Phase 2 versus Phase 3
	Entry points for software (using data flow diagrams [DFDs])
	Percent of risk accepted versus mitigated
	Percent of initial software requirements redefined
	Percent of software architecture changes
	Percent of software development life cycle (SDLC) phases without corresponding software security testing
	Percent of software components with implementations related to privacy controls
	Number of lines of code
	Number of security defects found using static analysis tools
	Number of high-risk defects found using static analysis tools
	Defect density (security issues per 1000 lines of code)

Design and Development (A4): SDL Activities and Best Practices	Percent compliance with company policies (updated)
	- Percent of compliance in Phase 3 versus Phase 4
	Number of lines of code tested effectively with static analysis tools
	Number of security defects found through static analysis tools
	Number of high-risk defects found through static analysis tools
	Defect density (security issues per 1000 lines of code)
	Number and types of security issues found through static analysis, dynamic analysis, manual code review, penetration testing, and fuzzing
	- Overlap of security issues found through different types of testing
	- Comparison of severity of findings from different types of testing
	- Mapping of findings to threats/risks identified earlier
	Number of security findings remediated
	- Severity of findings
	- Time spent (approximate) in hours to remediate findings
	Number, types, and severity of findings outstanding
	Percentage compliance with the security test plan
	Number of security test cases executed
	- Number of findings from security test case execution
	- Number of retests executed
Ship (A5): SDL Activities and Best Practices	Percent compliance with company policies (updated)
	- Percent of compliance in Phase 5 versus Phase 4
	Number, type, and severity of security issues found through vulnerability scanning and penetration testing
	- Overlap of security issues found through different types of testing
	- Comparison of severity of findings from different types of testing
	- Mapping of findings to threats/risks identified earlier
	Number of security findings remediated (updated)
	- Severity of findings
	- Time spent (approximate) in hours to remediate findings
	Number, types, and severity of findings outstanding (updated)
	Percentage compliance with security and privacy requirements
Post-Release Support (PRSA1–5)	Time in hours to respond to externally disclosed security vulnerabilities
	Monthly FTE (full-time employee) hours required for the external disclosure process
	Number of security findings (ranked by severity) after the product has been released
	Number of customer-reported security issues per month
	Number of customer-reported security issues not identified during any SDL activities

a step-by-step process for software security that is relevant to today's technical, operational, business, and development environments. We have focused on what humans can do to control and manage a secure software development process in the form of best practices and metrics. Although security is not a natural component of the way industry has been building software in recent years, the authors believe that security improvements to development processes are possible, practical, and essential. We believe that the software security best practices and model presented in this book will make this clear to all who read the book, including executives, managers, practitioners, and students.

When it comes to cyber security, we believe it is all about the software and whether it is secure or not. You can have the world's best client, host, and network security, including encrypted transmission and storage of data, but if software application vulnerabilities exist and can be exploited, your defense-in-depth security approach has just become a speed bump to the inevitable. As the old adage goes, you are only as good as your weakest link, and in today's world, that is still the software; and software permeates everything we do, from defense to medicine, industry, banking, agricultural, transportation, and how we manage and live our lives. This is a very serious and daunting vulnerability. You only have to look at how many years the same software vulnerabilities have remained on the CVE Top 25 or OWASP and SANS Top 25 to realize that organizations are still not taking software security seriously. Even worse, experienced and professional adversaries will target vulnerable software and don't necessarily need it to be Internet-enabled to be at risk—that just makes the exploitation easier. But software is still the primary target because if you can own the software, you can own the data and the processes that it controls. In today's world, this can result in life-threatening and serious local, regional, and global consequences. Throughout this book, we have described the SDL best practices and metrics to optimize the development, management, and growth of a secure software development life cycle (SDLC) and program to maximize the mitigation of this type of risk. Managing software security is an area that the authors live in on a daily basis, and this book is based on our real-world experiences. We have worked with Fortune 500 companies and have often seen examples of the breakdown of security development lifecycle (SDL) practices. In this book, we have taken an experience-based approach to applying components of the best available SDL models in dealing with the problems described above in the form of an SDL software security best practices model and framework. Most important, our SDL best practices model has been mapped to the standard model for an SDLC, explaining how you can use this to build and manage a mature SDL program. Although security issues will always exist, the purpose of this book has been to teach you how to maximize an organization's ability to minimize vulnerabilities in your software products before they are released or deployed, by building security into the development process. We hope you enjoyed reading this book as much as we have writing it, as we are passionate about our efforts to help alleviate the risk of vulnerable software in the world at large and, specifically, in our our readers' organizations.

References

1. Trapani, K. (2018, May 22). What Is AGILE?—What Is SCRUM?—Agile FAQ's. Retrieved from https://www.cprime.com/resources/what-is-agile-what-is-scrum/
2. Vashishtha, S. (2012, August 3). "Agile vs DevOps: Demystifying DevOps." Retrieved from http://www.agilebuddha.com/agile/demystifying-devops/

3. Maccherone, L. (2017, March 19). "DevSecOps Cycle" [Diagram]. Retrieved from https://twitter .com/lmaccherone/status/843647960797888512

4. REST API Tutorial. (2017, June 5). "What Is REST: Learn to Create Timeless RESTful APIs." Retrieved from https://restfulapi.net/

5. Epstein, J. (2009, June 18). "Jeremy Epstein on the Value of a Maturity Model." Retrieved January 7, 2022, from https://www.opensamm.org/2009/06/jeremy-epstein-on-the-value-of-a-maturity-model/

6. OWASP. (2017, April 14). "OWASP SAMM v1.5 Released." Retrieved January 7, 2022, from https:// www.opensamm.org/2017/04/owasp-samm-v1-5-released/

7. Migues, S., Steven, J., and Ware, M. (2021, September). "Building Security in Maturity Model." Retrieved January 13, 2022, from https://www.bsimm.com/

8. SANS Institute. (2021, December 8). "Practical Risk Analysis and Threat Modeling Spread-sheet." Retrieved January 10, 2022, from https://www.sans.org/blog/practical-risk-analysis-and -threat-modeling-spreadsheet/

9. "Security/OSSA-Metrics." (n.d.). Retrieved from https://wiki.openstack.org/wiki/Security/OSSA -Metrics#DREAD

10. MITRE Corporation (Ed.). (n.d.). "MITRE ATT&CK®." Retrieved January 6, 2022, from https:// attack.mitre.org/

11. Ibid.

Appendix A

Case Study for Chapters 3 Through 8 Exercises

The following case study forms the basis for the exercises you'll find in Chapters 3 through 8.

Revvin' Engines Auto Parts is a statewide retail and commercial supplier of auto parts throughout Illinois. They have a robust business from walk-in traffic and from their auto repair shops close to their retail locations. Six months ago, the owners decided it was time to open their catalog of items they sell to customers across the United States.

They hired a local Schaumburg software development company to design an Internet E-commerce site, implement an online shopping cart, and permit credit card payments for online orders. They even slapped together a mobile app for both iOS® and Android® devices.

Once the system was implemented, Revvin' Engines decided it was time to bring in a new staff of development team members to take over the applications for enhancements and maintenance. They hired three local people and two remote employees for the new team:

- 2 C# programmers for .NET Core
- 1 tester
- 1 designer
- 1 lead engineer who handles the architecture and engineering of the application and the corresponding system.

The team is relatively new, comprising people who have not worked together before and who had no direct experience beyond programming courses they completed and some freelance application development.

Future plans for the applications include expansion of capabilities and rewriting the applications as cloud native, composed of a series of microservices and application programming interfaces (APIs) using web services based on representational state transfer (REST).

The new site and mobile apps became wildly popular. Local customers appreciated the convenience of ordering from home or their place of business. In addition, the rare auto parts Revvin' Engines often carries gained national attention, and new orders began coming in from across the United States. Management was ecstatic about the site and decided it was time to expand the catalog and the marketing of their business to areas never considered before.

One morning, the owners and employees came into work at HQ and found a huge number of voice messages on their answering service and hundreds of email messages with complaints. People were outraged that right after a purchase on the Revvin' Engines website, their credit card issuers began sending alerts of out-of-pattern purchases using their credit cards in other cities, states, and countries throughout Eastern Europe.

Management was at a loss as to what to do and wound up calling NoMoreHacks Security Consultants to come in and perform a forensics analysis on the site and the databases and an analysis of how they're protected. NoMoreHacks viewed web logs, server logs, application logs, and Windows Event logs to see what may have happened. They found several critical and high-level vulnerabilities in the web application and a severe lack of proper controls on SQL Server databases. Some of the critical vulnerabilities included SQL injection, wherein the attackers were able to learn about the structure of the database and all of its tables. They found a series of SQL statements that the application dynamically generated that located the database of credit card details, followed by an extract of all the credit card data. Since stolen credit card data has a short shelf life, the attackers began using it right away, before the cards could be reported stolen or compromised.

A postmortem of the incident led management to temporarily shut down the site and the mobile applications while they took appropriate action to mitigate the damage and rebuild the application to stand up to hostile and malicious criminals on the Internet.

One of these measures is to focus on how Revvin' Engines develops or procures software, and you've been called in to advise them and help them to build a security consciousness for their development team and help them to establish a security development lifecycle (SDL) that's culturally appropriate and effective in producing secure software that management trusts will stand up to attacks from malicious hackers on the Internet or by internal, knowledgeable insiders.

Appendix B

Answers to Chapter Quick-Check Questions

Appendix B provides the questions from each chapter's Quick-Check with the correct answers shown in **bold** to help you check your own understanding.

Chapter 1

1. The costs to remediate security flaws once a software product is released can run as much as _____ times the costs to remediate them while still in development:

   a. 50
   b. **100**
   c. 500
   d. 1500

2. Defective software is:

   a. A network security problem
   b. An operating system security problem
   c. A user-caused problem
   d. **A software development and engineering problem**

3. The three goals of the security development lifecycle are:

   a. Reliability, efficiency, and maintainability
   b. Speed, quality, and continuous releases
   c. **Confidentiality, integrity, and availability**
   d. Availability, reliability, and portability

4. Threat modeling and attack surface analysis is most effective when it's conducted:

   a. Post-release
   b. **During product inception/product backlog development**
   c. During integration testing phase(s)
   d. Prior to code development/commitment

Chapter 2

1. The paradigm of Building Security In begins with the:

   a. Analysis phase
   b. Design phase
   c. **Specification phase**
   d. Development phase

2. The objectives of an SDL are to achieve all of the following except:

   a. To reduce the number of security vulnerabilities in software
   b. To reduce the severity of security vulnerabilities in software
   c. To eliminate threats to the software
   d. **To document a complete understanding of the vulnerabilities in software**

3. The fundamental approach to security in which an object has only the necessary rights and privileges to perform its task with no additional permissions is a description of:

   a. Layered security
   b. **Least privilege**
   c. Role-based security
   d. Clark-Wilson model

4. Which of the following statements best describes BSIMM?

   a. BSIMM is used to measure the maturity of a software assurance program by looking for evidence of security best practices in the SDLC.
   b. BSIMM is used to measure the maturity of a software assurance program by looking for evidence of security procedures in the SDLC.
   c. **BSIMM is used to measure the maturity of a software assurance program by looking for evidence of security activities in the SDLC.**
   d. BSIMM is used to measure the maturity of a software assurance program by looking for evidence of security requirements in the SDLC.

Chapter 3

1. The purpose for the discovery meeting with stakeholders early in the development life cycle is to:

   a. Discover who is on the development team

  b. Discover what budgets and resources are available to the initiative
  c. **Discover how security can be built into the development process from the start**
  d. Discover which platforms and languages will be used for development of the application

2. A Privacy Impact Assessment (PIA) is needed to:

  a. Identify laws and regulations related to the controls needed for the application
  b. Identify the data elements and their sensitivity for proper selection of security controls
  c. Identify communications and platform controls to apply to data in acquisition, processing, and storage
  d. None of the above
  e. **All of the above**

3. A threat profile developed in Phase A1 serves as input to which subsequent development activities?

  a. Requirements gathering
  b. **Threat modeling**
  c. Static analysis
  d. Post implementation sign-offs

Chapter 4

1. Threats are identified using a process described by this mnemonic:

  a. THREATEXPOSE
  b. **STRIDE**
  c. DREAD
  d. CAPEC

2. Risk is calculated for each identified threat to prioritize findings and needs for remediation using which technique?

  a. RISKCOMPUTE
  b. DANGER
  c. **DREAD**
  d. THREATORDER

3. Which of the following is not a mitigation method for threats identified in threat modeling?

  a. Redesign to eliminate vulnerability
  b. Apply a standard mitigation
  c. **Change the security requirements to eliminate the threat**
  d. Accept the vulnerability

4. The preferred security mitigation to use during threat modeling is:

   a. A custom control created specifically for the threat
   b. Encryption from an approved library to prevent information disclosure
   c. Acceptance of the vulnerability
   d. **Standard enterprise-level security controls in common use**

Chapter 5

1. The use of standardized design functions for similar or repeated functionality is referred to as:

   a. Psychological acceptability
   b. Complete mediation
   c. Open design
   d. **Economy of mechanism**

2. Logging of errors and failure information should be designed to protect:

   a. **Sensitive information**
   b. Availability through resilient controls
   c. Separation of duties
   d. Fail-safe designs

3. Designing a system so all parties can easily understand design objectives and maintaining a simple design embrace the principle of:

   a. Single point of failure
   b. Least common mechanism
   c. Fail-safe
   d. **Open design**

4. The security principle of fail-safe is related to:

   a. Session management
   b. **Exception management**
   c. Complete mediation
   d. Single point of failure

Chapter 6

1. The following are primary mitigation methods except:

   a. Locking down the environment
   b. Input validation
   c. **Use of deprecated libraries for legacy code**
   d. Output validation

2. Elements of defensive coding include all the following except:

   a. **Custom cryptographic functions to avoid algorithm disclosure**
   b. Exception handling to avoid program termination
   c. Interface coding efforts to avoid API-facing attacks
   d. Cryptographic agility to make cryptographic functions stronger

3. Static analysis can be used to check for:

   a. Approved function/library calls, examining rules and semantics associated with logic, and thread performance management
   b. Syntax, approved function/library calls, and race conditions
   c. **Syntax, approved function/library calls, and memory management**
   d. Syntax, approved function/library calls, and examining rules and semantics associated with logic and calls

4. Automated testing has the following advantages over manual code review except:

   a. Detection of unsafe or deprecated function calls
   b. **Identification of obfuscated routines**
   c. Speed of analysis
   d. Integration into the IDE

Chapter 7

1. The post-release plan should have a policy to allow:

   a. Rules
   b. **Deviations**
   c. Procedures
   d. Practices

2. Management reviews recommend:

   a. Best practices
   b. Roles
   c. Accountability
   d. **Corrective or remedial action**

3. The aim of black-box testing is to confirm that a given input:

   a. Is correct
   b. Can be processed accurately
   c. **Produces a predictable output**
   d. Will not cause a defect

4. Configuration management exercises:

   a. Rational control over the code

b. Rational control over the design
c. **Rational control over the change process**
d. Enforcement of the change process

5. The management level authorized to approve changes must be:

a. As high as possible
b. As simple as possible
c. **Clearly defined**
d. Approved

Chapter 8

1. Product deployment and post-release assurance requires:

a. Secure coding
b. Object-oriented management
c. **Problem resolution**
d. Configuration management

2. Incident response processes should be:

a. **Routinely executed and tested**
b. Operationally complex
c. Strategically planned
d. Totally constrained

3. The incident management team is:

a. A strictly technical operation
b. Composed of the best programmers
c. Strictly composed of managers
d. **Often a diverse bunch of people representing all relevant disciplines**

4. The operations and management processes are lumped together into sustainment because:

a. They are at the end of the life cycle.
b. **They are the major activities during the software use life cycle period.**
c. They are neither development nor acquisition.
d. They are strictly control processes for sustaining assurance.

Glossary

API	Application programming interface
ASF	Application Security Frame
BCO	Basic Center of Operations
BSI	Build Security In
BSIMM	Building Security In Maturity Model
CERT®	Carnegie Mellon Computer Emergency Readiness Team
CIA	Confidentiality, integrity, and availability
CI/CD	Continuous integration/continuous deployment
CISO	Chief Information Security Officer
COPPA	U.S. Children's Online Privacy Protection Act of 1998
COTS	Commercial off-the-shelf
CPO	Chief privacy officer
CR	Code Review
CRM	Customer relationship management
CSDL	Cisco Secure Development Lifecycle
CSIAC	Cyber Security and Information Systems Information Analysis Center
CSO	Chief Security Officer
CVE	MITRE Corporation Common Computer Vulnerabilities and Exposures
CVSS	Common Vulnerability Scoring System
CWE	Common Weakness Enumeration
DAST	Dynamic application security testing
DFD	Data flow diagram
DHS	U.S. Department of Homeland Security
DIACAP	U.S. Department of Defense (DoD) Information Assurance Certification and Accreditation Process
DoD	U.S. Department of Defense
DR	Design Review

DREAD	Damage potential, Reproducibility, Exploitability, Affected users, and Discoverability
EG	Education and Guidance
EH	Environment Hardening
FIPS	Federal Information Processing Standards
FIRST	Forum of Incident Response and Security Teams
FISMA	The Federal Information Security Management Act
FUD	Fear, uncertainty, and doubt
GPL	General Public License
GRC	Governance, risk management, and compliance
HIPAA	Health Insurance Portability and Accountability Act of 1996
HMAC	Hashed message authentication code
HR	Human Resources
IA	Information assurance
IaaS	Infrastructure as a Service
IAC	Information Analysis Center
IATAC	Information Assurance Technology Analysis Center
IEC	International Electrotechnical Commission
ISO®	International Organization for Standardization
M&A	Merger and acquisition
MSIAC	Modeling and Simulation Information Analysis Center
NCSD	National Cyber Security Division
NFR	Nonfunctional requirements
NIAC	National Infrastructure Advisory Council
NIST	National Institute of Standards and Technology
NSA	National Security Agency
NVD	U.S. National Vulnerability Database
OCTAVE®	Operationally Critical Threat, Asset, and Vulnerability Evaluation
OE	Operational Enablement
OEM	Original equipment manufacturer
OpenSAMM	OWASP's Open Software Assurance Maturity Model
OWASP®	Open Web Application Security Project
PaaS	Platform as a Service
PASTA	Process for Attack Simulation and Threat Analysis
PC	Policy and Compliance
PCI-DSS	Payment Card Industry Data Security Standard

PIA	Privacy Impact Assessment
PII	Personally identifiable information
PITAC	U.S. President's Information Technology Advisory Committee
PSIRT	Product Security Incident Response Team
QA	Quality assurance
RDT&E	Department of Defense Research Development Test and Evaluation
REST	Representational state transfer
ROI	Return on investment
SA	Secure Architecture
SaaS	Software as a Service
SAMM™	OWASP® Software Assurance Maturity Model
SANS	SysAdmin, Audit, Network, and Security
SAST	Static application security testing
SB	Security bulletin
SCAP	Security Content Automation Protocol
SDL	Security development lifecycle
SDLC	Software development life cycle
SEI	Carnegie Mellon University's Software Engineering Institute
SLA	Service-level agreement
SOHO	Small office/home office
SM	Strategy and Metrics
SME	Subject matter expert
SR	Security Requirements
SSC	Software security champion
SSE	Software security evangelist
SSG	Software security group
SSI	Software security initiative
ST	Security Testing
TA	Threat Assessment
TCP/IP	Transmission Control Protocol/Internet Protocol
TLS	Transport Layer Security
U.S.	United States
US CERT	Department of Homeland Security United States Computer Emergency Readiness Team (US-CERT)
VM	Vulnerability Management
XSS	Cross-site scripting

Index

Printed in the United States
by Baker & Taylor Publisher Services

Printed in the United States
by Baker & Taylor Publisher Services